GREAT EDITORIALS

Masterpieces of Opinion Writing

GREAT EDITORIALS

Masterpieces of Opinion Writing

By Wm. David Sloan, Cheryl Watts, and Joanne Sloan

ISION PRESS

P.O. Box 1106   3230 Mystic Lake Way   Northport, AL 35476

Vision Press
P.O. Box 1106
3230 Mystic Lake Way
Northport, Alabama 35476

Library of Congress Cataloguing-in-Publication Data

Great Editorials / [compiled by] Wm. David Sloan,
    Cheryl S. Watts, C. Joanne Sloan.
        p.   cm.
    ISBN 0-9630700-0-2
    1. American newspapers--Sections, columns, etc.--
Editorials. 2. Journalism--United States. I. Sloan,
W. David (William David), 1947-   . II. Watts,
Cheryl Sloan, 1968-   . III. Sloan, C. Joanne
(Cheryl Joanne), 1947-   .
PN4853.G74   1991
070.4'42--dc20   91-33806
                                                   CIP

Printed in the United States of America

"Men with actual capacity of certain sorts for acceptable writing have been frightened off from doing natural and vigorous work by certain newspaper...doctrinaires who are in distress if...the temper and blood of the writer actually show in his work."

—Charles Dana, New York *Sun*

Acknowledgments

A number of people helped us in the preparation of this book. We first would like to thank the editorial writers whose work is included here and who either provided material for us or were kind enough to give us permission to reprint their editorials: John Harrison of the New York Times Company, Theo Lippman Jr. of the Baltimore *Sun*, Ann Daly Goodwin of the St. Paul (Minn.) *Pioneer Press*, Samuel Francis of the Washington *Times*, and especially Paul Greenberg of the Pine Bluff (Ark.) *Commercial*. Mr. Greenberg provided us with stacks of editorials and biographical material and patiently responded to every request we made.

Many other individuals, including a number of winners of national awards for editorial writing, provided us with material and made our job of selecting and locating editorials much easier. We extend our special appreciation to Prof. Charlie Marler of Abilene (Tex.) Christian University; Jonathan Freedman, formerly of the San Diego *Tribune*; Richard Aregood of the Philadelphia *Daily News*; James Klurfield of *Newsday*; Jay Ambrose and Linda-Ann Salas of the Denver *Rocky Mountain News*; Asa Cole of the Harte-Hanks Community Newspapers in Massachusetts; John R. Alexander of the Center for Creative Leadership in Greensboro, N.C.; Jack Rosenthal of the New York *Times*; Robert L. Bartley of the *Wall Street Journal*; Bailey Thomson of the Orlando (Fla.) *Sentinel*; Robert Fisher of Little Rock, Ark.; Hap Cawood of the Dayton (Ohio) *Daily News*; Donald F. Brod, executive secretary of the International Society of Weekly Newspaper Editors; Prof. Garrett W. Ray of Colorado State University; Robert H. Estabrook of the Lakeville (Conn.) *Journal*; Phil McLaughlin of the Miami (Kan.) *Republican*; Dan Hicks Jr. of the Madisonville (Tenn.) *Democrat-Observer*; Jack Fuller of the Chicago *Tribune*; Lee Dembart of the San Francisco *Examiner*; and Mary Lou Marusin of the Scripps Howard Foundation.

For helping us obtain permission to reprint editorials, we thank William Hilliard and Judson Randall of the Portland *Oregonian*; James K. Cazalas of the Greenville (Miss.) *Delta Democrat-Times*; F.T. Weaver of the Jackson (Mich.) *Citizen Patriot*; Charles E. Brown of the Mercantile Library of St. Louis; Kathleen Bailey and Geneva Overholser of the Des Moines *Register and Tribune*; and Ronald A. Bartizek of the Dallas (Penn.) *Post*.

For assistance in preparing the manuscript, we especially thank Lisa Bailey.

CONTENTS

• The Professional Era, 1900-Present / 126 •

GREAT EDITORIALS

Masterpieces of Opinion Writing

Learning from the Masters

When was the last time you clipped an editorial from a newspaper and saved it so you could reread it again and again? If you have written editorials yourself, when was the last time one of your newspaper's readers told you that he or she had clipped one and taped it to a lunchbox to be read at lunch break?

If you never have had that happen, you are not alone.

If ever there were an ephemeral work, it is the editorial. In its day, it is (if fortunate) occasionally considered worth reading or perhaps even important—but good only for the day or the week. Most editorials are read one day and forgotten the next. Because of this unhappy fate, we begin to think that editorials possess little quality and certainly no lasting value.

Yet, in the history of editorial writing there are scores of editorials that exercised major importance during their day, there are even more that are not only highly readable but are writing gems, and there are others that had a universal appeal at the time they were written and even today still are able to speak to us about eternal truths. All of them make excellent reading. They also can provide excellent models for writers who wish to develop their own effective style.

Learning from such masterpieces is the principle underlying this book. It is a truism in literature that if one wants to write well, one should read good writing. Although true in "creative" writing such as fiction and poetry, that principle is no less true in editorial writing. The best way one can develop an effective writing style is to read effective editorials.

Yet, who can name more than three or four editorials? For a journalist today to be able to name more than a handful of great journalists from the past is rare enough. Even more rare is the person who can name an editorial by one of those journalists. Can we imagine that being the case with poetry? How many poets or teachers of English literature could name no more than three or four poems? Although many journalists may recall that William Cullen Bryant wrote poetry, few know that he devoted most of his life to editing the New York *Evening Post*. Even fewer realize that his stature as an editor comes almost solely from his editorial writing. Hardly anyone can name even one editorial he wrote. How many of today's journalists can identify E. L. Godkin or know that Horace Greeley's major place in history resulted not from his 1872 campaign for the United States' presidency but from his editorship of the New York *Tribune*? And how many journalists realize that Godkin and Greeley probably exercised more influence over public opinion than any other journalist in America's past? It is not surprising to find that few editorials by either Godkin or Greeley are familiar to journalists and students.

What Is an "Editorial"?

It is possible, however, to write excellent editorials, ones that people *want* to read. Several key principles are involved. To begin, let's look at what an "editorial" is. Over the years, the nature of editorials has changed, and "editorial" has been defined differently by various observers. Some definitions are relatively straightforward. In an early textbook on editorial writing, Leon Flint said an editorial "is the published expression of the opinions of an editor." (*The Editorial*, 1931.) Curtis MacDougall, another textbook author, said it is "that part of a publication which management dedicates to the purpose of influencing the thoughts, opinions and actions of its readers." (*Principles of Editorial Writing*, 1973.) Both of those definitions contain two key points: an editorial (1) is a statement of or by a newspaper staff member in an authority position and (2) deals in some manner with opinion.

Other writers have constructed more detailed definitions in an attempt to be more precise and more exclusive. Typical are the following two definitions, both of which are taken from textbooks on editorial writing:

•An editorial may be defined as a presentation of fact and opinion in concise, logical, pleasing order for the sake of entertaining, of influencing opinion, or of interpreting significant news in such a way that its importance to the average reader will be clear.... [I]t usually consists largely of individual opinion and makes no pretense to being unbiased. (Lyle M. Spencer, *Editorial Writing: Ethics, Policy, Practice*, 1924)

•[T]he editor's comment as distinguished from the news stories written by reporters and the "letters" contributed by readers.... It is, in other words, a serious comment in essay form about those present happenings which are important and significant to society.... The editorial... is a compact essay of exposition or argumentation, is seldom more than three or four hundred words in length, contains virtually no elements of narration, and represents the opinion of an institution—the newspaper—rather than that of the individual writer.... This definition does not take into account the entertaining type of editorial. (Chilton R. Bush, *Editorial Thinking and Writing*, 1941)

William Allen White, the renowned editor of the Emporia (Kan.) *Gazette*, was more human in his definition. He said simply that an editorial is "a free expression upon the news of the day, written briefly and bravely by a wise kindhearted man."

These definitions, just a few of many that could be quoted, were written in the past half century or so. As recent definitions, they therefore describe characteristics of contemporary editorials and may be inappropriate as descriptions of editorials of earlier times. Today, an editorial is presumed to be a piece of writing by a member of the newspaper's staff published at least ostensibly as the view of the editor, editorial staff, or owner of the newspaper. In earlier times, this was not necessarily the case. Throughout the 18th century, newspaper operators were mostly printers rather than editors, and "editorials" usually were written by contributors not officially associated with the newspaper. The loose affiliation the early writers had with newspapers may present the question of why a syndicated column of today is not an "editorial." The primary difference between early contributions and contemporary columns, in terms of definition, is that the former were printed as the opinion of the newspaper, whereas the latter are presented only as the view of the columnist.

As a definition that applies broadly and across time, we may say that an editorial is *a piece of writing originally published in a newspaper which is indicated by the newspaper as an editorial or is published as the opinion of the newspaper.*

Achieving Editorial Quality

Writers may do several things to assure that their editorials are of superior quality. The first thing is to recognize that *people are not interested in an editorial writer's opinion!*

That is a basic principle that all editorial writers should adopt. Not only should they adopt it, but they should underline it. With that principle in mind, they would avoid one of the most common causes of poor writing.

Editorial writers tend to think that people are eagerly waiting to hear what a writer's opinion is. The writer then assumes that his or her function is to tell readers what that opinion is. The result is that the writer gets caught up in the fervor of sharing the opinion—overlooking the fact that *how* the opinion is presented is just as important as what the opinion is.

Most readers, however, are not impressed by other people's (especially anonymous editorial writers') opinion. If you doubt that, ask yourself how impressed you are with the opinion of your hometown newspaper's editorial writer. On important issues, do you wait to make up your mind until you have a chance to read his or her editorials? Do you eagerly turn to the editorial page every day just to find out what the writer's opinion is? If you do, your newspaper has a rare gem writing its editorials. Now, if you are not a devout student of your newspaper's editorial writer, why should you think that any readers will be eager seekers after your opinion? Unless you are extraordinarily brilliant, they won't be.

How, then, can you get them to read your editorials?

The key is to cast aside any belief that they are interested in your opinion and to concentrate instead on writing editorials in a masterly style. Be concerned about focusing the editorial on a well-defined theme, about how the beginning introduces the theme and grabs the reader's interest, how the body of the editorial gives flesh to the theme, and how you structure your sentences and choose your words. Concentrate on making your editorials interesting to read. If you do that on a daily basis, after a while readers will want to read your editorials—and, in the process, they will start to pay attention to your opinions as well.

But how does one determine what a "good" editorial is? Part of the problem in answering that question is simply that there are no established, generally agreed-on guidelines about what constitutes editorial quality. Traditionally, the quality of editorials has been judged primarily on editorial effectiveness, that is, an editorial's capacity to influence a reader's opinion or behavior, that is, to persuade. Some observers still hold this view. The Walker Stone Awards for editorial writing, for example, which are given by the Scripps-Howard Foundation, are based on "the effectiveness of the editorials as measured by results."

In the last few years, however, editorial writers have suggested an editorial's capacity to explain or interpret as a criterion to augment persuasiveness. More and more editorials are being written ostensibly to explain or interpret rather than simply to persuade. Still, even such editorials as these often do attempt to influence opinion, and a large number of others are aimed transparently at attempting to persuade. Effectiveness (persuasiveness) must be considered then as a criterion when judging many editorials. Alone, however, it is inadequate. To be able to judge editorial quality, one must use a broader range of criteria.

Awards programs for editorial writing offer some guidelines. The widely quoted criteria for the Pulitzer Prize in editorial writing are "clearness of style, moral purpose, sound reasoning and power to influence public opinion in what the writer conceives to be the right direction." The last of the four criteria has been changed from the original one of "power to influence public opinion in the right direction," adding the phrase "... what the writer conceives...," a clear indication that the Columbia University trustees who set up the standards feel it is difficult, if not impossible, to determine precisely what is "right." Such an acceptance of values as relative rather than as absolute may account for the lack of moral force in many editorials today. If an editorial writer has no faith that any values are right, it is unlikely he or she can write powerfully about them. Other editorial contests are not so detailed in what standards, if any, are used in selecting their winners. No standards are stated for the Golden Quill Award of the International Society of Weekly Newspaper Editors. Although early promoters of the award suggested that it be given for "good editorial writing" and for a "good piece of writing," deciding the basis for the award is left to the discretion of the judges, who vary from year to year. The Society of Professional Journalists, Sigma Delta Chi, also relies on judges' standards. Typical perhaps of these standards is the statement of judges in selecting the 1946 award: "relative brevity, directness, and freedom from technicalities or vocabulary exhibitionism." In its "Basic Statement of Principles," the National Conference of Editorial Writers declares that the "chief duty" of editorial writers is to "provide the information and guidance toward sound judgments that are essential to the functioning of a democracy." Therefore, the NCEW states, editorial writers "should present facts honestly and fully... draw fair conclusions from the stated facts... [and] have the courage of well-founded convictions."

Considering the diversity of views—and their occasional absence—what, then, are the qualities that account for an editorial being superior? When one reduces the reasons to the most fundamental principles, one finds four standards. They are *effectiveness*, *artistry*, *thematic significance*, and *truth*. Let's look at each one.

Effectiveness

Traditionally, effectiveness has been the standard test for judging editorials. Although there is little means by which one can gauge effectiveness, a common lament is that editorials are no longer as influential as they were during the "golden age" of journalism in the 1800s. For more than a century, critics have been lamenting the editorial's decline. In the 1830s, political editors bewailed the frivolity and inanity of the penny press. In the 1870s, the passing of giants such as Horace Greeley and Henry Raymond was moaned. In the 1920s, men such as the late Joseph Pulitzer, Charles Dana, and E. L. Godkin were hailed as the last of the great personal editors. More recently, Henry Watterson and William Allen White have been honored as the last of the editors who spoke with authority and had the ear of their readers.

Whether editorials at any time in the past were influential is uncertain. Most beliefs about editorial influence originated with contemporary observers. If we assume that the observers, lacking sophisticated knowledge about newspaper persuasiveness, drew naive conclusions, then we may dismiss their faith in editorial power. On the other hand, it also is possible that their observations were correct.

The preponderance of present research indicates that mass communication works in combination with a variety of factors, rather than alone, in influencing attitudes. The early "bullet theory" concept of mass media persuasiveness (suggesting that all a mass communicator had to do to persuade an audience was to "shoot" a message into it), later was replaced with that of the "obstinate audience," an audience that appears only remotely susceptible to mass media persuasion. Today, theoreticians accept a more complex concept that combines parts of those ideas with other factors such as the cultural environment and the nature of the medium and the message.

In general, however, theoreticians and editorial writers both argue that a belief that editorials have an automatic, direct effect on attitude or behavior change is unrealistic. At most, they say, editorials act as catalysts to trigger an existing predisposition. On the other hand, a volume of research indicates that in some situations mass communication may directly affect both attitudes and behavior. A salient example of this research is that dealing with television and children. Moreover, a number of experiments have found that specific aspects of a message itself contribute to persuasiveness. These include order of arguments, strength of the language, statement of a conclusion, and the like. Furthermore, some studies of editorial influence on voting have found a correlation between editorial endorsements and electoral behavior. These findings should not necessarily be accepted, however, as conclusive evidence that editorials influence elections. It may simply be that the editors' views happened to coincide with voters' views. At the least, however, these studies do show a correlation between editorial endorsements and voting. Even though some theoretical studies have questioned the influence of mass communication, it is not unrealistic to suppose that occasional editorials have acted as exceptions and actually did exercise direct influence. This might especially have been true in the age of "personal journalism" when the editor may have been viewed as an opinion leader rather than a mass communicator.

If it is true, however, that editorial influence has declined from what it was during the "golden age," is there an answer to the question of "Why the decline?"

The reason may be simply that, as many editorial writers argue, the purpose of today's editorials is not to persuade. A large percentage of recent editorials tend more toward a presentation of facts with an emphasis on interpretation rather than intense argument. Almost 50 years ago, the author of a textbook on editorial writing pointed out: "The argumentative editorial shows a tendency to 'tone down.' There is more effort to gather convincing facts for the reader than to try to convince by formal logic. The flamboyant periods and oratorical perorations of a few years ago are less common, even in presidential election years." (Robert W. Jones, *The Editorial Page*, 1930.) This statement typifies 20th-century concepts of the function of editorials.

Still, it should not be presumed that newspapers never run editorials intended to persuade. Editorials may not be as caustic as a century ago, but most newspapers do run editorials aimed at affecting reader opinion. The difference between editorials of the "golden age" and of today is that whereas the earlier ones frequently attempted to persuade by trenchant opinion, many of today's editorials rely on exposition of fact.

The change in the approach to editorial writing and in the possible influence of editorials probably results from a number of factors. In *Editorial Writing* (1924), Dr. M. Lyle Spencer listed several factors, including the "phenomenal development of the news-gathering department," editors' failure to train editorial writers, "the failure of editorial writers to keep in practical touch with readers," increased speed in newspaper production, "the transfer of the editorial function to the news columns," and "the territorial expansion of the United States."

A frequently mentioned reason for the change is increased education of readers. As readers have become better educated, it is presumed that they are less susceptible to persuasion. Many editorial writers agree with Prof. Spencer's analysis that whereas readers during William Cullen Bryant's and Horace Greeley's day "were prone to accept as their own the ready-made opinions furnished them by their favorite editors, nowadays they are rather inclined to ask for the facts from which they may form their own opinions." Because readers today possess an "increased education and a growing spirit of individualism," they have become "more independent. Instead of turning to the editorial page to learn how to vote," Prof. Spencer reasoned, "they look to it—if they look at all—to see whether the opinions expressed there agree with their own. If the opinions differ, they may suspect an ulterior motive on the part of the editor; or, no matter how effective the reasoning, they may decide that he knows no more about the question than they do." In a similar vein, Charles Merz, then editor of the editorial page of the New York *Times*, wrote in 1942:

"The modern editorial page is dealing with readers who are incomparably better informed about everything that is happening in the world than newspaper readers used to be. These readers have formed the habit of thinking for themselves. And if the editorial page is arbitrary, or if its conclusions do not seem to follow the known premises in any given case, it will not move opinion.

"No doubt," Merz declared, "it is true that in the old days... editorials were more personal and passionate and sweeping than most editorials today. But these qualities would not in themselves convince the busy and well-posted people for whose attention the editorial page must now compete. A little research in the past will do much to deflate the tradition of the great "personal" editors. A reader who now turns back to the editorials of the early giants—Horace Greeley, for example—will be impressed by his discovery of how much of them consists of mere rhetoric and invective. There is little approaching the reasoned argument and the careful documentation that one expects today." ("The Editorial Page," *The Annals of the American Academy of Political and Social Science* [January, 1942]: 139.)

The nature of 20th-century education differs from earlier education on an important point relevant to editorial influence.

While formal logic and intuition earlier were considered the basis of much knowledge, modern education has stressed empiricism, an approach that places less importance on opinion and more on facts and experience. In regard to editorial influence, this change in the basis of discovering knowledge means that readers rely less on editors' opinions and place more trust in editorial statements of facts. Regarding this point, the publisher Raymond Clapper wrote in 1929 that "today we live in different times, in a new world of which it may be said generally that uncertainties have replaced certainties. Diversity and complexity have succeeded general optimism on religious, political, social, industrial, moral, and economic questions." Because of the complicated nature of modern life, he declared, "it is not a time for dogmatism or the closed mind. The old-time editorial writer, however effective for another age, would not fit well, and would perhaps not readily adjust himself in an age of widening knowledge and of bewildering change." Such observations should be instructive to today's editorial writer wishing to influence readers.

Oddly enough, considering what is perceived to be a stronger education among readers, a frequent complaint of editorials is that the language is not simple enough. Although today's editorial sentence structure is not as complex and the vocabulary not as erudite as they were in Greeley's time—when readers were said to be less sophisticated and editorials more influential—editorial writers constantly are urged not to write above the heads of today's more educated reader. This makes one wonder if editorial writers underestimate the education of readers—or is the claim that editorials have become more interpretive because of higher reader education simply a rationalization for the decline of editorial influence?

The 20th-century trend toward corporate newspapers also has affected editorial influence. Whereas a number of editorials in the 1700s and 1800s were credited with influencing national events, it is difficult to find recent editorials that exercised a major impact. Although some apparently have helped bring about small changes on the local level, influence on important national issues is nearly absent. The corporate trend in newspaper ownership may be the reason. In the 1800s, owners served as editors rather than publishers and were less interested in the business operation of their newspapers than the editorial. Their name also was identified with their newspaper, and readers recognized them as personal editors. With corporate ownership, editorship became anonymous and impersonal. Editorial writers, being employees rather than owners, lost the power to speak with the newspapers' personal authority. Owners, more concerned with the financial well-being of their newspaper properties than with editorial influence, favored objective news over editorial opinion. Middle-of-the-road editorials seemed safer than powerful ones. To be powerful, editorials frequently must take a stand. That means they may be controversial—and that they might anger readers or advertisers.

The corporate growth of newspapers also led to a professionalization of journalists. Editorial effectiveness was one of the victims of professionalization. Like other journalists, editorial writers began to adopt the standardized thinking of the profession. That included detachment from the surrounding community and, sometimes, a commitment that was stronger to the standards of the profession than to the values of the community. That change could be seen, for example, in journalists' interpretation of the meaning of the First Amendment, in their opposition to established institutions such as government, and in their secularized views on religion. As the gap between journalists' values and those of the general public widened, editorial writers lost touch with the readers' views, and editorial influence naturally diminished.

Despite the diminished influence of recent editorials, this anthology includes a number of editorials selected because of their effectiveness. Thomas Paine's "The Crisis," for example, was credited by colonists with reviving their determination during the American Revolution, and Joseph Pulitzer's "Shall Jay Gould Rule This Country?" was considered partially responsible for Grover Cleveland's election as president. In making decisions about effectiveness, we have considered primarily an editorial's success in bringing about a desired result. Success has been determined by examining opinions of contemporaries of the editorial and evaluations of historians. We hope that these editorials will provide lessons on how editorial writers may be effective.

Artistry

The second standard for evaluating editorial writing is artistry. The usual measure of artistry in an editorial has been that of literary quality. When judged by that standard, editorials more often than not fall short—but defenders of editorial writing should not be, as they sometimes have been, apologetic. Literary quality for a number of reasons is inadequate as a test of editorial quality. Even though the best editorials indicate that, given time or the inspiration, the editorial writer can match talent with the best of essayists, we need to discard the notion of "literary quality" in evaluating editorials. Not only does the phrase connote standards inappropriate for editorials; peculiar conditions make it impossible for most editorials to be of high literary quality.

One of the most obvious impediments is that editorials are written under restrictive time demands. As the columnist James Kilpatrick has pointed out: "Good writing takes time. There may be geniuses here and there who can produce superb paragraphs, full of pithy thought and subtle epigram, as popcorn flows from the nickel machine. But you will find few of them in the editorial offices of daily newspapers. For most of us, good writing comes like good cabinet-making—slowly, and with infinite writing and rewriting, with a rubbing and sandpapering and polishing of rough phrases."

The huge volume of editorials written also dictates that many will be of poor quality. It is as unrealistic to expect the thousands of editorials written each week to be of high literary character as it would be to expect thousands of poems, if written under the same kind of time restrictions, to be good.

Unfortunately, the attitudes of editorial writers are partly to blame for the lack of quality in their work. Many writers feel that editorials should be so reasoned that their style becomes dry, pontifical, somber. The result is editorials that are deadly dull. One editorial writer surmised, "Alas, something seems to freeze in us when we sit down to write an editorial. All the passion, all the poetry fly out the window and our words become dry, detached, desiccated, dreary." Editorial writing undoubtedly would improve if editorial writers did not begin their task assuming that they must be mechanical, detached, and formal to the point of dullness.

Despite the artistic shortcomings of most editorials, however, writing quality has never been the sole measure of an editorial's worth. Few of America's famous editorials are known only for their literary merit. Most of our notable editorials have endured for some reason in addition to their writing quality. Most editors would even say that high literary attempts are inappropriate for the editorial page. Still, a number of editorial writers have displayed true literary ability. Godkin, Greeley, William Cobbett, William Cullen Bryant, Frank Cobb, and William Allen White are examples. They should attest to the fact that even though few editorials may achieve literary perfection, writers always should place a premium on good writing.

A measure other than literary quality should, however, be used in evaluating editorial writing. The meaning of the phrase is vague, and usually it simply refers to that quality found in writing genres normally associated with the word "literature." Thus, "literary quality" is the characteristic found in good fiction, autobiography, and poetry. To measure the quality of editorial writing by a standard more appropriate to "literature" is as unrealistic as to judge poetry or fiction by the characteristics of good editorial writing.

The primary criterion for judging writing should be "Does the style suit the purpose?" The purpose of editorials is specific. Editorials are expressions of opinion. They comment on facts. Their purpose normally is to comment, persuade, explain, or interpret. The quality of their writing style needs to be evaluated by how well it performs those functions.

The audience also is a necessary consideration when judging whether style is suitable. The editorial generally is intended for a nonexclusive mass audience. Because readers spend only a short time with a newspaper, they are not expected to analyze an editorial slowly and carefully. A number of limitations are thus imposed on editorial writing. It is expected, for example, to be understandable to the general reader on the first reading. It therefore should be lucid and easy to understand. It should avoid verbosity, tedious length, and obtuseness. The editor of the Anniston (Ala.) *Star* wrote in *The Masthead*, the journal of the National Conference of Editorial Writers, in 1949 that he considered the "worst" editorial writing that in which "editors are wont to parade their French, Latin or other esoteric words and phrases that cannot be interpreted by the fellow on the other side of the railroad tracks." Such considerations are almost synonymous with readability, a characteristic that has received considerable attention from researchers. Readability, however, does not assure that an editorial will be artistic. Indeed, language or style alone is not the same as artistry. Other characteristics of the entire editorial must also be considered.

Over the years, writers have proposed a number of guides for achieving editorial quality. Reuben Maury, a Pulitzer Prize winner, and Karl G. Pfeiffer suggested that "effective editorial writing" is achieved through use of such techniques as short sentences, simple sentence structure, simple and familiar words, active words, and concrete rather than abstract words and phrases. (*Effective Editorial Writing*, 1960). In an anthology of news stories entitled *20th Century Reporting at Its Best* (1964), Bryce Rucker listed a number of characteristics of "excellent writing": "vivid, powerful, accurate verbs and crisp, specific nouns," "simplicity in sentence, paragraph, and story structure," "change of pace in sentence length and structure to avoid monotonous, singsongy, juvenile prose," "similes, metaphors, examples, anecdotes, etc., which heightened communication," and "clear organization."

The student should take to heart all such advice. To understand the foundation of editorial artistry, however, one needs to recognize the broad principles not only of style, but of structure also. There are four criteria that are most important in contributing to editorial artistry. They are *unity, complexity, intensity,* and *clarity.*

Unity. This is the characteristic of a work that is well-organized, is formally perfect, and has, as Monroe Beardsley described it, an "inner logic of structure and style." (*Aesthetics: Problems in the Philosophy of Criticism*, 1958.) Beardsley provides the most original discussion of these characteristics of artistry and can be consulted fruitfully by the student looking for a thoughtful explanation of the essentials of quality in artistic composition. The concept of unity has two distinguishable components: *completeness* and *coherence.* A work has completeness when it seems to need nothing outside itself. It is coherent if it seems to fit together and contains nothing that does not belong.

Coherency is promoted by such factors as compositional scheme, balance, similarities among parts, harmony, and consistency of style. To be unified, an editorial thus needs to exhibit a designed order. *It should be built around one central theme* (a main idea or point), with its various elements or parts clearly and definitely related to each other. (That point is so important that it bears repeated emphasis.) It needs a clear expository or narrative structure containing all necessary elements with no irrelevancies introduced.

Complexity. Unity alone, however, does not assure that an editorial will be artistic. A one-word editorial might have pure unity but little artistry. The complement to unity is *complexity*. Complexity increases when a work is developed on a larger scale, is rich in contrasts (variety), and is subtle and imaginative. The complexity of an editorial is dependent on such factors as number of parts and differences between them, spatial and temporal scope, the range of experience encompassed, abundance of detail, number of ideas and logical distinctions, richness, depth, and magnitude or size.

Obviously, unity and complexity may be at odds. As complexity increases, unity tends to decrease. Complexity is increased by differences of parts, unity by similarities. The artistry of an editorial becomes greater when complexity increases without sacrificing unity.

Intensity. Intensity usually will be greater when a work is full of vitality, when it is vivid and forceful. Words such as "powerful," "beautiful," "ironic," "tender," "tragic," "comic," and "graceful" frequently are associated with the type of writing designated by the term *intense*. Intensity may be influenced by an editorial's subject, its style, or the attitude of the writer. A subject of high emotional appeal will be more intense than one without it. Intensity will increase if the style exhibits forcefulness and vigor, qualities imparted by easily understood, pungent, specific, concrete words and phrases rather than obscure, pedantic, or general ones. Intensity tends to decrease when there is pretentiousness, sentimentality, pompousness, banality, or gaudiness. If a writer's strong emotion shows in the writing, or if forceful logic is apparent, or if he or she writes with positiveness and authority—rather than with tentativeness (indicated by the use of "perhaps," "on the other hand," and other such phrases) or pure dogmatism—intensity tends to increase.

Clarity. The fourth criterion, *clarity*, is necessarily an aspect of intensity. It deserves, however, special attention in editorial writing because of the audience. Readers usually do not analyze editorials word by word. Editorials, therefore, must be immediately understandable on a single reading. Clarity may be increased by such things as well-structured reasoning or narration, lucid presentation of argument, short sentences, and short and familiar words.

Some editorial writers have been noted for their style, and students who take them as models will be better for the mentoring. E. L. Godkin's style was forceful, incisive, and concise. Godkin himself declared that Horace Greeley possessed "an English style which, for vigor, terseness, clearness, and simplicity, has never been surpassed except, perhaps, by [William] Cobbett." Many of William Cullen Bryant's editorials are models of reasoned prose, eloquence, clarity, and force. Frank Cobb wrote with a combination of simplicity and power rarely equalled. William Allen White was a master of unencumbered description and narrative. Today, they have their peers in writers such as Paul Greenberg of the Pine Bluff (Ark.) *Commercial* and the columnist James Kilpatrick.

Although the value of great editorials does not rest on artistry alone, no editorial becomes outstanding without some semblance of artistry. Artistry can be irrelevant to the criteria of thematic significance and truth; but without artistry, an editorial will be routine or worse—and it probably cannot be effective.

Thematic Significance and Truth

The final two standards for evaluating editorials—thematic significance and truth—are subjective and cannot be measured even with the nebulous precision applied to effectiveness and artistry. The nature of thematic significance and truth thus will be hinted at only briefly here.

Thematic significance refers primarily to the *importance* of the editorial's subject. When determining significance, one can consider such factors as magnitude of consequence, number of people concerned, universality, and timelessness. A war (the subject of, for example, Henry Watterson's "Vae Victus") normally would be more significant than an automobile accident, a presidential election (the subject of Pulitzer's "Shall Jay Gould Rule This Country?") more significant than a city council election. Yet in some instances the death of a relatively obscure person (as in William Allen White's "Mary White") may be extremely meaningful because death is universal.

Originality is also important to thematic significance. It usually is found in new treatment of a theme. Often, editorials derive their force from writers' ability to look at common subjects in new ways. Arthur Brisbane's "Those Who Laugh at a Drunken Man" provides a perfect example. It points out that finding humor in the sight of a drunk going home to a family "whose life he has made miserable" demonstrates inhumanity on the part of those who laugh at his drunkenness. Many of the memorable editorials are those that were first to treat a topic in a certain manner. Take, for example, editorials dealing with race relations. A number of editorials that have won the Pulitzer Prize argued during the midst of racial troubles that the rule of law is supreme. The most memorable of these is Harvey Newbranch's "Law and the Jungle," the prize winner in 1920 and the first to discuss racial relations or the rule of law. Likewise, although William Allen White's "To An Anxious Friend" is widely quoted on the topic of freedom of the press, it simply mirrored typical arguments for press freedom. More original is Joseph Pulitzer's "Lese-Majesty," which argued for freedom of the press and was published 15 years before White's editorial.

The concept of *truth* is broad and is not limited to objectively verifiable knowledge. It may include, along with factual truth, accuracy of interpretation and explanation, and moral rightness. Although one may claim that some truth is subjective, the concept plays a key, perhaps *the* key role in editorial quality. Clearly, editorials based on falsity are of no merit. The propaganda preceding the Spanish-American War that appeared in the Hearst newspapers, although influential, holds little respect from anyone and thus fails when evaluated as quality editorial writing. On the other hand, Francis Church's "Is There a Santa Claus?" falls short when measured by a standard of objective factual truth, but it succeeds on a higher plane. Church's chief aim was not to answer the question of whether Santa Claus physically exists but to touch a philosophical truth that transcends surface facts.

Moral good sometimes can be equated with truth. In many cases, this standard can be applied as part of the test of effectiveness: Is the effect of an editorial morally good? The opposite of that principle is that when the end sought by an editorial is reprehensible, that editorial fails on the standard of truth. For example, Ambrose Bierce's quatrain about the assassination of William Goebel, governor-elect of Kentucky, may have influenced the assassin of President William McKinley; but because of the morality of the action suggested by the editorial, its merit is nil. It read:

The bullet that pierced Goebel's breast
Cannot be found in all the west.
Good reason: it is speeding here
To lay McKinley in his bier.

On the other hand, some editorials fall within a nebulous area of morality. Some question may exist as to whether the end sought is good or bad. Examples are Henry Watterson's editorials calling for and celebrating America's entry into World War I. There is still some question whether entry was the proper moral course. A similar factor, the value of the end achieved by an editorial, also is important. The New York *Tribune* editorial "Forward to Richmond," for example, which prematurely advocated that the Union army attack the Confederates, helped accomplish that goal, but the attack resulted in military defeat at Bull Run. Some might say that this editorial was influential because it persuaded the army to attack; but because its ultimate goal of the defeat of the Confederates was not achieved, one must question the value of its achievement.

Learning from the Masters

In the following collection, the student will find true masterpieces of editorial writing. They range from the historically significant, such as Benjamin Franklin's essay in the 1750s warning American colonists to "Join or Die," to literary gems such as Ben Hur Lampman's description of "Where To Bury a Dog." The student will find demonstrated in them the most important principles and techniques.

For the student determined to be an excellent editorial writer, no better means exists than to begin by reading the best works from the best writers. If one is content to be an ordinary writer, one should read ordinary editorials. If, on the other hand, one wishes to rise above the routine, if one wishes to be a good writer, one will find in these *Great Editorials* many valuable lessons. Besides that, many are just good, fun reading!

The Partisan Era, 1690-1833

Although American newspapers have almost always carried news, for most of their history their editors believed that their most important function was to express opinion. In the beginning, many newspapers were intended principally as a means of publishing political opinion rather than news.

For the first century and more after the founding of America's first newspaper in 1690, newspaper "editors" were usually only printers and had little time—or, frequently, ability—to pen editorial opinion. What opinions their papers carried were usually submitted by contributors under pen names, although occasionally enterprising printer-editors would write letters to themselves, signing the pieces "from a correspondent" or with some other such identification. Seldom did the editor or another member of the staff actually write the material which appeared as the opinion of the newspaper. In some instances, a group of like-minded individuals would devise a plan to publish a newspaper, contract with a printer-publisher, and agree to provide written contributions.

More frequently, a newspaper's "editorials" (although they were not called such) were contributed by writers not officially associated with the newspaper. A contributor might be a sponsor who occasionally provided financing for the paper but who did not actually work for it (such as Alexander Hamilton in his relation with the *Gazette of the United States* around the turn of the 19th century) or a writer with no connections to a paper but who sometimes presented material for publication (such as Thomas Paine in his association with the *Pennsylvania Journal* in the Revolutionary era). In either case, the "editorial" writer was at most loosely connected with the publishing of the newspaper. Because newspapers, along with pamphlets, were the favored medium for writers wishing to publish their views, we find in newspapers some of the most important works in early American history, including such classics as John Dickinson's "Letters from a Farmer in Pennsylvania," a series of essays that were published in the *Pennsylvania Chronicle and Universal Advertiser* in 1767 and were instrumental in the American colonies' opposition to British parliamentary power; Thomas Paine's "Crisis" papers (*Pennsylvania Journal*, 1776 and 1777) that helped rally colonists' morale during the American Revolution; and the

"Federalist Papers" (New York *Independent Journal*, 1787 and 1788) that argued for adoption of the U. S. Constitution and today are recognized as the greatest work on political science ever produced in the United States.

The Revolutionary crisis brought an increase in the activity of contributors, mostly agitators and political philosophers. Their writings frequently resembled the form of pamphlets and were published a section at a time in successive issues of newspapers. Two of the selections in the first part of this anthology formed a part of the independence movement.

The colonies' victory in the Revolution did little to change the characteristics of newspaper opinion. In the decade after independence, it remained the domain primarily of the contributor and its nature that of the pamphlet. A significant event in the development of the editorial occurred, however, during the 1780s. It was at that time that the editorial in its modern form appeared. During the Revolution, a few isolated printers began to italicize their opinions to differentiate them from other parts of news accounts, and others began to print the news they gathered themselves or their brief comments on the news under a hometown heading. Whereas earlier opinion had been dispersed throughout the pages of newspapers, in the early 1780s some newspapers began to separate their opinion statements from the news and to reserve a specific place for the opinion. The editors Noah Webster and James Cheetham began publishing a separate section of short paragraphs they had written. Other editors began to place a specific caption over the opinion, indicating that the opinion was that of the editor rather than of a contributor.

These two practices—opinion separated from news, and a typographical designation of an opinion to indicate that it was the newspaper's—came together for the first time in Hartford's *Connecticut Courant* in 1783. During the early part of the Revolution, the *Courant's* George Goodwin began to place local material beneath a Hartford heading. In the 1780s, he and his partner, Barzalai Hudson, began to reserve that space for their own writing and reporting. Whenever they wished to express themselves and have it known that a particular opinion in the *Courant* was that of the paper's ownership, they printed it in the Hartford column.

With the rise of strong partisan feeling during the presidency of George Washington, the nature of editorializing began to change. During the Revolutionary crisis, publicists had recognized the growing importance of the newspaper in influencing public opinion. In the early Constitutional period party leaders such as the Federalist Alexander Hamilton and Republican Thomas Jefferson saw fit to establish organs to espouse their party sentiments. The group that controlled a paper had none of the characteristics, however, of a modern corporation. Few of its members, one historian has observed, "had any very vivid expectation of earning a direct return upon a definite investment, or even of getting their money back, but all stood to gain in social prestige, literary reputation, political influence, or in the form of a better job if the paper succeeded—that is, if the party won the next election."[1]

Although politicians still contributed essays to the papers, journalists with the essential features of the modern editor, who did their own writing, began to appear. As political factions developed after the Revolution, newspapers quickly became important as partisan mouthpieces. Previously, most newspapers were conducted by owners who were printers only and who thought of themselves primarily as mechanics and publishers. They did little in the way of imaginatively selecting news to be published or composing their own writings. However, as the newspaper in the new Republic came to play a critical role in the political process, there was a growing need for individuals who could voice their faction's views in an effective manner. By the time the first parties appeared around 1790, the position of editor already was well-established, and newspapers were viewed no longer as simply the mechanical product of their printer-conductors but the expression of the editors' views. Noteworthy were such Federalists as John Fenno of the *Gazette of the United States*, William Cobbett of *Porcupine's Gazette*, Noah Webster of the *American Minerva*, and William Coleman of the New York *Evening Post*. Leading Republicans included Benjamin Franklin Bache and William Duane of the Philadelphia *Aurora*, Philip Freneau of the *National Gazette*, and James Cheetham of the *American Citizen.*

By the early 1800s, the editorial had been accorded an established position in many newspapers, but its effectiveness as a literary form was handicapped by several characteristics. Throughout the entire period of the party press' dominance of American journalism, which ended around 1860, the hallmarks of newspaper opinion were extreme vituperation, personal abuse, and domination by political subjects. These features frequently repel the modern reader, but partisan editorial writers, on the other hand, exhibited a number of enviable strengths. Many of them held key posts in local, state, and national politics and thus possessed an intimate and detailed knowledge of political issues. As a result, their editorials often revealed a keen understanding of the intricacies involved in public affairs. Because newspapers and editors were so closely tied to politics, it can be argued that at no other time in the history of editorial writing in the United States has the newspaper's editorial role been of such critical importance to the functioning of the nation's political system.

Before editorials developed their modern form, 18th-century newspapers published most of their opinion pieces in the form of essays. Because the newspaper columns were open to contribu-

---

[1]Eric W. Allen, "Economic Changes and Editorial Influence," *Journalism Quarterly* 8 (Fall 1931): 346.

tors, one thus finds that outsiders wrote many of the early statements of opinions that newspapers published. These essays served as the equivalent of today's editorials. Occasionally, the owner-editors themselves wrote opinion material for their newspapers. As an introduction to this early history, we've begun this anthology with two prominent forerunners of the editorial written by editors.

BENJAMIN FRANKLIN COINS
A SLOGAN FOR A REVOLUTION

America's first widely circulated "editorial" also included the nation's first newspaper political cartoon. An illustration of a severed snake with the caption "JOIN, or DIE," the cartoon is probably the most famous in American history.

At the time the editorial was written in 1754, France had embarked on a plan to enlarge its territory and extend its power in America. It sent expeditions into the Ohio Valley to enforce its territorial claims and to construct forts to keep out advancing colonists. In April a French force attacked a small garrison of colonial volunteers and forced its surrender. Word of the capitulation reached the towns on the Atlantic coast about two weeks later. In the meantime, a conference had been called for delegates of the colonies to devise a plan of defense against the French advances. Benjamin Franklin, however, was already thinking of a plan of union.

On May 9 he published in his *Pennsylvania Gazette* a report of the French attack and appended to it his views on the necessity of colonial union. To emphasize his point, he added the illustration of the divided snake. It was based on the legend that the glass snake could break itself into fragments when attacked and later recombine and survive. The eight snake parts represented the colonies. Despite the fact that numerous newspapers reprinted the editorial and cartoon, Franklin's plan for union did not gain approval. Only one colonial assembly recommended it. Colonial jealousies remained; and union, at least for the time being, had died.

Franklin's exhortation, however, would survive and play a role in eventual union. During the Stamp Act crisis of 1765, many colonial newspapers reprinted the "Join or Die" motto and the snake emblem, creating immense furor among authorities. Again, in 1774, when Britain invoked the "Intolerable" Acts in retaliation for the Boston Tea Party, the motto and snake reappeared. Numerous newspapers used them in various forms, with Isaiah Thomas' *Massachusetts Spy* running a standing nameplate composed of a snake confronting a dragon symbolizing England and the motto "Join or Die." With the onset of the Revolution, Franklin's devices proliferated in both newspapers and broadsides, becoming the most popular symbols of the revolt. Although his editorial had failed to bring about a union in 1754, it provided the motto of a Revolution more than two decades later.

[UNTITLED]
(Benjamin Franklin; *Pennsylvania Gazette*; May 9, 1754)

Friday last an Express arrived here from Major [George] Washington, with Advice, that Mr. [Edward] Ward, Ensign of Capt. [William] Trent's Company, was compelled to surrender his small Fort in the Forks of Monongahela to the French, on the 17th past; who fell down from Venango with a Fleet of 360 Battoes and Canoes, upwards of 1000 Men, and 18 Pieces of Artillery, which they planted against the Fort; and Mr. Ward having but 44 Men, and no Cannon to make a proper Defence, was obliged to surrender on Summons, capitulating to march out with their Arms, &c. and they had accordingly joined Major Washington, who was advanced with three Companies of the Virginia Forces, as far as the New Store near the Allegheny Mountains, where the Men were employed in clearing a Road for the Cannon, which were every Day expected with Col. Fry, and the Remainder of the Regiment— We hear farther, that some few of the English Traders on the Ohio escaped, but 'tis supposed the greatest Part are taken, with all their Goods, and Skins, to the Amount of near £20 000. The Indian Chiefs, however, have dispatch'd Messages to Pennsylvania, and Virginia, desiring that the English would not be discouraged, but send out their Warriors to join them, and drive the French out of the country before they fortify; otherwise the Trade will be lost, and to their great Grief, an eternal Separation made between the Indians and their Brethren the English. 'Tis farther said, that besides the French that came down from Venango, another Body of near 400, is coming up the Ohio; and that 600 French Indians, of the Chippaways and Ottaways, are coming down Siota River, from the Lake, to join them; and many more French are expected from Canada; the Design being to establish themselves, settle their Indians, and build Forts just on the Back of our Settlements in all our Colonies; from which Forts, as they did from Crown-Point, they may send out their Parties to kill and scalp the Inhabitants, and ruin the Frontier counties. Accordingly we hear, that the Back Settlers in Virginia, are so terrify'd by the Murdering and Scalping of the Family last Winter, and the Taking of this Fort, that they begin already to abandon their Plantations, and remove to Places of more Safety.—The confidence of the French in this Undertaking seems well-grounded on the present disunited State of the British Colonies, and the extreme Difficulty of bringing so many different Governments and Assemblies to agree in any speedy and effectual Measures for our common Defence and Security; while our Enemies have the very great Advantage of being under one Direction, with one Council, and one Purse. Hence, and from the great Distance of Britain, they presume that they may with Impunity violate the most solemn Treaties subsisting between the two Crowns, kill, seize and imprison our Traders, and confiscate their Effects at Pleasure [as they have done for several Years past], murder and scalp our Farmers, with their Wives and Children, and take an easy Possession of such Parts of the British Territory as they find most convenient for them; which if in the Destruction of the British Interest, Trade and Plantations in America.

ISAIAH THOMAS CALLS HIS FELLOW COLONISTS TO ARMS

Following the attacks of British troops at Concord and Lexington, Patriot printers helped spread the alarm throughout the colonies. Foremost among the printers was Isaiah Thomas of the *Massachusetts Spy.*

Many printers, like most colonists, in 1775 remained neutral or only lukewarm to the Patriot cause. Thomas, however, wrote with a revolutionary fervor. Historians believe that the Sons of Liberty met in his printing shop and that, after his employees had gone home, he printed the fiery group's handbills. He gained notoriety with the British authorities, who referred to his printing operation as a "sedition foundry."

Learning that the British had placed him on their list of 12 "most wanted" Patriots, to be captured and hanged, Thomas shipped his printing equipment from Boston to Worcester. The outbreak of hostilities on April 19, 1775, however, delayed his plans to resume publication of his newspaper. Just where Thomas was on the historic days of April 18 and 19 and what he was doing have been open to varying speculation. Some biographers have claimed he was the "friend" who Paul Revere said hung the signal lanterns from Christ Church. Others have declared that he was one of the messengers who, like Revere, rode during the night of April 18 warning Patriots of the British movement. Others have said he participated in the Battle of Lexington the following day. Good historical evidence suggests, however, that men other than Thomas shone the lantern and joined in the midnight ride. His own memoirs include no record of what he did the following day, but a friend said he joined the militia at daybreak, and his account of the battle hints of details witnessed by the author.

On the eve of the battle, the colonists were divided on independence, without resolve. The rebel forces were weak. The British foray to destroy the Patriot ammunition stores at Concord probably was intended as a simple, symbolic maneuver. But Lexington changed all that.

The Patriot leaders and printers quickly spread the news of the battle. The Committees of Correspondence dispatched letters on the same day of the battle, and within a week 15 newspapers from New Hampshire to New York had published accounts.

None, however, made more political mileage out of it than Thomas. Nor was any account more eloquent than his. Because of the interruption of his newspaper's publication, he did not print anything about the battle until May 3, but he still was the first printer to take full advantage of the propaganda possibilities of the battle and to use his account as a clarion call for independence. Above the nameplate on page one, each issue of the *Spy* carried the legend "Americans!—Liberty or Death!—Join or Die!" In the text below, parts of several paragraphs have been omitted for the sake of space, but Thomas' eloquent approach remains clear.

WORCESTER, MAY 3
(Isaiah Thomas; Massachusetts *Spy*; May 3, 1775)

AMERICANS! Forever bear in mind the BATTLE OF LEXINGTON!—where British troops, unmolested and unprovoked, wantonly and in a most inhuman manner, fired upon and killed a number of our countrymen, then robbed, ransacked, and burnt their houses! Nor could the tears of defenseless women, some of whom were in the pains of childbirth, the cries of helpless babes, nor the prayers of old age, confined to beds of sickness, appease their thirst for blood!—or divert them from their DESIGN OF MURDER and ROBBERY!

The particulars of this alarming event will, we are *credibly* informed, be soon published by authority, as a committee of the Provincial Congress have been appointed to make special inquiry and to take the depositions, on oath, of such as are knowing in the matter. In the meantime, to satisfy the expectation of our readers, we have collected from those whose veracity is unquestioned the following account, viz....

About ten o'clock on the night of the 18th of April, the troops in Boston were disclosed to be on the move in a very secret manner, and it was found they were embarking on boats (which they had privately brought to the place in the evening) at the bottom of the Common; expresses set off immediately to alarm the country, that they might be on their guard.... The body of the troops, in the meantime, under the command of Lieutenant Colonel Smith, had crossed the river and landed at Phipp's Farm. They immediately, to the number of 1,000, proceeded to Lexington, about six miles below Concord, with great silence.

A company of militia, of about eighty men, mustered near the meetinghouse; the troops came in sight of them just before sunrise. The militia, upon seeing the troops, began to disperse. The troops then set out upon the run, hallooing and huzzaing, and coming within a few rods of them the commanding officer accosted the militia, in words to this effect, "Disperse, you damn'd rebels!—Damn you, disperse!" Upon which the troops again huzzaed and immediately one or two officers discharged their pistols, which were instantaneously followed by the firing of four or five of the soldiers; and then there seemed to be a general discharge form the whole body.

It is to be noticed they fired on our people as they were dispersing, agreeable to their command, and that we did not even return the fire. Eight of our men were killed and nine wounded. The troops then laughed, and damned the yankees, and said they could not bear the smell of gunpowder.

A little after this the troops renewed their march to Concord, where, when they arrived, they divided into parties, and went directly to several places where the province stores were deposited. Each party was supposed to have a Tory pilot. One party went into the jailyard and spiked up and otherwise damaged two cannon, belonging to the province, and broke and set fire to the carriages. Then they entered a store and rolled out about a hundred barrels of flour, which they unheaded and emptied about forty into the river.

At the same time others were entering house and shops, and unheading barrels, chests, etc., the property of private persons. Some took possession of the town house, to which they set fire, but was extinguished by our people without much hurt. Another party of the troops went and took possession of the North Bridge.

About 150 provincials who mustered upon the alarm, coming toward the bridge, the troops went and fired upon them without ceremony and killed two on the spot! (Thus had the troops of Britain's king fired FIRST at two separate times upon his loyal American subjects, and put a period to two lives before one gun was fired upon them.) Our people THEN fired and obliged the troops to retreat, who were soon joined by their other parties, but finding they were still pursued the whole body retreated to Lexington, both provincials and troops firing as they went.

During this time an express from the troops was sent to General Gage, who thereupon sent out a reinforcement of about 1400 men, under the command of Earl Percy, with two fieldpieces. Upon the arrival of this reinforcement at Lexington, just as the retreating party had got there, they made a stand, picked up their dead, and took all the carriages they could find and put their wounded thereon. Others of them, to their eternal disgrace be it spoken, were robbing and setting houses on fire, and discharging their cannon at the meetinghouse....

Deacon Joseph Loring's house and barn, Mrs. Mulliken's house and shop, and Mr. Joshua Bond's house and shop, in Lexington, were all consumed. They also set fire to several other houses, but our people extinguished the flames. They pillaged almost every house they passed by, breaking and destroying doors, windows, glass, etc., and carrying off clothing and other valuable effects.

It appeared to be their design to burn and destroy all before them, and nothing but our vigorous pursuit prevented their infernal purposes from being put into execution. But the savage barbarity exercised upon the bodies of our unfortunate brethren who fell is almost incredible. Not content with shooting down the unarmed, aged, and infirm, they disregarded the cries of the wounded, killing them without mercy, and mangling their bodies in the most shocking manner.

We have the pleasure to say that notwithstanding the highest provocations given by the enemy, not one instance of cruelty that we have heard of was committed by our militia; but, listening to the merciful dictates of the Christian religion, they "breathed higher sentiments of humanity."

...[Here Thomas gives a list of Patriots killed and wounded.]...

The public most sincerely sympathize with the friends and relations of our deceased brethren, who sacrificed their lives in fighting for the liberties of their country. By their noble intrepid conduct, in helping to defeat the force of an ungrateful tyrant, they have endeared their memories to the present generation, who will transmit their names to posterity with the highest honor....

THE CONNECTICUT COURANT PUBLISHES THE FIRST EDITORIAL

What was the first editorial, in the modern sense of the term, ever to be published in an American newspaper? Although it is difficult to pinpoint such a landmark, an argument can be made for a column that appeared under the local "Hartford" head in the October 28, 1783, issue of the Connecticut Courant. It was in the Courant, one may recall, that practices associated today with the editorial form first combined. In the October 28 issue, editors George Goodwin and Barzalai Hudson printed for the first time a synopsis and comment on action taken by the state assembly and published the piece under the local column heading. The author was Noah Webster, the Courant's "official" contributor.

Previously, the paper had included only titles of laws. For their innovation of summarizing legislative action and commenting on it in the Hartford column, Goodwin and Hudson were widely criticized. In response, they argued forcefully for the right of the public to be informed about the conduct of their representatives.

At issue in the legislative debate was the question of "commutation": whether the United States Congress was to approve giving officers of the former Continental Army full pay for five years. When the lower house of Connecticut's General Assembly proposed remonstrating to Congress about the Act, the *Courant* challenged the house, arguing that a remonstrance could have no remedial effect.

Reprinted here is the *Courant's* column, one that represents perhaps the first use of an editorial, in the modern sense, by an American newspaper. The text as printed here omits a brief first paragraph about the arrival in America of an official delegation from Holland.

HARTFORD, OCTOBER 28
(Noah Webster; *Connecticut Courant*; October 28, 1783)

... By authentic accounts from New Haven, we learn, that his Excellency the Governor has resigned the Supreme executive authority of the State; and that the Honorable Oliver Wolcott, Samuel Huntington, Richard Law, and Oliver Ellsworth, Esquires, have resigned their places in Congress, which resignations are all accepted by the General Assembly.

Nothing of consequence has transpired this session, except an Address to Congress upon the Civil [... ?], in which the convulsions and embarrassments of the State, produced by commutation, will be mentioned. The Lower House urges a Remonstrance to Congress upon commutation, which is opposed in the Upper House; the Upper House urges an Impost to alleviate the public burthens, which is opposed in the Lower House.

A Correspondent begs leave to enquire, what salutary effect can be expected from Remonstrance to Congress upon commutation? The Assembly of Massachusetts remonstrated last spring upon the same subject, and received for an answer, that it was not in the power of Congress to make any alterations in their arrangements, or revoke a promise which had received the sanction of the United States, and that if the Legislature were unwilling to allow the officers the full value of the grant, the only measure they could take was to purchase their securities and give them state notes to a less amount, and to this Congress had no objection. If the Assembly of Connecticut should remonstrate, they must expect the same answer, which would leave them in their present situation. But when a people, so much enlightened as the inhabitants of this State, suffer themselves to be duped out of their senses by the foes of our independence and British emissaries, who are scattering the seeds of discord in the regions of tranquility, it seems the design of heaven to punish their blindness by some fatal catastrophe, and harden them, like Pharaoh of old, till they plunge themselves into an ocean of difficulties.

PHILIP FRENEAU WAGES THE CRUSADE THAT OPENED SENATE DOORS

The United States government initially was controlled by men who believed they should be shielded from the whims of the public. The nation's affairs, they argued, were best run by "the choice sort of men"—men of principles who would not, as one Federalist said, stoop to conduct "government by the passions of the multitude." The stronghold of this aristocratic faction was the Senate, which prided itself on its independence from the "common" people. Behind closed doors and away from prying eyes, Federalist senators declared, policies and questions critical to the future of the infant nation could best be decided.

Into this situation in 1791 stepped the ardent Anti-Federalist editor Philip Freneau—better known today as the "Poet of the Revolution" than as an editor—and out of his partisan crusade emerged the right of the people to know what the United States Senate was doing. As editor of the *National Gazette*, the official newspaper organ of the national Anti-Federalist leadership, Freneau served as the spokesman of Anti-Federalist views and provided the guide for partisan thinking and writing.

Among the Federalists' actions, perhaps none, Freneau thought, epitomized more clearly their disdain for democracy than conducting Senate business in secret. In 1792 he therefore began a crusade for opening the Senate's doors based on the theme that despots desire to keep their subjects in ignorance. Federalist reaction was derision, with Senators boasting that they would rather be right than popular. When in 1793 the Senate for a second time defeated a proposal to open its doors to the public, Freneau reported, "So it was AGAIN lost—and the PEOPLE are to remain ignorant of the proceedings of their Senators!" In the same issue of the *National Gazette* he wrote his most impassioned plea for open sessions. Entitled "To the Freemen of America," the editorial asked with scathing satire whether citizens of the United States should have any right to know what their officials were doing. That editorial is reprinted below.

Freneau kept up his crusade; and, with public pressure mounting, the Senate finally approved in February 1794 a measure to open its sessions. The ultimate achievement of the crusade was increased popular participation in the affairs of the government. Although Freneau's efforts were founded on partisan motives, his accomplishment should not be diminished. In his editorial campaign for opening Senate doors, he also opened the way to citizens playing a greater role in how their nation is run.

TO THE FREEMEN OF AMERICA
(Philip Freneau; *National Gazette*; February 13, 1793)

The Secrecy of the Senate of the United States in their legislative deliberations. A motion for opening the doors of the Senate chamber has again been lost by a considerable majority, in defiance of instruction—in defiance of every principle which gives security to freemen! What means this conduct? Which expression does it carry strongest with it, contempt for you, or tyranny? Are you freemen who ought to know the conduct of your legislators, or are you an inferior order of beings, incapable of comprehending the sublimity of senatorial functions, and unworthy to be trusted with their opinions? How are you to know the just from the unjust steward when they are covered with the mantle of concealment? Can there be any questions of legislative import, which freemen should not be acquainted with? What are you to expect when the stewards of your household refuse to give an account of their stewardship? Secrecy is necessary to design and a masque to treachery; honesty shrinks not from the public eye. The PEERS of America disdain to be seen by vulgar eyes; the music of their voices is harmony only for themselves, and must not vibrate in the ravished ears of an ungrateful and uncourtly multitude. Is there any congeniality, excepting in the administration, between the government of Great Britain, and the government of the United States? The Senate supposes there is, and usurps the *secret privileges* of the House of Lords—but whom do the lords represent? Not a free people, but a nobility; and whom does the Senate represent? Not a free people, not a nobility as yet, but *themselves.*—If they represent a free people they would hold themselves bound to listen to their opinions, and attend to their instructions; but as they are an *insulated body*, the *would be sovereign* of the United States, they disdain every other influence. Shall the master listen to the lispings of the servant? This would be changing the current of nature indeed, and converting *the right honorable Senators* into the mere representatives of a free people.—This surely is a character too insignificant for beings (I dare not call them men; it would lessen their quality) who move in a sphere above the lot even of regenerated humanity.—Remember, my fellow citizens, that you *still* are freemen; let it be impressed upon your minds that you depend not upon your representatives, but that *they* depend upon you; and let this truth be ever present to you, that secrecy in your representatives is a worm which will prey and fasten upon the vitals of your liberty.

MASTERS OF THE EDITORIAL

WILLIAM COBBETT:
MASTER OF POLITICAL ATTACK

The United States was a new nation in the 1700s, still struggling with growing pains. The Federalists and the Republicans, under the leadership of those two great thinkers Alexander Hamilton and Thomas Jefferson, fought for control of the new government. More often than not, they fought their battles with the pen. It was, after all, the age of the partisan press.

Into this situation stormed William Cobbett, an Englishman who fought for the memory of monarchial England and against the reality of revolution. Through numerous pamphlets and newspapers, including the highly successful *Political Register* and *Porcupine's Gazette*, he became the most effective journalist of his day. His stature rested on his outspoken personality, incisive analytical ability, and powerful writing style.

During an era of ardent partisanship, Cobbett possessed unarguable talent. One of England's greatest essayists, he also was one of history's most prolific journalists, writing scores of political pamphlets and countless books, and founding at least 14 periodicals. During the half-century when the party press dominated American journalism, he was without peer as a battling political commentator.

Born in England in, by most accounts, 1762, he experienced a simple upbringing with almost no formal education. His parents were countryfolk, and his childhood world revolved around family matters and rural happenings. In 1783, he joined a British infantry unit. It was during his term in the military that his courage to question authority first became evident. He accused a superior officer of a court-martial offense. When he realized, however, that he would not emerge from the case triumphant, he and his wife fled to France. The revolutionary situation in France, however, did not provide the solace they desired, and in 1792 they sailed to America.

In this country, Cobbett became, as one historian has put it, "a passionate defender of the Old Order." He battled for the old, monarchial way of life and against the violence of change. Dismayed by the confusion revolution had created in France, he feared that the American dispute between the Federalists and the Republicans would erupt into chaos and perhaps into civil war.

Already known as an eloquent speaker in defense of his beliefs, Cobbett, soon after his emigration to America, turned to the printed word as his avenue of expression. He began to author political pamphlets, a popular medium of the day. His first,

"Observations on the Emigration of Dr. Joseph Priestley" (1794), reached a wide audience and thrust him into the public eye. It had three reprints and was also published in England. Several pamphlets followed, including "A Prospect from the Congress Gallery," to which he was assigned in 1795 by a Philadelphia publisher. After a dispute with his employer, Cobbett quit and started his own monthly publication, *Political Censor*. It became the daily *Porcupine's Gazette* in 1797.

During his career, Cobbett published a huge number of periodicals. Along with the *Censor* and the *Gazette*, his most successful was Philadelphia's *Daily Advertiser*. In addition to 14 successful newspapers and hundreds of political commentaries, he began more than a few dailies and weeklies that never got off the ground or were short-lived. He also published a wide array of books, on every topic from the French language, to farming, to family life, to religious history. At his death, a contemporary credited Cobbett with being "by far the most voluminous writer that has lived for centuries."

Cobbett's writing success lay in several fundamental characteristics of style. As "Peter Porcupine" (his successful alter ego), he wrote in a manner that scorched his enemies and that endeared him to his faithful readers. He was known as a conscientious, emotional writer. His unswerving system of beliefs fueled the passion that is so evident in his editorials. When he felt strongly, he wrote with a fervor rarely matched by other editors. He produced large and lengthy amounts of material in a short amount of time. Often his first draft was his final one.

Although the haste and fervor with which he wrote probably accounts for the crudity of some of his pieces, Cobbett was also an eloquent writer. To today's reader, early writing may appear lofty and intellectual because of the use of lengthier sentences and erudite vocabularies. At the same time that Cobbett's writing bore those characteristics, his style separated him from his contemporaries. He was a master wordsmith. The individual words he chose were ideal for their purpose.

While sometimes eloquent and even ceremonious, he also wrote with humor and wit. He was an expert with plays on words and with melodramatic techniques. His nickname itself was an act of melodrama. Originally, it was a derogatory term given to him by opponents. He adopted it with pride. He also used such techniques as simile and metaphor, repetition, and historical and literary allusions.

His most effective techniques, however, were sarcasm and caricature. During a period when much editorial writing was loaded down with heavy-handed insult, Cobbett wielded ridicule as a sharp rapier. In the editorial "A Toad-Eater," for example, he painted editors as the humorous, animal-like caricature in the title. In newspapers, he argued, rogues of all types could find a means for communicating their messages. He wrote: "For a subscription, or the insertion of an advertisement, he finds mouths of all sizes, and gullets of all dimensions, distended to receive his *toad*, with as much joy and gratitude as the young ones of the crow receive the carrion from her bill."

Cobbett's editorializing often got him into trouble with opponents. Within a short time after beginning his American career, he became the Republicans' biggest target. His most famous confrontation was with Dr. Benjamin Rush, a Philadelphia physician. Rush used the popular practice of bleeding his patients and purging them with mercury to help "rid" them of the yellow fever. Cobbett disagreed with the practice and never disguised his disgust for Rush. "[I]n that emphatical style which is peculiar to himself," Cobbett wrote, Dr. Rush "calls mercury the 'Samson of medicine.' In his hands, and in those of his partisans, it may, indeed, be justly compared to Samson: for I verily believe they have slain more Americans with it than ever Samson slew of the Philistines. The Israelite slew his thousands, but the Rushites have slain their tens of thousands." Rush sued for libel in 1797. Cobbett lost in a trial tinged with partisanship and was fined $5,000. Even more disillusioned by the American political system, he fled to New York and then to England.

Reflecting on his American career, in 1800 he wrote an open letter to his readers. It provides his definition of a newspaper's purpose and illustrates his undying belief in the rightness of his cause. "I must congratulate myself," he declared, "on having established a paper, carried it to a circulation unparalleled in extent, and preserved this circulation to the last number, without the aid of any of those base and parasitical arts by which patronage to American newspapers is generally obtained and preserved;—I congratulate myself on having, in the progress of this paper, uniformly supported, with all my feeble powers, the cause of true religion, sound morality, good government, and real liberty; I congratulate myself on having... persisted in openly and unequivocally avowing my attachment to my native country and my allegiance to my king.... "

Cobbett's home country was, however, no refuge. He was soon disillusioned with its system also and began catering his publications to the working class. Officials continuously attacked his writing, and in 1817 he fled once again to America. He became dissatisfied once again and returned to England, for the final time, in 1819. His editorial voice continued to be one of the strongest in the nation. In 1835, however, he suffered a fatal heart attack while delivering a fiery message in Parliament.

•The editorial "Medical Puffing" is one of the pieces of writing for which Dr. Rush sued Cobbett for libel. It demonstrates Cobbett's ability to use wit and satire as part of his arsenal of attack.

MEDICAL PUFFING
(*Porcupine's Gazette*; September 1796)

"The times are ominous indeed,
"When quack to quack cries, *Purge* and *bleed.*"

Those who are in the habit of looking over the Gazettes which come in from the different parts of the country must have observed, and with no small degree of indignation, the arts which our remorseless *bleeder* is making use of to puff off his preposterous practice. He has, unfortunately, his partisans in every quarter of the country. To these he writes letters, and in return gets letters from them: he extols their practice, and they extol his; and there is scarcely a page of any newspaper that I see which has the good fortune to escape the poison of their prescriptions. Blood, blood! still they cry, More blood! In every sentence they menace our poor veins. Their language is as frightful to the ears of the alarmed multitude as is the raven's croak to those of the sickly flock.

Among all these puffs I do not recollect a more shameless one than the following from *Dr. Tilton*:

Extract of a letter from Dr. Tilton, of Wilmington, to Dr. Rush, dated September 12.—"We have had repeated instances of *your fever* at this place. The infection has generally been taken in Philadelphia. I am not acquainted with any instances where the contagion has been received at Wilmington; but at Newcastle and Newport there are unequivocal examples of the contagion being received from those who brought it from the city.

"In the treatment of the fever we use *copious* blood-letting in the beginning, and active *mercurial purges.* I have conceived, however, that mercury is useful not merely as a cathartic, but as a *specific against all kinds of contagion.* There is no contagious disease in which its use is not acknowledged; not only small-pox, measles, dysentery, &c., but scarlatina and influenza yield to its specific virtues. You probably remember, as well as I, that it was given with advantage in the hospital and camp fever. In short, I have established it as a maxim to give mercury as soon as I know a disease to be contagious."

The mercurial purges, too, Dr. Tilton must break forth in praise of! Mercury is good for everything that is contagious! Is it good for sansculottism, Doctor? If it be, in the name of goodness, take a double dose of it twice a day, till it has wrought a cure.—Dr. Rush, in that emphatical style which is peculiar to himself, calls *mercury* the "*Samson* of medicine." In his hands, and in those of his partisans, it may, indeed, be justly compared to *Samson*; for I verily believe they have slain more Americans with it than ever Samson slew of the Philistines. The Israelite slew his thousands, but the Rushites have slain their tens of thousands.

•Being the Federalists' most prominent writer made Cobbett the target of numerous attacks. He could not, he explained, respond to *all* the attacks, choosing instead to note several of them in the following single editorial.

REMARKS ON THE PAMPHLETS
(*Political Censor*, September 1796)

"Dear Father,—when you used to set me off to work in the morning, dressed in my blue smock-frock and woollen spatterdashes, with my bag of bread and cheese and bottle of small-beer swung over my shoulder on the little crook that my old godfather Boxal gave me, little did you imagine that I should one day become so great a man as to have my picture stuck in the windows, and have four whole books published about me in the course of one week."—Thus begins a letter which I wrote to my father yesterday morning, and which, if it reaches him, will make the old man drink an extraordinary pot of ale to my health. Heaven bless him! I think I see him now, by his old-fashioned fire-side, reading the letter to his neighbours. "Ay, ay," says he, "*Will* will stand his ground wherever he goes."—And so I will, father, in spite of all the hell of democracy.

When I had the honour to serve King George, I was elated enough at the putting on of my worsted shoulder-knot, and, afterwards, my silverlaced coat; what must my feelings be then, upon seeing half-a-dozen authors, all *Doctors* or the devil knows what, writing about me at one time, and ten times that number of printers, bookbinders, and booksellers, bustling, running, and flying about in all directions, to announce my fame to the impatient public? What must I feel upon seeing the newspapers filled from top to bottom, and the windows and corners of the houses placarded, with, a *Blue Shop for Peter Porcupine*, a *Pill for Peter Porcupine*, *Peter Porcupine detected*, a *Roaster for Peter Porcupine*, a *History of Peter Porcupine*, a *Picture of Peter Porcupine?* The public will certainly excuse me, if after all this, I should begin to think myself a person of some importance.

It is true, my heroic adversaries do all set out with telling their readers, that I am a contemptible wretch *not worth notice*. They should have said, not worth the notice *of any honest man*, and, as they would all naturally have excluded themselves by such an addition, they would have preserved consistency at least: but, to sit down hammering their brains for a fortnight or three weeks, and at last publish each of them a pamphlet about me and my performances, and then tell the public that *I am not worth notice*, is such a gross insult to common sense that nothing but democratic stupidity can be a sufficient excuse for it.

At the very moment that I am writing, these sorry fellows are hugging themselves in the thought that they have silenced me, *cut me up*, as they call it. It would require other pens than theirs to silence me. I shall keep plodding on in my old way, as I used to do at plough; and I think it will not be looked upon as any very extraordinary trait of vanity to say, that the *Political Censor* will be read, when the very names of their bungling pamphlets will be forgotten.

I must now beg the reader to accompany me in some few remarks that I think it necessary to make on each of their productions, following the order in which they appeared.

"A Roaster For Peter Porcupine."

What can I say worse of this blustering performance, than that it bears all the internal evidence of being written by the blunderbuss author who disgusted the city with *Rub from Snub*?

"The Blue Shop; or *Humorous* Observations, &c."

The inoffensive and unmeaning title of this pamphlet is fully expressive of the matter it is prefixed to, excepting that the word *humorous* was, perhaps, never before so unfortunately applied. Every one who has been taken in with this quarter-dollar's worth, whether a friend or an enemy of Peter Porcupine, curses it for the most senseless and vapid piece of stuff that ever issued from the press. The author, I hear, retorts, and swears the Americans are a set of stupid jackasses, who know not what true humour is. 'Tis pity he had not perceived this before, he might then have accommodated his *humour* to their understandings. It is now too late to rail against their ignorance or want of taste, for, in spite of his railing and fretting, *James Quicksilver* will, by them, ever be looked upon as a most leaden-headed fellow.

"Porcupine, A Print."

This is a caricature, in which I am represented as urged on to write by my old master King George (under the form of a crowned lion), who, of course, comes accompanied with the devil. The *Jay*, with the treaty in his back, is mounted on the lion's back, though, by-the-by, it has ever been said, by the democrats, that the lion rode the *Jay*. His Satanic Majesty holds me out a bag of money, as an encouragement to destroy the idol, Liberty, to which he points. The American Eagle is represented as drooping his wings in consequence of my hostility, and America herself, on the same account, weeps over the bust of Franklin. This is almost the only part of the print of which I find fault; for, if by America the people of America be to be understood, I believe most of those who have read my essays will do me the justice to say, that I have endeavoured to make America laugh instead of weep.

Perhaps I ought to take some notice of the quarter whence this *caricature* and the *Blue Shop* issued, as it furnishes an instance, among thousands, of that degradation which the first movers in the French revolution have long been, and still are exhibiting to the world. These poor miserable catch-penny pictures and pamphlets are published by a man of the name of *Moreau*, who was one of those whom Tom Paine and his comrades Price and Priestley called, "the great illuminated and illuminating National Assembly of France."—Goddess of Liberty! and dost thou permit this thy "great illuminated and illuminating" knocker-down of Bastiles to wage a puny *underhand* war with one of King George's red-coats? Dost thou permit one of those aspiring "legislators of the universe!" who commanded the folding doors of the *Louvre* to fly open at their approach, and who scorned to yield the precedence to Princes and Emperors, to dwindle down into a miserable *marchand d'estampes*? If these be thy tricks, Goddess of French Liberty, may the devil take Peter if ever thy bloody cap and pike entice him to enlist under thy banners.

Mr. Moreau, to his other misfortunes, adds that most calamitous one of thinking he can write. He is cursed with the scribbling itch, without knowing how to scratch himself with a good grace. As this is torment enough in itself, I do not wish to add to it by mentioning particular instances of his want of taste and talents. The greatest punishment I wish my enemies, is, that *Moreau* may be obliged to write all his lifetime, and that the rest may be obliged to read his productions....

•The following editorial epitomizes one of Cobbett's favorite weapons, wit dripping with sarcasm. Cobbett frequently used the technique of coining words or using words in a unique way to describe opponents. He wrote this editorial to explain why he used the word "blunderbuss" in reference to "Citizen" Adet, the French foreign minister to the United States who worked secretly in league with some Republicans to defeat the Jay Treaty.

REMARKS ON THE BLUNDERBUSS
(*Political Censor*, November 1796)

When we see an unprincipled, shameless bully, "A dog in forehead, and in heart a deer," who endeavours, by means of a big look, a threatening aspect, and a thundering voice, to terrify peaceable men into a compliance with what he has neither a right to demand, nor power nor courage to enforce, and who, at the same time, acts in such a bungling, stupid manner, as to excite ridicule and contempt in place of fear; when we see such a gasconading, impudent bluff as this (and that we do every day), we call him a *Blunderbuss*. But, the reader will not, I hope, have conceived me so devoid of all decency and prudence, as to imagine, even for a moment, that it is in this degrading sense that the name of *Blunderbuss* has been given to the invaluable collection which I here present to the public. Indeed, it is so evident that I could mean no such thing, that this declaration seems hardly necessary; but, as my poor old grandmother used to say, "A burnt child dreads the fire," and after the unrelenting severities of misconception and misconstruction, that a humane and commiserating public have so often seen me endure, they will think it very natural for me to fear, that what I really intended as a compliment, would, if left unexplained, be tortured into insult and abuse, if not into the horrid crime of leze-republicanism, at the very idea of which my hair stands on end, and my heart dies within me.

"But," cry the democrats, "in what sense, then, do you apply the word *Blunderbuss*? Come, come, Mr. Peter, none of your shuffling."—Silence, you yelping devils; go, growl in your dark kennel; slink into your straw, and leave me to my reader: I'll warrant I explain myself to his satisfaction.

Writings of a hostile nature are often metaphorically expressed, in proportion to the noise they make, by different instruments that act by explosion. Thus it is, for instance, that an impotent lampoon is called a *Popgun*; and that a biting paragraph or epigram, confined to a small circle, is termed a *squib*; and thus it is, that, rising in due progression, the collection of Citizen Adet's Notes and Cockade Proclamation is denominated a *Blunderbuss*, a species of fire-arms that exceeds all others, manageable by a single hand, in the noise of its discharge.

If we pursue the metaphor, we shall find the application still more strikingly happy. The *first Note* is a kind of preparative for the *Cockade Proclamation*, and this latter adjusts matters for the *grand explosion*; or, in the military style,—

Make Ready!
Present!
Fire!

To be sure we are not dead, but this circumstance, instead of mutilating my metaphor, renders it complete; for of all the long list of fire-arms, none is so difficult to adjust, or makes so much noise and smoke, with so little execution, as a *Blunderbuss*....

•Benjamin Franklin Bache, the Republican editor of Philadelphia's *Aurora*, was one of Cobbett's harshest antagonists. The following editorial profile of Bache shows Cobbett's virulent lampooning in its most cutting form.

THE MARKET STREET SCOUNDREL
(*Porcupine's Gazette*; November 16, 1797)

[The Market Street Scoundrel] Has, as usual, published a heathenish republican Calendar for the year 1788. At the head of one of the months he has placed the following:

"*Reign of blood before the Revolution.*

"In 1788, Louis XVI had *eight thousand persons murdered*, of both sexes and all ages, at Paris, in the Street Melet and the Pont

Neas."

Now, who ever heard of this before? Who ever heard of a massacre at Paris, while poor Louis retained his power as king? Never in his life did he authorize the shedding of a drop of human blood. Every one of any information knows that, had it not been for his unconquerable [?] aversion to shedding the blood of his radical subjects, he would this day have been alive, and king of France. And yet, the impudent scoundrel *Franklin* dares not only to accuse him of murder, but to name the number of his victims on a particular occasion, and the spot where they fell, without having even hearsay for a foundation to his charge.

This atrocious wretch (worthy descendant of *old Ben*) knows that all men of any understanding set him down as an abandoned liar, as a tool and a hireling, and he is content that they should do so. He does not want to be thought any thing else. He knows very well, that the story about the *eight thousand murdered people* will be believed by nobody, except by those ignorant creatures, who can scarcely comprehend what they read; but these are the very creatures the information is intended for. These are they whom his supporters [?] want to secure on their side.

As this *Gazette* is honored with many readers in foreign countries, it may not be improper to give them some little account of this miscreant.

If they have read the old hypocrite Franklin's will, they must have observed that part of his library, with some other things, are left to a certain *grandson*; this is the very identicle Market-Street scoundrel.—He spent several years in hunting offices under the Federal Government, and being constantly rejected, he at last became its most bitter foe. Hence his abuse of General Washington, whom, at the time he was soliciting a place, he panegyrized up to the third heaven.

He was born for a hireling, and therefore when he found that he could not obtain employ in one quarter, he sought it in another. The first effect of his paw being greased, appeared soon after Genet's arrival, and he has from that time to this been as faithful to the cut-throats of Paris, as ever dog was to his master.

He is an ill-looking devil. His eyes never get above your knees. He is of a sallow complexion, hollow-cheeked, dead-eyed, and has a *toute ensemble*, just like that of a fellow who has been about a week or ten days in a gibbet.

WILLIAM DUANE EXPOSES
THE 1800 ELECTION SCHEME

In the critical presidential election of 1800, the Republican editor William Duane published an editorial that not only helped save the victory for Thomas Jefferson, but also brought on the first attempt by the United States Senate to punish an individual for a breach of that body's privileges. From 1798 to 1822, when Duane edited the Philadelphia *Aurora*, he was the most important party newspaper editor in the nation, and he thus became the target of a variety of Federalist attacks.

Recognizing the 1800 election as a pivotal one in deciding the future of the American political system, Federalist senators, who made up a majority of their chamber's membership, devised a plan to give the election to John Adams in the face of the public will. In January of 1800, Sen. James Ross introduced a bill to establish a committee of 13 members—seven senators, seven representatives, and the chief justice of the United States—to count the electoral votes and announce the winner. Since both the Senate and House had Federalist majorities and all Supreme Court justices were Federalists, the committee would have been nothing more than an arm of the Federalist party. The bill provided that the committee was to meet in secret, decide which electoral votes to accept and which ones to throw out, determine who the new president was, and then announce its decision. The bill prohibited an appeal of the committee's decision.

Duane somehow managed to get a copy of the bill and the procedure by which it had been devised. He printed the entire text in the *Aurora* along with a scathing editorial attack. Republicans across the country were outraged.

Federalist senators were outraged also—but at Duane. They declared his editorial and publication of the bill "a daring and high-handed breach of the privileges" of the Senate and commanded him to appear before the Senate to answer for his conduct and be sentenced. Following his refusal to do so, the Senate declared him in contempt and issued a warrant for his arrest. Even though annoyed Federalists collected $300 which they paid 23 constables to capture the "obstinate democrat," Duane remained at large. When President Adams moved to have him prosecuted under the Sedition Act, Republicans claimed that the entire episode was part of a Federalist plot to destroy the Republicans' leading newspaper before the 1800 election.

The Ross election bill itself, however, after passing the Senate, was defeated in the House, in part because of the public protest raised by Duane. In the contest of paramount importance, the 1800 election, Jefferson won with 73 electoral votes to Adams' 65.

Following is Duane's editorial condemning the Ross bill.

[UNTITLED]
(William Duane; Philadelphia *Aurora*; February 19, 1800)

In our piece of the 27th ult. we noticed the introduction of a measure into the Senate of the United States, by Mr. Ross calculated to *influence* and *affect* the approaching presidential election, and to frustrate in a particular manner the wishes and interests of the people of the *Commonwealth of Pennsylvania.*

We this day lay before the public a copy of that bill as it has passed the Senate.

Some curious facts are connected with this measure, and the people of the Union at large are intermediately and the people of this state immediately interested to consider the *movement*, the *mode* of operation, and the *effects*.

We noticed a few days ago the Caucuses (or secret consultations) held in the Senate Chamber—An attempt was made in an evening paper to give a counter-action (for these people are admirable at the system of intrigue) to the developments of the Aurora, and to call those meetings *jacobinical*; we must cordially assent to the *Jacobinism* of those meetings—they were in the perfect spirit of a *jacobinical* conclave.

The plain facts we stated are, however, unquestionable; but we have additional information to give on the subject of those meetings. We stated that intrigues for the presidential election were among the objects. We now state it as a fact that cannot be disputed upon fair ground that the Bill we this day present was discussed at the *Caucus on Wednesday* evening last.

It is worthy to remark how this Bill grew into existence.

The opponents of independence and republican government, who supported *Mr. Ross* in the contest against governor *McKean* [of Pennsylvania], are well known by the *indecencies*, the *slander*, and the *falsehood* of the measures they pursued—and it is well known that they are all devoted to the *federal party* which we *dissected* on Monday. *Mr. Ross* proposed this in the federal senate (how confidently with the decency of his friends will be seen), a committee of five was appointed to prepare a bill on the subject, on this committee Mr. *Pinckney* of South Carolina was appointed,—on Thursday morning last (the *Caucus* held the preceding evening) Mr. Ross informed Mr. *Pinckney* that the committee had drawn up a bill on the subject, when in fact Mr. Pinckney had never been consulted on the subject, though a member of the committee! The bill was introduced and passed as below.

On this occasion it may not be impertinent to introduce an *anecdote* which will illustrate the nature of *Caucuses* and show that our popular government may in the hands of a faction be as completely abused as the French constitution has been by the self-created consuls.

In the summer session of 1798, when federal *thunder* and *violence* were belched from the pestiferous lungs of more than one despotic minion, a *caucus* was held at the house of Mr. *Bingham,* in this city. It was composed of members of the senate, and there were present *seventeen members.* The senate consisting of 32 members, this number was of course a majority and the session was a full one.

Prior to deliberation on the measures of *war, navy, army,* democratic prescription, &c. &c., it was proposed and agreed to that all the members present should solemnly pledge themselves to act firmly upon the measures to be agreed upon by the majority of the persons present at the *Caucus*.

The measures were perfectly in the *high tone* of that extraordinary session. But upon a division of the *Caucus* it was found that they were divided *nine* against *eight*. This majority, however, held the minority to their engagement, and the whole seventeen voted in Senate upon all the measures discussed at the *Caucus*.

Thus it is seen that a *secret self-appointed* meeting of 17 persons dictated laws to the United States, and not only that *Nine* of that seventeen had the full command and power over the consciences and votes of the other *eight*, but that nine possessed by the turpitude of the eight actually all the power which the constitution declares shall be invested in the majority only.

In other words, a minority of *nine members* of the Senate ruled the other *twenty three members*.

It is easily conceivable, as in the recent changes in France, that this spirit of *caucusing* may be conducted in progression down to two or three persons; thus *three* leading characters may agree to act upon measures approved by any two of them—these three may add two others, and they would be a majority of *five*; and those adding four others would be a majority of nine; and these nine posses all the power of a majority of 23!!!

Yet such is the way we are treated—by those who call themselves federalists.

The following Bill is an offspring of this spirit of faction secretly working; and it will be found to be in perfect accord with the outrageous proceedings of the same party in our state legislature, who are bent on depriving this state of its share in an election that may involve the fate of the country and posterity....
[Text of bill follows.]

WILLIAM LLOYD GARRISON ROUSES THE NATION AGAINST SLAVERY

William Lloyd Garrison was born into a poor family whose father, a heavy drinker, abandoned the family when his son was three years old. The son received little formal education but eventually became one of the central figures in the anti-slavery movement. His uncompromising stand and strident editorials pricked the conscience of many people and aroused the anger of others.

On January 1, 1831, he and another young printer launched *The Liberator*. In its small one-room office, they slept on mattresses in a corner in order to conserve their meager funds. The paper was printed in the beginning with borrowed type. Despite these circumstances, Garrison's salutary editorial was one of history's stirring social protests.

Because of its severity, trenchant language, and forthrightness, the editorial shocked many people. This type of writing, which Garrison was to employ throughout his career, was one reason *The Liberator* never gained a large circulation. Yet the editorial became one of the nation's most famous and widely quoted pieces of abolitionist literature.

It presented Americans with two new concepts about slavery: immediate emancipation and "impassioned intolerance." Before 1831, many Northerners and Southerners had agreed that slavery eventually would be abolished. Freeing the slaves, the logic went, would be a natural result as they were needed less and less in the South's economic system. But Americans saw no great urgency to free them. Even members of the anti-slavery movement were content to wait for time to take its course. Garrison presented a direct challenge to this attitude.

His language also provoked Americans. Critics accused him of using unnecessarily virulent language and thereby encouraging violence. Garrison, although an advocate of nonviolence, replied, "My language is exactly such as suits me; it will displease many, I know—to displease them is my intention." When a friend suggested that Garrison moderate his language because he was "all on fire," Garrison answered, "I have need to be all on fire, for I have mountains of ice about me to melt."

The response to Garrison naturally was fervent. His writing raised Southern hostility to the anti-slavery movement, and Southerners became defensive about slavery, while Northerners found they could no longer remain neutral on the issue. When in 1837 the abolitionist James G. Birney was praised for his moderation, he replied that only Garrison's "rude and ruffian-like shake" had been able to rouse the nation from its sleep. With the country awakened, compromise became more difficult. War eventually broke out. Part of the cause was Garrison, whose first *Liberator* editorial had helped start the chain reaction that led to the Civil War and the end of slavery.

TO THE PUBLIC
(William Lloyd Garrison; *The Liberator*; January 1, 1831)

In the month of August, I issued proposals for publishing *The Liberator* in Washington City; but the enterprise, though hailed in different sections of the country, was palsied by public indifference. Since that time, the removal of *The Genius of Universal Emancipation* to the Seat of Government has rendered less imperious the establishment of a similar periodical in that quarter.

During my recent tour for the purpose of exciting the minds of the people by a series of discourses on the subject of slavery, every place that I visited gave fresh evidence of the fact, that a greater revolution in public sentiment was to be effected in the free States—and particularly in New-England—than at the South. I found contempt more bitter, opposition more active, detraction more relentless, prejudice more stubborn, and apathy more frozen, than among slave-owners themselves. Of course, there were individual exceptions to the contrary. This state of things afflicted, but did not dishearten me. I determined, at every hazard, to lift up the standard of emancipation in the eyes of the nation, within sight of Bunker Hill and in the birthplace of liberty. That standard is now unfurled; and long may it float, unhurt by the spoilations of time or the missiles of a desperate foe—yea, till every chain be broken, and every bondman set free! Let Southern oppressors tremble—let their secret abettors tremble—let their Northern apologists tremble—let all the enemies of the persecuted blacks tremble.

I deem the publication of my original Prospectus unnecessary, as it has obtained a wide circulation. The principles therein inculcated will be steadily pursued in this paper, excepting that I shall not array myself as the political partisan of any man. In defending the great cause of human rights, I wish to derive the assistance of all religions and of all parties.

Assenting to the "self-evident truth" maintained in the American Declaration of Independence, "that all men are created equal, and endowed by their Creator with certain inalienable rights—among which are life, liberty and the pursuit of happiness," I shall strenuously contend for the immediate enfranchisement of our slave population. In Park-Street Church, on the Fourth of July, 1829, in an address on slavery, I unreflectingly assented to the popular but pernicious doctrine of *gradual* abolition. I seize this opportunity to make a full and unequivocal recantation, and thus publicly to ask pardon of my God, of my country, and of my brethren the poor slaves, for having uttered a sentiment so full of timidity, injustice, and absurdity. A similar recantation, from my pen, was published in *The Genius of Universal Emancipation* at Baltimore, in September, 1829. My conscience is now satisfied.

I am aware that many object to the severity of my language; but is there not cause for severity? I *will be* as harsh as truth, and as uncompromising as justice. On this subject, I do not wish to think, or speak, or write, with moderation. No! no! Tell a man whose house is on fire to give a moderate alarm; tell him to moderately rescue his wife from the hands of the ravisher; tell the mother to gradually extricate her babe from the fire into which it has fallen;—but urge me not to use moderation in a cause like the present. I am in earnest—I will not equivocate—I will not excuse—I will not retreat a single inch—AND I WILL BE HEARD. The apathy of the people is enough to make every statue leap from its pedestal, and to hasten the resurrection of the dead.

It is pretended, that I am retarding the cause of emancipation by the coarseness of my invective and the precipitancy of my measures. The charge is not true. On this question my influence,—humble as it is,—is felt at this moment to a considerable extent, and shall be felt in coming years—not perniciously, but beneficially—not as a curse, but as a blessing; and posterity will bear testimony that I was right. I desire to thank God, that he enables me to disregard "the fear of man which bringeth a snare," and to speak his truth in its simplicity and power, and here I close with this fresh dedication.

> "Oppression! I have seen thee, face to face,
> And met thy cruel eye and cloudy brow;
> But thy soul-withering glance I fear not now—
> For dread to prouder feelings doth give place
> Of deep abhorrence! Scorning the disgrace
> Of slavish knees that at thy footstool bow,
> I also kneel—but with far other vow
> Do hail thee and thy herd of hirelings base:—
> I swear, while life-blood warms my throbbing veins,
> Still to oppose and thwart, with heart and hand,
> Thy brutalizing sway—till Africa's chains
> Are burst, and Freedom rules the rescued land,—
> Trampling Oppression and his iron rod:
> *Such is the vow I take*—SO HELP ME GOD!"

The Popular Era, 1833-1900

During the period of the penny press, the editorial came to full flower. The revolution was not, however, effected instantaneously with the appearance of the first penny papers in the 1830s. It was not until 1853, when S. S. Cox published "A Great Old Sunset" in the Ohio *Statesman*, that editorials began their liberation from domination by political subjects. That editorial was reprinted nationwide, and its author thereafter was referred to as "Sunset" Cox. The sudden popularity of human interest subjects did not, however, mean that political editorials suddenly vanished. Even today they are the staple of editorial pages; but after the 1850s, editorials on non-political subjects appeared more and more frequently.

The years from the advent of the penny press in 1833 until the Civil War often have been referred to as the "Golden Age" of editorial writing. During these years the editorial gained a generally recognized importance. Emphasis on news gave papers a financial freedom they had not experienced during the partisan era. Political independence grew. Yet editors, gaining their political freedom, did not become slaves of the newspaper dollar. Although many made their living at journalism, they did not view their papers simply as a business. Tied to neither political control nor the profit motive, editorial writers enjoyed full freedom to express themselves. As a result, the prestige of the editorial writer grew.

Conditions were ideal for editorial writing. Many editors were intricately involved in public affairs, but not under the direction of politicians or parties. Although the function of newspapers as journals of news had increased in importance, editors still considered the editorial to be the heart of the newspaper. Since most editors owned their own newspapers, the leading ones spent only a small proportion of their time dealing with business affairs. Consequently, they exercised complete editorial control without deference to employers, and they focused their attention and energy on their newspaper's editorial operations. Under these conditions, the public thought of the editorial not simply as the policy statement of a newspaper institution, but as the voice of its editor. In the hands of the great personal editors of the age, Leon Flint, an early textbook writer, remarked, the editorial "enjoyed a kind of conspicuity and prestige it is likely never again to attain. This was not solely because of the special genius of the great editor as writer or thinker, but also, and perhaps chiefly, because of the nature of his office and its place in the social and political life of the period. But there is also to be taken into account the fact that under the simple conditions of the old-time newspaper its editor was able to write almost always in the line of his own personal convictions, with all the tonic sense of his own direct accountability, and with full freedom to wreak his personality upon his literary form in all its whims, its inconsistencies, even its extravagances. This gave his work its gusto, its reality, its human appeal." (*The Editorial*, 1931).

The legend of editorial writing of this "Golden Age" is in large part the shadow of one man, Horace Greeley. As editor of the New York *Tribune* from 1841 to 1872, Greeley consistently fought for the causes he felt would aid mankind. He became one of the most influential figures of his age and, many historians believe, the most influential journalist ever. He was one of the leading proponents of many of the most important movements in American society in the mid-1800s, and it was said that thousands of readers would wait to decide where they stood on issues until they heard what "Uncle Horace" had to say. Of him and the *Tribune* the historian Allan Nevins wrote:

"To Horace Greeley's great newspaper we may unhesitatingly ascribe the development of the editorial page in its modern American character: that is, a page treating a wide variety of topics in a variety of manners, though pursuing a consistent policy; achieving a level of genuine literary merit; produced by a body of editors, not by a single man, and representing their united judgment and information; and earnestly directed to the elevation and rectification of public opinion.

"The New York *Tribune* for a whole generation, the fateful generation in which the struggle against slavery rose to a climax, stood preeminent among the organs of opinion in the United States; it was one of the great leaders of the nation." (*American Press Opinion*, 1928).

If Greeley could be criticized, it would be for his naïveté and eccentricity on some causes and for his passion. Such was not true of Henry Raymond. Founder of the New York *Times* in 1851 and its editor until 1869, Raymond was Greeley's temperamental opposite. In the *Times'* opening statement, Raymond wrote that he did not intend to "write as if we were in a passion, unless that shall really be the case; and we shall make it a point to get in a passion as rarely as possible." Raymond lived up to his promise. His editorials were temperate, objective, rational, cautious. Partially because of his moderation, Raymond exercised less power than Greeley and contemporaries such as William Cullen Bryant and Samuel Bowles II and his son. His writing had neither the force of Greeley's nor the stylistic appeal of Bryant's, but it was he who set the tone for the rational, dispassionate, impersonal editorial style of today.

With the departure of several of the great names—such as Greeley, Raymond, Bryant, and the senior James Gordon Bennett—around 1872, many observers noted the passing of the "Golden Age" of journalism. The dirges, however, were premature. Under such editors as Charles Dana, E. L. Godkin, and Joseph Pulitzer, American editorial pages by 1900 were to achieve a freshness, a depth, and a practical influence greater than ever.

Dana, editor of the New York *Sun* from 1868 to 1897, brought to editorial writing a liveliness, a freshness, and a sparkle it had never exhibited. Human-interest, brief literary essays, humor, and biting phrases became the hallmark of the *Sun's* editorial page. A cynic, however, Dana encouraged levity and perversity on the page also. As a result, editorially he was never as effective as he might have been otherwise. Still, he created a model of pungency, lightness, and wit in editorial writing, and the *Sun's* casual editorial essays remain the best examples of sensitivity to fundamental human concerns combined with sophisticated tongue-in-cheek humor.

Dana's chief rival for editorial fame was E. L. Godkin, editor of the *Nation* from 1865 to 1899 and of the New York *Evening Post* from 1883 to 1899. He was the foremost leader of public opinion in his day. The philosopher William James wrote of him: "To my generation, his was certainly the towering influence in all thought concerning public affairs, and indirectly his influence has assuredly been more pervasive than that of any other writer of the generation, for he influenced other writers who never quoted him, and determined the whole current of discussion." Godkin's readership was not large, as the circulation of the *Nation* and the *Evening Post* never exceeded 35,000; but it was composed of the leaders of public opinion—teachers, ministers, and judges, for example—and his ideas were disseminated through them.

Two factors accounted for Godkin's influence: his intellect and his writing style. Possessing an analytical and critical mind, he was concerned with the underlying principles of issues rather than their superficial surfaces. He thus offered penetrating insight into public questions. As for his writing, it exhibited versatility of style, lightness of touch, and pungency. Witty and ironic, it also could be devastatingly cold and cutting. Of Godkin's style, the editor Oswald Garrison Villard observed: "His English was clear and straightforward, wonderfully powerful, free from all unnecessary verbiage. No one else, no Bowles, or [Henry] Watterson, or Raymond, has approached that style in our press except occasionally. For one thing, it was the writing of a completely educated man, polished by travel and the society of intellectual leaders everywhere, who wrote only with profound conviction, who till the last of his long career burned at injustice with the ardor of youth. To this he added a power of irony and sarcasm never equaled by anyone else, almost too great at times." (*Some News-*

papers and Newspapermen, 1926). Godkin's only real handicap as an editorial writer, liberal critics claimed, was his disdain for the common man. Even his admirers remarked that his biting writing style occasionally was too much for even his intellectual, upper-class readers.

Of a different bent was Joseph Pulitzer. He made his fortune and journalistic fame by his New York *World's* outright appeal to the lower classes. Although catering to less sophisticated readers through news sensationalism, Pulitzer considered a respected editorial page to be the heart of his paper. He made it into a constructive, accurate, crusading instrument against social and governmental ills. Despite the fact that the *World's* readership probably limited the paper's editorial influence, no other newspaper has matched its record for observable editorial accomplishments, from presidential elections to insurance reform to foreign policy to civic improvement. The *World* took the lead in these and other causes for what Pulitzer conceived to be the public good. Once Pulitzer determined the issue, he and the World's editorial writers pounded at it day after day in a writing style marked by clear, forceful language.

MASTERS OF THE EDITORIAL

WILLIAM CULLEN BRYANT: MASTER OF LITERATE STYLE

Historians have bestowed on William Cullen Bryant two titles of vast importance: the "father of American poetry" *and* the "father of 19th-century American journalism." The fact, however, that Bryant was one of America's most notable poets has obscured the fact that the second title is as meaningful as the first. In his 50 years as editor of the New York *Evening Post,* he wrote more than 10,000 editorials, a volume of journalistic work that far surpassed his poetic output. His editorials, written with simplicity, spoke on every important issue of the day and positioned his newspaper as the most literary in American history.

Bryant was born in Cummington, Massachusetts, on November 3, 1794, into a family that encouraged academic pursuits. His father, Peter Bryant, was a physician and, later, a state legislator; his mother, Sarah, a woman who taught her family to condemn social injustices. Early in his life, Bryant discovered a love for words. A voracious reader, he began to pen verses when he was only nine years old. After attending college for one year at the age of 15, he began to study law under the tutelage of local attorneys and soon began his own practice. While practicing law for the next decade, he also published numerous poems in national literary periodicals.

He changed his professional course in 1825, when he became editor of the New York *Review and Atheneum Magazine*. In 1826, he began editing the *United States Review*, while also serving as an editorial assistant at the *Evening Post*. In little over a year, he became an associate editor at the *Post* and, on July 13, 1829, following founder William Coleman's death, took the helm as editor-in-chief. He also served as one of the newspaper's co-proprietors.

For the next 50 years, he established himself as one of America's preeminent editorial writers and spokesmen on political issues. His international reputation as a poet and literary critic also grew.

Bryant's success as a journalist can be attributed, in one sense, to the high standards he expected in his own writing. At the *Evening Post*, he developed a literary style characteristic of the "double life" he led as a journalist *and* as a poet. He insisted that the newspaper be a model of literate English, and he was careful to print nothing that might compromise his own reputation as a poet.

He believed journalism tends to make its practitioners superficial in their understanding, "since the necessity of attending to many subjects prevents the journalist from thoroughly investigating any." As a result, journalism "begets desultory habits of thought, disposing the mind to be satisfied with mere glances at difficult questions and to dwell only upon plausible commonplaces." The editorial writer, he argued, had to look more deeply than at day-to-day occurrences. He has to exercise sound judgment and an unwavering courage in maintaining it, especially in the face of an erratic public opinion that might change with each day. The editorial writer's devotion has to be to truth that does not change with years. The duty of a journalist, he wrote, is to be "a commentator on the events of the day and the various interesting questions which they suggest," and his "business is to enforce important... truths, and to refute what seem to him errors, just as the occasions arise." It is clear that Bryant believed the higher purpose of newspapers was not simply to provide news but to give direction on important public issues.

In presenting his views to the reader, Bryant perhaps was exceeded by no American editorial writer in his concern for the quality of his writing. Having already fully developed his sensitivity to literary quality before he joined the staff of the *Evening Post*, he insisted on attention to language at the newspaper. One of the hazards that journalism presents, he once said, is that a writer's style tends to "become, in consequence of much and hasty writing, loose, diffuse, and stuffed with local barbarisms and the cant phrases of the day."

He gave close attention to his own editorials, writing slowly and carefully, and editing them fastidiously. His copy usually went to the typesetter with numerous changes, erasures, and corrections. Asked how his daily editorials, written under much haste, showed such perfection, he replied, "If my style has fewer defects than you expect, it is for the same reason, I suppose, which Dr. Johnson gave Boswell for conversing so well: I always write my best." Historian W. H. Prescott observed, "Frequently in Bryant's editorials, I see the same qualities that mark his poetry, the peculiar stillness of great passion not merely controlled, but utterly vanquished, and the power of making common epithets tell."

This love for the English language manifested itself in another of Bryant's beliefs: the conviction that foreign expressions were useless. English, he believed, provided enough flexibility, utility, and beauty that to resort to other languages would be frivolous. He often quoted from the wide array of English poetry he so ravenously read and studied. This belief was evident in all of his editorials, even those not considered his most eloquent. In 1862, the Hartford *Press*' Charles Dudley Warner commented, "Some of its ordinary editorials are magnificent specimens of English."

Although Bryant prescribed no formula for good writing, he placed a premium on simplicity, directness, and clearness of expression. Although believing that editorials should be understandable within the experiences of ordinary people, he also could write with urbanity, wit, refined humor, irony, and scathing satire; and, learned as he was, he often illustrated points with classical allusions and quotations from poems. He always insisted, however, on purity of diction: short words and precise meaning. "Be simple, unaffected," he advised one young, hopeful writer; "be honest in your speaking and writing.... Elegance of language may not be in the power of us all, but simplicity and straightforwardness are." His readers never misunderstood his meaning; his language was always simple and unassuming. On the impact of this writing style on readers, he said, "When a short word will do, you will always lose by a long one: you lose in clearness, you lose in honest expression of meaning, and, in the estimation of all men who are capable of judging, you lose in reputation for ability."

Bryant's success as a journalist rested also on his farsightedness in examining issues. He explained that an editor plays the following role: "To the more thoughtful among his readers he offers serious topics of reflection. He combats error in all shapes and disguises, and perceives with satisfaction that through his efforts the empire of truth is extending its sway." His professional role was to report and, more importantly, to give a studied opinion on the day's news. It is said that he never wanted to be remembered as a journalist; instead, he desired that his legacy be one of affecting human action and attitudes.

The *Evening Post* had been founded, a quarter century before, as the political mouthpiece of Alexander Hamilton. As editor, Bryant converted the paper—which had been the leading national journal of the conservative Federalist cause—into a preeminent supporter of the Jacksonian Democrats. He brought a strong moral nature, combined with classical English liberalism, to his job of interpreting the political, social, and economic issues of the day. In the many years that he stood near the top of American journalism, he was one of the nation's foremost advocates of free speech, low tariffs, international copyright, labor unions, low postage rates, and democracy. As pro-slavery elements gained more and more control of the Democratic party, he shifted his allegiance to the Whig party; and with the appearance of the Republican party in 1848, he gave it the full support of the *Evening Post* and argued forcefully for the abolition of slavery. As the nation drew near civil war, he was one of its most consistent advocates of the inviolability of the Union.

Bryant's talent as an editorial writer reached its peak during the dispute over slavery and the Civil War. The two issues of ultimate importance during his journalistic career were human freedom and the integrity of the Union. He staunchly believed the Southern secessionists were traitors, yet he believed in dealing with them moderately when the War was over. His 1861 editorial "The Union, Now and Forever!" (included in this anthology), written after the Confederate bombing of Fort Sumter, was one of his most intense and majestic pieces. In it, one sees Bryant's eloquence of phrasing. The same tone is visible in 1865's "Glory to the Lord of Hosts." Written after General Robert E. Lee's surrender on April 9, the editorial reveals Bryant's belief in justice in his call for a peaceful reconstruction.

The Civil War and post-War years were fruitful ones for Bryant. They were not, however, the only times when his talent was obvious to the American public. Years before, an editorial caught the attention of the majority of New Yorkers in its call for a peaceful refuge in the heart of the city. He believed that citizens needed an escape from the sultry, crowded streets of Manhattan; and members of the public, other newspapers, and political candidates took up his cause. The origin of the idea that eventually led to the creation of Manhattan's Central Park can be traced to his 1844 editorial, "A New Public Park." The editorial's stance typified the beliefs of the Romanticists of the early 19th century, an influence, also, on his poetry. The Romanticists believed that "civilization," epitomized at its worst by city life, degraded the human spirit, whereas nature revitalized it. Along with the influence that Romantic thought had on Bryant's poetry, one can see it also in his editorial writing.

Today, Bryant's words are read in literature classes, and his verses are found in anthologies of great American poetry. His work as an editorial writer was, however, just as important for the field of journalism. His simple, yet eloquent style of prose writing positioned him as perhaps the most literary editor in American history.

•Among the Democratic leadership in New York were three men with the names Slamm, Bangs, and Ming. The Whig newspapers grabbed on to that interesting combination of names as a device for lampooning. Bryant responded with the following editorial that demonstrated his talent for humor and satire.

NEW YORK BIRD-CATCHERS
(New York *Evening Post*, June 2, 1838)

In the first volume of "Hone's Table-book" is an engraving of a London Bird-Catcher in the year 1827, and under it are printed the calls, or *jerks*, as they are technically called—the peculiar sounds and articulations of the voice by which the people of this profession allure wild birds within their reach. Our readers will perhaps be amused with a sample of these *jerks*:

Tuck-Tuck-Fear.
Tuck-Tuck-Fear-Ic,Ic,Ic.
Tuck-Tuck-Fear-Ic quake-e weet.
   (This is a *finished jerk*.)
Tolloc, Ejup, R-weet, weet, weet.
Tolloc, Tolloc, cha-Ic,Ic,Ic.
Lug, Lug, G-cha,cha.
Lug, Lug-Orchee, weet.

New York has its bird-catchers as well as London. One of these goes under the name of the "Express." He has established himself at the corner of Wall and Water Streets, where he practices his jerks diligently every morning for the catching of such foolish birds as he finds in that neighborhood. Here is a sample of his jerks:

Slam Bang-Slam Bang-Slam Bang & Co.
Slam Bang-Slam Bang-Slam Bang Ming & Co.
   (This is a *finished jerk*.)
Loco Foco, Loco Foco-Jacques, mob-Eli.
Loco Foco, Loco Foco-Eli Hart's flour store-
Flour riot, Flour riot.
Agrarians, Agrarians-Fanny Wright, Fanny Wright,
Levellers, Levellers, Levellers-Jack Cade, Jack Cade, etc., etc.

The birds allured and taken by means of these calls are chiefly of the kinds called gulls, boobies, noodles, doddrels, and geese, which do mostly affect maritime places. Plenty of lame ducks which haunt the neighborhood where the bird-catcher has established himself are also taken, being more easily made prisoners on account of their disabled state; and that fiercer fowl, that bird of prey, the kite, which delights to hover over and swoop upon his victims in the atmosphere of Wall Street, is often by these calls decoyed into the net. When caught, the birds are made to practice the jerks which we have given, until they become quite perfect in their parts, when you will hear the boobies, noodles, lame ducks, geese, kites, etc., call out "Slam Bang, Slam Bang, Jack Cade, Jack Cade," etc., all at once, with astonishing energy and correctness of accent. A friend of ours heard the words Slam, Bang, Ming & Co. pronounced by one of these birds the other day in Broadway, not far from Leonard Street, as distinctly as the bird-catcher himself could have uttered it. A great black and white bird called the "Journal of Commerce," from its coming out every morning and hovering over the shipping, was once caught, and for two or three mornings uttered the words Slam, Bang & Co. as distinctly as a human being, of which there are at present several living witnesses.

•The origin of the plans for Central Park in New York City can be traced to the following editorial. One may find in the editorial the strong influences of Romanticism with its emphasis on the wholesome effects of nature.

A NEW PUBLIC PARK
(New York *Evening Post*; July 3, 1844)

The heats of summer are upon us, and while some are leaving the town for shady retreats in the country, others refresh themselves with short excursions to Hoboken or New Brighton, or other places among the beautiful environs of our city. If the public authorities, who expend so much of our money in laying out the city, would do what is in their power, they might give our vast population an extensive pleasure ground for shade and recreation in these sultry afternoons, which we might reach without going out of town.

On the road to Harlem, between 68th Street on the south and 77th Street on the north, and extending from Third Avenue to the East River, is a tract of beautiful woodland, comprising 60 or 70 acres, thickly covered with old trees, intermingled with a variety of shrubs. The surface is varied in a very striking and picturesque manner, with craggy eminences and hollows, and a little stream runs through the midst. The swift tides of the East River sweep its rocky shores, and the fresh breeze of the bay comes in, on every warm summer afternoon, over the restless waters. The trees are of almost every species that grows in our woods—the different varieties of oak, the birch, the beech, the linden, the mulberry, the tulip tree, and others. The azaleas, the kalmia and other flowering shrubs are in bloom here at their season, and the ground in spring is gay with flowers. There never was a finer situation for a public garden of a great city. Nothing is wanted but to cut winding paths through it, leaving the woods as they are, and introducing here and there a jet from the Groton aqueduct, the streams from which would make their own waterfalls over the rocks, and keep the brook running through the place always fresh and full. In the English Garden at Munich, a pleasure ground of immense extent, laid out by our countryman Count Rumford, into which half the population pours itself on summer evenings, the designer of the grounds was obliged to content himself with artificial rocks, brought from a distance and cemented together, and eminences painfully heaped up from the sand of the plain. In the tract of which we speak, nature has done almost everything to our hands except the construction of paths.

As we are now going on, we are making a belt of muddy docks all around the island. We should be glad to see one small part of the shore without them, one place at least where the tides may be allowed to flow pure, and the ancient brim of rocks which borders the waters left in its original picturesqueness and beauty. Commerce is devouring inch by inch the coast of the island, and if we rescue any part of it for health and recreation it must be done now.

All large cities have their extensive public grounds and gardens; Madrid and Mexico City their Alamedas, London its Regent's Park, Paris its Champs Elysees, and Vienna its Prater. There are none of them, we believe, which have the same natural advantages of the picturesque and beautiful which belong to this spot. It would be of easy access to the citizens, and the public carriages which now rattle in almost every street of this city would take them to its gates. The only objection which we can see to the plan would be the difficulty of persuading the owners of the soil to part with it—and this rich city can easily raise the means.

If any of our brethren of the public press should see fit to support this project, we are ready to resign in their favor any claim to the credit of originally suggesting it.

•Bryant wrote the following editorial after President Lincoln delivered the proclamation of war in the wake of the Confederate bombing of Fort Sumter. Although the editorial was intense and eloquent, it also demonstrates the problems even the best of writers sometimes face, that of shortsightedness because of zeal. As indicated here, Bryant, caught up in the fervor of the moment, boasted idly about the quick success that Union armies would have.

THE UNION, NOW AND FOREVER!
(New York *Evening Post*; April 15, 1861)

The President's proclamation proves him worthy to be the head of the nation. His honest words find an echo in millions of loyal hearts this day. Only these words were needed to seal the speedy doom of treason.

To-day, who is not for the Union is against it. To-day he whose heart does not throb and whose blood does not stir with patriotic fire is a vile traitor. The rebels have chosen war. They have done their best to slay a loyal garrison. Without a single cause of complaint, they have turned their arms against the Union and against the lives of loyal citizens. From to-day dates the extermination of treason from the land. The people will not rest, the nation will not be satisfied, while a traitor is left in arms.

The measures the President has taken and proposes to take are the wisest and most prudent that could be devised. Already he has the band of traitors in his net. Charleston is blockaded. As we write, news comes that Fort Pickens is attacked by the traitors—but Fort Pickens was reinforced on Saturday! Washington is safe—and even if the disappointed General at Charleston should venture to bring his army northward, a hundred thousand loyal freemen of Pennsylvania would sweep the traitors from the face of the earth.

Let us thank God that we shall hear no more of "conditional loyalty." If the traitors of Virginia choose to secede let them do so quickly. It is no time for half measures. The loyal men of the border states must speak out, and put down the treason which has grown rampant in their midst. To-day the nation demands to know who are is enemies; and it will lose no time in driving them out.

The President will "re-possess the forts, places and property which have been seized from the Union." If he calls for only seventy-five thousand men it is because he knows that he can have a million if he needs them. But he judges rightly, that every loyal arm is a match for ten traitors.

Charleston is already blockaded. Within a week every port in the rebel states will have its mouth guarded by United States armed ships. Within ten days, unless they sue for peace and lay down their traitorous arms, the rebels will find themselves in the face of a hundred thousand men determined to maintain with their lives a government under which we have prospered and been happy for eighty years, and a constitution made for us by Washington, Jefferson, and the host of patriots who gathered about them.

"God speed the President" is the voice of millions of determined freemen to-day.

•The following editorial, written after Lee had surrendered to Grant to end the Civil War, demonstrates Bryant's ability to write eloquently and, at the same time, to express his ideas clearly.

GLORY TO THE LORD OF HOSTS
(New York *Evening Post*, April 10, 1865)

The great day, so long and anxiously awaited, for which we have struggled through four years of bloody war, which has so often seemed to "stand tip toe on the misty mountain tops" but which dawned only to go down in clouds and gloom; the day of the virtual overthrow of the rebellion, of the triumph of constitutional order and of universal liberty—of the success of the nation against its parts, and of humane and beneficent civilization over a relic of barbarism that had been blindly allowed to remain as a blot on its escutcheon, in short, the day of PEACE, has finally come. It has come, as every wise lover of his country wished it to come, not as a weak compromise between the government of the people and its enemies, not as a concession to an exhausted yet vital power of revolt, not as a truce between two equal forces which lay down their arms for the time, to resume them as soon as they should repair damages and recover strength—but as the result of a stern, deliberate, unyielding determination to vindicate the supremacy of the organic law over the entire territory and people of the nation.

The issue raised by the insurgents was a distinct one; it arraigned the right of the Union to exercise its authority over states which chose to assert a right of secession; the appeal was made to the arbitrament of arms; for four weary years "the weary hours toiled heavy with the unresting curse they bore"; and all the strength, the valor, the endurance, the pride, the energy, the sentiment, the passion and earnest conviction of duty of either side, was put forth in the terrible conflict of principles, in an awful and gigantic wrestle for the mastery. Now, when the trial has been made, when the victory abides with us, when the vital question has been decided, when the insane leaders of the slave states and their ignorant followers have been shown what the sovereign people demand as to the integrity of the nation and its government, the peace that must follow will be a peace founded upon establishing and enduring principles.

Glory, then, to the Lord of Hosts, who hath given us this final victory! Thanks, heartfelt and eternal, to the brave and noble men by land and sea, officers and soldiers, who by their labors, their courage, their sufferings, their blood and their lives, have won it for us! And a gratitude no less deep and earnest to that majestic, devoted and glorious American People, who through all these years of trial have kept true to their faith in themselves and in their institutions, have maintained themselves steady and self-respectful amid all the excitements of an unexampled civil war, who have never given way to despair or terror on one hand, or dashed out wildly on the other in a spirit of vengeance and fury, but through every vicissitude of the times have stood calm, self-reliant, determined, indomitable, conscious of strength, and in the deep prophetic instinct which that strength lent, assured of success.

We need not admonish such a people as to the manner in which they should rejoice in the signal successes of the day. They who are capable of grand achievements in the field are no less capable of magnanimous feeling toward the fallen foe. They will exult in no petty or insolent feeling of triumph over a prostrate enemy, but in a cheerful and generous sentiment of the great general ends accomplished; in a sense of the calamities escaped, of the burdens removed, of the feuds closed, of the blood staunched, of the animosities laid aside, and of the kindly feelings restored; in the prospect of a speedy recovery of our wasted energies, of the return of industry to its wonted channels, of the establishment of our institutions on a basis more indestructible than ever before; of the elevation of the national heart to all the heights of heroism, of the diffusion of liberty to all races; and in the hope of a securer, broader, nobler development of whatever is just and free in our society, until the example of the great republic shall purify and redeem all the nations of the earth. By the overrulings of the Divine Providence it has come to pass that the sacred Palm Sunday, celebrated in the offices of the Church as the day of the Savior's entry into Jerusalem, was the day of our cessation from active strife. A new, a Holy Week begins for us, which may bring us sorrows and even crucifixion, but which, if we adhere to the high duty God has imposed on us, will bring also a resurrection for ourselves and salvation for all mankind.

'SUNSET' COX STARTS A NEW APPROACH TO EDITORIAL WRITING

In 1853 Samuel Sullivan Cox offhandedly wrote an editorial that changed the course of editorial writing. Until then, editorials were dominated by political subjects. Although occasional non-political editorials had been written prior to 1853, none had been able to change journalistic attitudes. Cox's editorial blazed the trail for human interest topics.

At the age of 29 Cox was gaining stature as a leading Democrat in Ohio, and he bought part interest in the state's official Democratic organ, the *Ohio Statesman* in Columbus. With an interest in and considerable talent for writing, he became its editor. Late one afternoon, as occasionally happened on small newspapers in the 1800s, the foreman of the *Statesman's* composing room discovered that he lacked enough copy to fill the front page. The solution in such instances was simply to ask the editor to dash off some additional editorial opinion, and the foreman sent word to Cox's home with the request. Despite a heavy spring rainfall, Cox dutifully returned to the office, arriving just as the rain ended and the sun was setting brilliantly. The beauty of the sunset displaced for the moment all editorial concern for politics, and as the composers waited for copy Cox wrote out a florid description of the scene.

When published the next day, the editorial captured the attention of readers and, through a series of reprintings in other newspapers, created a sensation. It broke completely and abruptly with the political tradition in editorial writing. Opposition Republican editors, however, locked onto the editorial, with its odd subject matter and ornate style, as a means to criticize its Democrat creator. Across the state, they greeted it with a wave of derisive laughter. The *Ohio State Journal* published it along with ridiculing annotations. The Circleville editor wrote a parody, "A Great Old Henset." The editor of the local competing newspaper, taking advantage of Cox's initials, got in what he thought was the best gibe of all by referring to the author as "Sunset" Cox. Ironically, the catchy nickname gained widespread popularity, was adopted by Cox himself, and proved to be a valuable asset in his later political life.

Even though Cox had no other claim to journalistic fame than this one editorial, he was a polished, successful author with a solid intellect and education. He published more than 20 books and wrote for a variety of newspapers. His educational background included study of the arts, religion, philosophy, science, and law.

The success of "A Great Old Sunset" was no accident. The editorial was greatly influenced by Cox's deep religious beliefs and by Romanticism, a view of the world that pervaded philosophy in the 1800s and that placed primary emphasis on nature and the interrelationship of nature, God, and man. The topic of "A Great Old Sunset" found a receptive audience in the mid-19th century. The vividness of the editorial's description, although overdone by today's standards, was enhanced by Cox's sensitivity to colors, smells, the effect light has on a scene, and ordinary sights.

After leaving the *Ohio Statesman*, Cox successfully used the sobriquet from his editorial in his political career. Elected to the United States Congress in 1856, he became one of the Democrats' leading national figures, serving with only short interruptions until his death in 1889. During his lifetime, most voters and public officials knew him only by his nickname, and many historians still assume that the "S.S." of his initials really did stand for "Sunset."

A GREAT OLD SUNSET
(Samuel Sullivan Cox; *Ohio Statesman*; May 19, 1853)

What a stormful sunset was that of last night! How glorious the storm and how splendid the setting of the sun! We do not remember ever to have seen the like on our round globe. The scene

opened in the west, with a whole horizon full of golden interpene-
trating lustre, which colored the foliage and brightened every object into its own rich dyes. The colors grew deeper and richer until
the golden lustre was transfused into a storm cloud full of the
finest lightning, which leaped in dazzling zigzags all around over
the city.

The wind arose with fury, the slender shrubs and giant trees
made obeisance to its majesty. Some even snapped before its
force. The strawberry beds and grass plots turned up their whites
to see Zephyrus march by. As the rain came and the pools formed
and the gutters hurried away, thunder rolled grandly and the fire-
balls caught the excitement and rang with hearty chorus.

The South and the East received the copious showers, and the
West all at once brightened up in a long polished belt of azure,
worthy of a Sicilian sky. Presently a cloud appeared in the azure
belt in the form of a castellated city. It became more vivid, revealing strange forms of peerless fanes and alabaster temples and glories rare and grand in this mundane sphere. It reminds us of
Wordsworth's splendid verse in his "Excursion":

The appearance instantly disclosed
Was of a mighty city—boldly say
A wilderness of building, sinking far
And self-withdrawn into a boundless depth,
Far sinking into splendor—without end.

But the city vanished, only to give place to another isle, where
the most beautiful forms of foliage appear, imaging a paradise in
the distant and purified air. The sun, wearied of the elemental
commotion, sank behind the green plains of the West. The "great
eye of heaven," however, went not down without a dark brown
hanging over its departed light. The rich flush of the unearthly
light had passed, and the rain had ceased when the solemn church
bells pealed, the laughter of children rang out loud and, joyous after the storm, was heard with the carol of birds; while the forked
and purple weapon of the skies still darted illumination around
the Starling College, trying to rival its angles and leap into its
dark windows.

Candles were lighted. The piano strikes up. We feel it good to
have a home, good to be on earth where such revelations of beauty
and power may be made. And as we cannot refrain from remind-
ing our readers of everything wonderful in our city, we have begun
and ended our feeble etching of a sunset which comes so rarely
that its glory should be committed to immortal type.

MASTERS OF THE EDITORIAL

HORACE GREELEY: MASTER OF EDITORIAL INFLUENCE

Horace Greeley, more than a hundred years after his death, is best remembered for the phrase "Go West! young man. Go West." The phrase had an immense influence on Americans. The fact that it was penned by an Indiana editor and not by Greeley, who received the credit, is illustrative of Greeley's incredible effect on the public consciousness. His influence was apparent also in the fact that the weekly edition of his New York *Tribune* developed a higher circulation than any American newspaper up until its time. His writing desk became a pulpit from which he spoke on every paramount issue of the day.

Today, most laymen remember that one, immortal phrase, overlooking his other achievements. Throughout his career, however, he was a strong proponent of freeing the slaves; he ran for president in 1872; and he founded the most influential newspaper of his time, perhaps of all time. Critics and historians recollect his powerful writing style and his unbending stance on political issues. Rural readers were said to have valued the weekly *Tribune* "next to the Bible" and waited to make a decision on an issue until after they had read "what Uncle Horace said." No other editorial writer in American history seemed to exercise so much authority on major national issues as Greeley.

His editorial stature rested on his intense commitment to ideas that benefited large numbers of the populace, his incisive and economical writing style, and his ability to present arguments in a well-organized and cogent manner. He never swayed in his political conviction, and the *Tribune's* pages became home to his opinions on every major issue of the day, including abolition, capital punishment, temperance, and westward expansion. Benjamin Poore, a contemporary journalist, observed, "He was a man of intense convictions and wielded an incisive, ready pen, which went straight to the point without circumlocution or needless use of words.... [T]here was a 'method in his madness,' and his heretical views were evidently the honest convictions of his heart. Often egotistical, dogmatic, and personal, no one could question his uprightness and thorough devotion to the noblest principles of progressive civilization."

The cold day of February 3, 1811, threw Greeley into the world. His mother and father, a hapless farmer and day worker in Amherst, New Hampshire, were destitute and provided their son with no material amenities. They were also heavy drinkers, an influence years later on their son's untiring campaign for temperance. He rarely attended school, and most of his knowledge was self-taught. His love for books developed into a desire to become a printer, and in 1826 he was apprenticed to the printer of the *Northern Spectator* in a small Vermont town.

Five years later he moved to New York City, where he would remain for the rest of his life. He worked at various printing posts and then, at the age of 21, experienced his first major career setback. He and a partner founded a print shop in 1833, and their first job was to print New York's first penny paper, the *Morning Post.* The editor was unable to pay for the printing, and Greeley and Co. was barely able to stay afloat.

In 1834 he founded the *New-Yorker*, a journal of both literary and political interests. With it, he attracted the attention of Whig politicians, who discovered that the editor's opinions ran close to their own. Whig leaders Thurlow Weed and William Seward enticed him to edit the party newspaper, the *Jeffersonian.* Following that, he edited the *Log Cabin*, a campaign weekly for presidential candidate William Henry Harrison. Greeley's influence on state politics that year seemed evident; the Whigs won the governor's and lieutenant governor's seats and a majority of the assembly and senate in New York. Greeley would remain a Whig until 1854, when he broke with the party and joined the newly formed Republican opposition.

Until 1841, Greeley's influence was in party newspapers with selective audiences. The market around him, however, had changed. New York City was in the throes of a penny newspaper war, as James Gordon Bennett's *Herald* and Moses Beach's *Sun* fought for readers. Often, the fighting got ugly, and both papers employed sensationalist tactics. Amidst this situation, Greeley saw the need for a cheap but respectable Whig-oriented daily. On April 10 he printed the first issue of the New York *Tribune*, and he soon began a weekly edition. Although he founded the newspaper as an outlet for Whig views, it was never Whig-controlled.

With the *Tribune*, he established a newspaper that evidenced his own values on journalism and that provided a forum for his political views. He believed in the timeliness of news and catered to his readers' needs in that area. "The fact," he explained, "that certain journals have the earliest news soon becomes notorious and almost everyone wants his newspaper with his breakfast, delivered between the hours of five and half past seven. They take the morning papers to read with their breakfast." He also catered to their desire for an inexpensive newspaper. At the time, all of the Whig papers cost $10 a year; the other, general-circulation newspapers cost a mere cent an issue. The *Tribune* followed in their footsteps and cost only a penny.

Circulation grew; and, as the Civil War broke out, the *Tribune* was the most powerful newspaper America had ever known. Greeley's impact was especially evident in the westward migration of America and the anti-slavery movement. On the first, he printed the counsel to move west so frequently that by the 1830s he had been tagged with the nickname "Go West Greeley." He continued to urge westward movement once he founded the *Tribune*. He had a deep interest in internal improvements and agriculture, and trips later in his life began to take him farther and farther west. As part of his overall program for westward expansion he had proposed a transcontinental railroad and western telegraph lines before 1850. He also supported land reform to divide western land more equitably so that entrepreneurs could not monopolize it. He urged the establishment of a public university with agricultural education as a main area of study. He wrote on techniques of productive farming and worked his own small garden.

Should anyone ask him, as many did, on the merits of moving to the city or engaging in farming, his answer was certain. All these themes were tied in to his advice to "Go West." He wrote, for example, in the editorial "Go to the West": "If any young man is about to commence in the world, with little in his circumstances to possess him in favor of one section above another, we say to him publicly and privately, Go to the West; there your capabilities are sure to be appreciated and your industry and energy rewarded." Similarly in the 1853 editorial "To Aspiring Young Men," he answered the constant inquiries he received: "'I want to go into business,' is the aspiration of our young men: 'can't you find me a place in the city?' their constant inquiry.... If you have no family or friends to aid you, and no prospect opened to you there, turn your face to the Great West, and there build up a home and fortune."

And the nation *was* moving west, with families looking for their fortunes on free land. By the end of the 1840s, a mighty surge was carrying the nation westward. This westward movement was one of the most momentous events in American history, at least partially as a response to Greeley's counsel. No editor probably ever played a more decisive role in an issue of such national moment.

In the anti-slavery movement, Greeley likewise provided a leading voice. He long had been a staunch advocate of abolition. With the onset of the Civil War, he and many other Northerners felt that emancipating the slaves was the union's surest way of defeating the South. Greeley's most overt influence on abolition came from his 1862 editorial "The Prayer of Twenty Millions." It confronted President Lincoln with the demand to enforce the nation's law by declaring slaves free. Although Lincoln had already decided to issue his Emancipation Proclamation before Greeley published his editorial, the fact that he did issue it only a few days after the editorial led most people to think that it was the editorial that had prompted Lincoln to act. Despite indications that the editorial's influence was less than people thought, the editorial does indicate that Greeley saw earlier than the president did that gradual emancipation was unrealistic and unworkable.

Today, Greeley's work can serve as a model for the most important aspects of editorial writing—understanding and taking stands on major issues, presenting well-reasoned exposition and argument, and gaining the respect of and influence with readers.

•Greeley believed that Sen. Stephen Douglas was one of the most treacherous public officials of the antebellum period. The following editorial demonstrates one of the devices he used to attack him.

[STEPHEN DOUGLAS, HANGMAN]
(New York *Tribune*, February 22, 1854)

Some years ago, several localities of the south were terribly agitated on the subject of Abolitionism. It was at the time that Mr. Van Buren sanctioned the opening of private letters and packages by postmasters in their search for "incendiary documents." In a place we care not to name the opposition to the anti-slavery sentiment ran so high that a Committee of Safety was appointed, and before this dread and irresponsible tribunal were arraigned all who could in any way be suspected of entertaining anti-slavery sentiments. Our soul sickens at the scenes of brutality that were witnessed there; but the reign of terror was for the moment triumphant.... A poor, miserable, half-witted and degraded wretch, who consorted with the negroes because he found no other willing associates, and what is most singular, a native born citizen of the very place we write about, was arrested and tried for using inflammatory expressions before the negroes. The poor creature could not comprehend his situation; born and reared in the place, he had no idea that any harm was intended him; and he listened to the charges in the trial with a silly laugh, and heard himself condemned to be hanged as if it were a joke.

The moment that sentence was pronounced, there went up a clamor for the execution, and from the tribunal the prisoner was hurried to the fatal tree. In a few moments a limb was selected, the rope adjusted, and the cart was driven beneath it. So far, all had been action, and consequently there was a want of time for reflection; but the moment that an executioner was needed, the moment that the fearful responsibility of taking life could not be distributed out among the multitude, there was a holding back, an irresolution, a fear that the act was not right.

In the meanwhile the victim sat on the edge of the cart, his hands tied behind his back, almost able to see the miserable cabin in which he was born, silent—speechless with terror. His life was trembling in the balance. A moment more and there would have gone up in the crowd a cry, "Let him go," "Let him go"; but at this critical moment a person unknown to the crowd was seen to move toward the cart. Springing upon it and rudely seizing the dangling rope, he turned round to the astonished spectators and said: "If none of you will act as hangman, I will. Damn the Abolitionists!" In another instant the fatal cord was adjusted, the cart driven off, and there was seen suspended between heaven and earth the trembling—the dead—form of an innocent man. The body in due time was dispersed with horror depicted upon their faces, and dark and before unknown passions of destruction awakened in their hearts.

Now who was this hangman? Who was this fierce defender of the peculiar institution? Was he a Southern man? No. Was he a citizen identified with the South? No. It was on the contrary a Northern man, from a free State—in fact, one who had been but two days in the place. It seemed as if, suspecting his own principles, revolting in his heart at slavery and afraid that in the excitement of the hour he might next be arraigned, he took this fearful and terrible office of executioner in order to place himself, as he supposed, on "high Southern ground." Thus, by one glaring act, wherein he violated his conscience—his early education—every law, in fact, of God and man—he thought to identify himself as a defender of slavery, and have his soundness placed above suspicion.

And here is to be seen reflected the true picture of Mr. Douglas's turpitude. Southern men may have in the madness of the hour conceived such iniquity as is embodied in the Nebraska bill. They may have prepared the halter for the neck of the Missouri Compromise—but the last fatal act would never have been undertaken had not the Senator from Illinois volunteered to act as executioner, been willing to mount the scaffold, and call down the infamy of murdering liberty upon his own head.

Thus it has ever been in Congress whenever the rights of man have been violated. Southerners, from the necessity of defending their local interests, are compelled to advocate principles repugnant to their consciences, but they would never press them upon the people of the North if there had not always been volunteers, like Douglas, willing to do the foul work that Southern men themselves revolt at, while feeling toward these ready tools of tyranny a contempt that is ever extended toward the traitor, whatever may be the advantages they reap from the treason enacted.

•In 1854 Anthony Burns, an escaped slave, was arrested in Boston in accordance with the Fugitive Slave Act and escorted to a ship to be remanded to his Southern owner, at a cost to taxpayers of $40,000. Bostonians' opposition to the action indicated the growing Northern revolt against enforcement of the law.

SLAVE-CATCHER'S TRIUMPH
(New York *Tribune*; June 3, 1854)

The fugitive Burns is delivered into slavery. A man as much

entitled to his freedom as any other man on the soil of Massachusetts has been seized in that State by other men, manacled, and consigned to hopeless bondage. The people of that great Commonwealth, containing a million of inhabitants, every one of them knowing the act to be a gross and unpardonable exercise of tyrannical power, a criminal outrage upon the inalienable rights of man, have suffered it to be done without interposing force to prevent it. That there was opposition to the act is seen, however, in the means employed for its consummation. Burns was not torn from the soil of freedom and consigned to slavery by any ordinary methods of imprisoning malefactors. He was not taken by a constable or sheriff, or even a whole police force of a great city. All these were insufficient. It took all the police of Boston, three companies of United States troops, one company of cavalry, and an entire battalion of militia, together with several pieces of artillery, to secure the capture of this citizen and remand him to slavery. It is said that this was an experimental case of slave-catching, got up especially for the purpose of showing how readily the North would acquiesce in the Nebraska bill, and succumb to the aggressions of the slave power. We trust the managers of the performance are satisfied. What do they think of the prospect of performing the same feat over again?

This cowardly capture of an innocent man, and consigning him to the horrors of a servile bondage, necessarily provokes some reflection. We desire to ask the principals in the affair, the leading Nebraska conspirators, and the Executive Government at Washington, what was the use of the ostentatious display of artillery charged with grape-shot that were planted in Court Square on the occasion? Do they not know that the discharge of that cannon upon the Boston multitude there assembled would have been the signal for fifty thousand men of Massachusetts to fly to arms? Do they not know that they did not dare discharge that artillery upon the friends of freedom in that commonwealth? Why, then, did they indulge in this piece of intimidation? Was it for the luxury of an unmeaning taunt? It may be that they cannot see that through all this Burns trial the public peace has been slumbering upon the edge of a volcano. If they cannot, perhaps they had better devote themselves to a closer scrutiny of the existing state of the popular pulse.

There has been the most imminent danger of a violent and armed outbreak during this late tragedy. And suppose it had taken place? Who would have quelled it? Who would have restored the public peace when once broken? Burns has been taken away, but let us tell the slave power that nothing has been accomplished by that capture but to deepen the resolution that slaves shall not be taken on the soil of the Free States. Nothing has been accomplished by it but to arouse the Northern mind to a determination to resistance to such scenes in the future. This time men have been unarmed. Another time it may be otherwise. We are but at the beginning of the resistance to the arrogant domination of the slave power. Things are but in the bud, in the gristle. Nothing has been done in this case but to declare against the proceeding. Not an arrangement to rescue the fugitive has been made. Nothing which savored of earnest resistance has been attempted. But it will not be so always. Some such even as a forcible rescue will yet take place, and when that takes place in Massachusetts, the fugitive will not be sent to Canada. He will be held upon her soil, and a note of defiance sounded to let them come and take him who dare.

The future is big with events such as these unless something is done to allay the public excitement produced by the proceedings of the slave power, backed by our rulers. The fugitive slave law, as it now stands, can no longer be enforced without jeopardizing the public tranquility to an alarming extent. We again call upon Congress to give their earnest and immediate attention to this grave subject. If there can be no repeal of the law at this session, which we think is quite certain, let us at least have the trial by jury. A modification of this sort is absolutely demanded unless the country is to be precipitated upon insurrection, and perchance civil war.

•While serving in the U. S. Senate for 30 years, Thomas Hart Benton of Missouri was one of the leading figures in American political life. Like Andrew Jackson, he demonstrated an aggressive frontiersman character. The following obituary editorial about him captures that personality and typifies Greeley's most effective style.

DEATH OF BENTON
(New York *Tribune*; April 12, 1858)

In the death of Mr. Benton the country loses one of its marked public characters. He was a man of great force, but that force was of a personal rather than of an intellectual nature. An intense individuality characterized all that he said and did. His frame was large, his health robust, his nature burly. He was truculent, energetic, intrepid, willful, and indomitable. He always wore a resolute and determined air, and, simply viewed as an animal, possessed a very commanding aspect. He strode into public life with these qualities all prominent and bristling. Whenever he shone he shone in the exhibition of them. His intellectual powers always appeared as subsidiary; they never took the lead, never appeared to be the propelling force in any of the marked epochs of his life. The leading points of his career were his land-reform measure; his opposition to the old United States Bank; his expunging resolution; his war on Mr. Calhoun after his disappointment in the succession to the Presidency; and his hostility to the Compromise measures of 1850. In all these contests, at least in all but that for the reform of the land system, he bore himself as a fighting man. He carried this so far as to allude, in one of his later senatorial exhibitions, to a pair of pistols, which he said had never been used but a funeral followed.

Mr. Benton had been ten years in the Senate before he was known to the country as a prominent debater. The discussion on the United States Bank question brought him out fully, and was of a character to exhibit his powers to the greatest possible advantage. It was a question that touched the feelings and the private interests of individuals deeply, and roused the intensest ardor of all partisan politicians. The debates were heated and fiercely personal. A hand-to-hand political encounter overspread the country. This contest suited Benton exactly. He loved the turmoil and the war, and he rose with each successive exigency until he became, par excellence, the champion of General Jackson's Administration in its contest with the Bank. On one occasion, in 1830-31, he made a speech of four days. At the close of the fourth day Mr. Calhoun sarcastically remarked that Mr. Benton had taken one day longer in his assault on the Bank than it had taken to accomplish the revolution in France.

The intellectual strength of Mr. Benton's efforts never impressed his great adversaries, Clay, Calhoun, and Webster. They never regarded him as belonging to their class intellectually. Yet they always appreciated and dreaded his great personal force. In no case did this peculiar Bentonian ability manifest itself more clearly or more offensively than in the passage of the expunging resolution. General Jackson had been censured by the Senate in a resolution drawn by Mr. Clay for acting "in derogation of the Constitution." Mr. Benton set about to remove the censure by expunging it from the records. He has told how he accomplished this in his "Thirty Years' View." The story is fairly told and illustrates the man perfectly. The whole transaction bears the marks of a haughty, domineering, and repulsive spirit. The reader, as he peruses Mr. Benton's account of it, feels the triumph to be of a coarse and vulgar character, the work of ill-temper and passion, with no single flash of intellectual or moral elevation in the whole proceeding.

In his political career Mr. Benton often showed himself a fierce and malignant, but never, we think, a generous adversary. It is said that on his deathbed he has done full justice to Mr. Clay in finishing his abridgement of the debates of 1850, and it is pleasant to hear it. We do not doubt that his temper was mollified in later years, as he found himself rapidly approaching the termination of his life. In that debate he came directly in collision with Mr. Clay, and was the only man, indeed, who offered or was able to offer anything like real practical resistance to the impetuous and overbearing march of that great parliamentary leader. In the great debate of 1850 in the Senate, Mr. Clay crushed at will all effective opposition but that of Mr. Benton. On that occasion Benton did not, however, furnish the brains of the debate any more than on previous occasions. Mr. Seward and others of the opposition had done that much more strikingly. But in parliamentary tactics, in the exhibition of personal intrepidity, and in individuality and manner—which in every legislative contest are important elements—Mr. Benton rose superior to every ally. His temper was roused, and he hurled wrath and defiance at his enemies. On a question of parliamentary law he came in immediate conflict with Mr. Clay, who had the majority of the Senate with him and was determined to carry his point. Mr. Benton met him with equal resolution, and with a bulldog ferocity that caused his antagonist to recede and yield the point from considerations of expediency. Mr. Benton was allowed his way after hours of violent struggle and a night's deliberation of the majority. It was, to a very great extent, a triumph of his fighting qualities. Foote, of Mississippi, entered very largely into that debate, and persisted in dogging and attacking Benton. Benton at last bade him stop; he would bear no more of his insults. Foote continued in the same strain. Benton rose from his seat and strode directly toward Foote, as if to throttle him on the spot. Foote fled, and Benton was checked; but Foote never referred to Benton afterward in the Senate. On another occasion Mr. Benton laid himself out to attack Mr. Calhoun. He did it with ability, but his bad blood, his ill-temper, his violence of manner and gross personaly were the predominant characteristics of the attack. There was no pleasure to be derived from it merely as an intellectual demonstration. On the contrary, it only impressed the hearer as repulsive and disgusting.

In all these examples we see where Mr. Benton's power lay as a parliamentarian, a debater, and a man. He never carried his point by winning or convincing, or by pure mental effort. He never reached his objects nor accomplished his successes by mere force of oratory or intellect. He never impressed his audience or the public by sheer strength of mind. It was his intense individuality and animal force, acting upon an intellect of common scope and character, that gave him all his triumphs. His industry was great and his memory remarkable. His knowledge was large, but it was in the domain of facts. He never rose to the consideration of scientific principles, and perhaps never even to the commoner field of philosophic generalization. For himself he claimed to be a man of "measures" rather than of principles or ideas. We should further qualify this claim by saying he was chiefly a man of "facts." His ideas of currency and the "gold" reform, which occupied him for many years, were very crude; and so far as we know, were never improved by after-study or reflection. They found expression in the existing sub-treasury system. Another favorite measure of his was a road to the Pacific, across the continent. His services in establishing the preemption system in the disposition of the public lands were conspicuous, and their results have been eminently beneficient, but we think the record of his principal "measures" must stop here....

Mr. Benton's moral character as a public man is deserving of very high praise. In his public acts we believe he always followed the dictates of an honest purpose. He did not legislate for popularity nor for pay, nor for any individual advantage in any way. He advocated and opposed public measures on the ground of what he considered to be their merits. His judgments may have been clouded by passion or partisan feeling, as no doubt at times they were, but we believe he was always true to his convictions. Of venality and corruption in legislation he had an instinctive abhorrence, and during the thirty years of his senatorial life we do not think the perfect integrity of his votes on all subjects, whether of a public or private character, was ever impugned. In this respect his example is worthy of the attention of all our rising public men, who, in these budding years of corruption, are likely to be tested by severer temptations than the statesmen of the past. Whatever else is unattainable in reputation to a legislator, the proud distinction of integrity is beyond no man's reach, and it is a virtue that is not likely to lose any of its lustre by being too common.

•When Greeley felt that Abraham Lincoln was being tardy in proclaiming the freedom of southern slaves, he wrote the president the following open letter. Soon afterward, Lincoln issued the Emancipation Proclamation; and the belief spread that it was this editorial that had spurred him to action. The editorial normally is considered among the five greatest ones ever published in American newspapers.

THE PRAYER OF TWENTY MILLIONS
(New York *Tribune*; August 19, 1862)

To ABRAHAM LINCOLN, president of the United States:

DEAR SIR: I do not intrude to tell you—for you must know already—that a great proportion of those who triumphed in your election, and of all who desire unqualified suppression of the Rebellion now desolating our country, are sorely disappointed and deeply pained by the policy you seem to be pursuing with regard to the slaves of the Rebels. I write only to set succinctly and unmistakably before you what we require, what we think we have a right to expect, and of what we complain.

I. We require of you, as the first servant of the Republic, charged especially and preeminently with this duty, that you EXECUTE THE LAWS. Most emphatically do we demand that such laws as have been recently enacted, which therefore may fairly be presumed to embody the *present* will and to be dictated by the *present* needs of the Republic, and which, after due consideration have received your personal sanction, shall by you be carried into full effect, and that you publicly and decisively instruct your subordinates that such laws exist, that they are binding on all functionaries and citizens, and that they are to be obeyed to the letter.

II. We think you are strangely and disastrously remiss in the discharge of your official and imperative duty with regard to the emancipating provisions of the new Confiscation Act. Those provisions were designed to fight Slavery with Liberty. They prescribe that men loyal to the Union, and willing to shed their blood in her behalf, shall no longer be held, with the Nation's consent, in bondage to persistent, malignant traitors, who for twenty years have been plotting and for sixteen months have been fighting to divide and destroy our country. Why these traitors should be treated with tenderness by you, to the prejudice of the dearest rights of loyal men, we cannot conceive.

III. We think you are unduly influenced by the counsels, the representations, the menaces, of certain fossil politicians hailing from the Border Slave States. Knowing well that the heartily, unconditionally loyal portion of the White citizens of those States do not expect nor desire that Slavery shall be upheld to the prejudice of the Union—(for the truth of which we appeal not only to every Republican residing in those States, but to such eminent loyalists as H. Winter Davis, Parson Brownlow, the Union Central Committee of Baltimore, and to *The Nashville Union*)—we ask you to consider that Slavery is everywhere the inciting cause and sustaining base of treason; the most slaveholding sections of Maryland and Delaware being this day, though under the Union flag, in dull sympathy with the Rebellion, while the Free-Labor portions of Tennessee and of Texas, though writhing under the bloody heel of Treason, are unconquerably loyal to the Union. So emphatically is this the case, that a most intelligent Union banker of Baltimore recently avowed his confident belief that a majority of the present Legislature of Maryland, though elected as and still professing to be Unionists, are at heart desirous of the triumph of the Jeff. Davis conspiracy; and when asked how they could be won back to loyalty, replied—"Only by the complete Abolition of Slavery." It seems to us the most obvious truth, that whatever strengthens or fortifies Slavery in the Border States strengthens also Treason, and drives home the wedge intended to divide the Union. Had you from the first refused to recognize in those States, as here, any other than unconditional loyalty—that which stands for the Union, whatever may become of Slavery—those States would have been, and would be, far more helpful and less troublesome to the defenders of the Union than they have been, or now are.

IV. We think timid counsels in such a crisis calculated to prove perilous, and probably disastrous. It is the duty of a Government so wantonly, wickedly assailed by Rebellion as ours has been, to oppose force in a defiant, dauntless spirit. It cannot afford to temporize with traitors nor with semi-traitors. It must not bribe them to behave themselves, nor make them fair promises in the hope of disarming their causeless hostility. Representing a brave and high-spirited people, it can afford to forfeit anything else better than its own self-respect, or their admiring confidence. For our government even to seem, after war has been made on it, to dispel the affected apprehensions of armed traitors that their cherished privileges may be assailed by it, is to invite insult and encourage hopes of its own downfall. The rush to arms of Ohio, Indiana, Illinois, is the true answer at once to the Rebel raids of John Morgan and the traitorous sophistries of Beriah Magoffin.

V. We complain that the Union cause has suffered, and is now suffering immensely, from mistaken deference to Rebel Slavery. Had you, Sir, in your Inaugural Address, unmistakably given notice that, in case the Rebellion already commenced were persisted in, and your efforts to preserve the Union and enforce the laws should be resisted by armed force, *you would recognize no loyal person as rightfully held in Slavery by a traitor*, we believe the Rebellion would therein have received a staggering if not fatal blow. At that moment, according to the returns of the most recent elections, the Unionists were a large majority of the voters of the Slave States. But they were composed in good part of the aged, the feeble, the wealthy, the timid—the young, the reckless, the aspiring, the adventurous had already been largely lured by the gamblers and negro-traders, the politicians by trade and the conspirators by instinct, into the toils of Treason. Had you then proclaimed that Rebellion would strike the shackles from the slaves of every traitor, the wealthy and the cautious would have been supplied with a powerful inducement to remain loyal. As it was, every coward in the South soon became a traitor from fear; for Loyalty was perilous, while Treason seemed comparatively safe. Hence the boasted unanimity of the South—a unanimity based on Rebel terrorism and the fact that immunity and safety were found on that side, danger and probable death on ours. The Rebels from the first have been eager to confiscate, imprison, scourge and kill: we have fought wolves with the devices of sheep. The result is just what might have been expected. Tens of thousands are fighting in the Rebel ranks to-day whose original bias and natural leanings would have led into ours.

VI. We complain that the Confiscation Act which you approved is habitually disregarded by your Generals, and that no word of rebuke for them from you has yet reached the public ear. Fremont's Proclamation and Hunter's Order favoring Emancipation were promptly annulled by you; while Halleck's No. 3, forbidding fugitives from Slavery to Rebels to come within his lines—an order as unmilitary as inhuman, and which received the hearty approbation of every traitor in America—with scores of like tendency, have never provoked even your own remonstrance. We complain that the officers of your Armies have habitually repelled rather than invited approach of slaves who would have gladly taken the risks of escaping from their Rebel masters to our camps, bringing intelligence often of inestimable value to the Union cause. We complain that those who *have* thus escaped to us, avowing a willingness to do for us whatever might be required, have been brutally and madly repulsed, and often surrendered to be scourged, maimed and tortured by the ruffian traitors, who pretend to own them. We complain that a large proportion of our regular Army Officers, with many of the Volunteers, evince far more solicitude to uphold Slavery than to put down the Rebellion. And finally, we complain that you, Mr. President, elected as a Republican, knowing well what an abomination Slavery is, and how emphatically it is the core and essence of this atrocious Rebellion, seem never to interfere with these atrocities, and never give a direction to your Military subordinates, which does not appear to have been conceived in the interest of Slavery rather than of Freedom.

VII. Let me call your attention to the recent tragedy in New Orleans, whereof the facts are obtained entirely through Pro-Slavery channels. A considerable body of resolute, able-bodied men, held in Slavery by two Rebel sugar-planters in defiance of the Confiscation Act which you have approved, left plantations thirty miles distant and made their way to the great mart of the South-West, which they knew to be the indisputed possession of the Union forces. They made their way safely and quietly through thirty miles of Rebel territory, expecting to find freedom under the protection of our flag. Whether they had or had not heard of the passage of the Confiscation Act, they reasoned logically that we could not kill them for deserting the service of their lifelong oppressors, who had through treason become our implacable enemies. They came to us for liberty and protection, for which they were willing to render their best service: they met with hostility, captivity, and murder. The barking of the base curs of Slavery in this quarter deceives no one—not even themselves. They say, indeed, that the negroes had no right to appear in New Orleans armed (with their implements of daily labor in the cane-field); but no one doubts that they would gladly have laid these down if assured that they should be free. They were set upon and maimed, captured, and killed, because they sought the benefit of that act of Congress which they may not specifically have heard of, but which was none the less the law of the land—which they had a clear right to the benefit of—which it was *somebody's* duty to publish far and wide, in order that so many as possible should be impelled to desist from serving Rebels and the Rebellion and come over to the side of the Union.

VIII. On the face of this wide earth, Mr. President, there is not one disinterested, determined, intelligent champion of the Union cause who does not feel that all attempts to put down the Rebellion and at the same time uphold its inciting cause are preposterous and futile—that the Rebellion, if crushed out tomorrow, would be renewed within a year if Slavery were left in full vigor—that

Army officers who remain to this day devoted to Slavery can at best be but half-way loyal to the Union—and that every hour of deference to Slavery is an hour of added and deepened peril to the Union. I appeal to the testimony of your Ambassadors in Europe. It is freely at your service, not at mine. Ask them to tell you candidly whether the seeming subserviency of your policy to the slaveholding, slavery-upholding interest, is not the perplexity, the despair of statesmen of all parties, and be admonished by the general answer.

IX. I close as I began with the statement that what an immense majority of the Loyal Millions of your countrymen require of you is a frank, declared, unqualified, ungrudging execution of the laws of the land, more especially of the Confiscation Act. That Act gives freedom to the slaves of Rebels coming within our lines, or whom those lines may at any time inclose—we ask you to render it due obedience by publicly requiring all your subordinates to recognize and obey it. The Rebels are everywhere using the late anti-negro riots in the North, as they have long used your officers' treatment of negroes in the South, to convince the slaves that they have nothing to hope from a Union success—that we mean in that case to sell them into a bitter bondage to defray the cost of war. Let them impress this as a truth on the great mass of their ignorant and credulous bondsmen, and the Union will never be restored—never. We cannot conquer Ten Millions of People united in solid phalanx against us, powerfully aided by the Northern sympathizers and European allies. We must have scouts, guides, spies, cooks, teamsters, diggers and choppers from the Blacks of the South, whether we allow them to fight for us or not, or we shall be baffled and repelled. As one of the millions who would gladly have avoided this struggle at any sacrifice but that of Principle and Honor, but who now feels that the triumph of the Union is indispensable not only to the existence of our country but to the well-being of mankind, I entreat you to render a hearty and unequivocal obedience to the law of the land.

WALT WHITMAN, THE REVOLUTIONARY POET, HOLDS A MIRROR TO AMERICA

Many major literary figures were journalists first. America's most revolutionary poet, Walt Whitman, was one of them. Even though he put more intensity into his poetic writing efforts than his newspaper work, his editorials bore the marks of a daily writer concerned about what he said and how he said it.

Whitman got his first experience in newspapers at the age of 12 when he was apprenticed to a Long Island printer and publisher. Over the next 60 years, until his death in 1892, he edited or co-edited a dozen newspapers and wrote for at least 15 others. His editorial writing was marked by many of the characteristics of subject matter and style found in his poetry.

His editorials fell into two broad categories: ideology and American life. In both, the "Poet of Democracy" identified intensely with the common man and fervently advocated "Americanism." On politics and other areas affecting the ordinary person, Whitman wrote independently and fearlessly. "We have never hesitated to assume an independent position," he told readers, "and to comment upon passing events freely and boldly.... We never intend to mince matters."

When not advocating a cause or excoriating a politician or editor on the other side, Whitman devoted his time to observing America. He liked nothing better than to take leisurely walking tours to see firsthand the exuberant, optimistic life of the American city, to experience and then describe the swirling center of the nation's melting pot. No nativist was Whitman, but a believer that America's greatness would grow out of its millions of individuals of diverse backgrounds and its independence from "the moth eaten systems of the old world." The newspapers that he edited were notable for their "sketches" and "photographs," as if holding a mirror to America.

In explaining effective editorial writing style, Whitman wrote: "[The writer] should have a fluent style: elaborate finish we do not think requisite in daily writing. His articles had far better be earnest and terse than polished; they should ever smack of being uttered on the spur of the moment, like political oratory.—In temper, Job himself is the lowest example he should take." He offered these guides on "How to Write for Newspapers": "Have something to write about.... Write short; to the point; stop when you have done.... Read it over, abridge, and correct it until you get it into the shortest space possible."

The following editorial, a good example of the sketches of city life Whitman wrote, illustrates the techniques and subject matter used by Whitman the poet as Whitman the editorial writer.

SATURDAY NIGHT—"ITEMS" MAKES A TOUR
(Walt Whitman; Brooklyn *Times*; December 6, 1858)

Made desperate by the plentiful lack of interesting local news of late, and foreseeing that unless a "dreadful murder," a "disastrous conflagration," or a "gigantic burglary" should turn up soon, his occupation would be gone and himself forced to retire temporarily to the shades of private life, Mr. Items sallied forth from the airy attic in which poets and police-reporters are traditionally supposed to reside, and fortified by a five-dollar overcoat and a blue cotton umbrella (borrowed for the occasion), proceeded to hunt up materials for a paragraph.

The night was rainy. Probably people are aware of that interesting fact. It was also muddy. Of that Mr. Items' boots soon afforded undoubted evidence. But the grocery stores were full of life, and the others ditto, in a diminished degree. Grand street on a Saturday evening presents quite a spectacle in the way of life and animation. On such occasions when good steady people or their servants are out "marketing" and when dissolute youths are busily squandering the week's earnings and making vigorous preparations for a "blue Monday," the swarms that fill the pave remind one more of Grand street in New York than of a thoroughfare of our own quiet 'Burgh. South 7th, with its hurrying crowds hastening from the ferry, and South 10th, with its procession of passengers on a smaller scale, also wear a busier aspect than usual.—People have the air of men who have finished the labors of the week and who are glad of it, and willing to let their contentedness be seen in their faces—of men who are going home with the vivid impression that

"—there's an eye will mark
Their coming, and grow brighter
When they come."

—of men, finally, who are blessed with good appetites and are looking forward to their suppers, not without having provided something extra for the Sunday dinner. The sight of the turkeys, chickens, geese, fish, and other edibles that travel up these streets on Saturday night is a capital appetizer—better than ye Bitters of Stoughton—though rather aggravating to poor devils, in commiseration for whose empty stomachs Items here drops a sympathizing tear.

The hotel bar-rooms do a thriving business. Young men with shining hats and garrote collars appear to be impressed with the firm conviction that the Water Works are a superfluous institution, and that the fluid from Baisely's Pond is religiously to be eschewed. Brandy and billiards appear to be the programme at these resorts on Saturday night.

At the Station House they are pretty busy in providing accommodations for inebriated Johns, intoxicated Pats and unfortunate Bridgets. A motley set they are—the debris of the North Side, wretched, sodden, degraded, but all occupying the same dead level. Rum, like poverty, makes strange bedfellows. And yet, at times there will occur cases of no little interest among this miscellaneous crowd of what are elegantly termed by the police—"bummers." Sometimes it is a broken-down business man whose love of conviviality has been his ruin; sometimes a used-up actor with a hoarse voice, a haggard visage and some remains of a stage-walk in his shambling gait; sometimes a "retired physician" whose "sands of life have nearly run out"—through the medium not of an hour glass but of a glass of grog; sometimes a forsaken woman "who has seen better days," and from whose poverty-pinched features, vice and gin have not yet removed all traces of earlier years. Queer things turn up occasionally among the common run of "drunks and disorderlies" that constitute the bulk of the "returns," and which are hardly glanced at by the newspaper reporter. And queer things sometimes fall from the lips of the miserable set the next morning when they stand before the police justice to receive their quantum of days or months in the Penitentiary, with shaking limbs and wild eyes. Sometimes, we say, but not often. Usually the "drunks" are prosaic and commonplace enough.

Among the Germans, Saturday and Sunday nights are marked by a little more than usual jollity. That hardworking and sensible people enjoy themselves after their own moderate fashion once a week, and we should like to know exceedingly who better earn the right. Winter evenings, however, are not favorable to the observation of our 16th Ward friends. Summer Sunday afternoons and evenings are the best time to see the elephant ["see the show"] in that locality. When the air is balmy, and laden with the grateful odor of the meerschaum; when half the population are outdoors and the rest sitting with open doors and windows; when the amber colored lager creams and mantles in the glass, and the piano and violin are making merry music on every side,—then should "Dutchtown" be visited by the benighted Southsider, who has never visited "Schneider's" or witnessed the performance of a Teutonic play at the theatre nearby. But at all times the bier saloons are lively enough. Passing along Meserole street, Items, ever willing to make a sacrifice on the altar of public good, looked in and took notes, to the no small discomfiture of some of the smaller saloon-keepers, who were persuaded that he was a spotter, or detective on the look-out for infractions of the license law. The amount of indignant virtue which was paraded when "schnaaps" or "whiskey skin" was asked for by a thirsty traveller was charming to behold. "We sells nothing but bier!" is invariably the response at this time, unless the enquirer is personally known to be safe. These houses are much the same, so far as externals go. A few round and square tables, round which the customers sit, perhaps a billiard table or two, a bar behind which stands the inevitable bier keg, a few pictures and prints which are not usually art treasures, and in every place of any pretensions a piano, which is nightly fingered by some aspiring amateur—all Germans are amateurs—and the establishment is complete. The burly landlord is civil and attentive, his wife efficiently aids and abets him in the exhibition of those qualities, and in the background there are glimpses of the small-fry and indubitable evidences of infantile life. Dominoes, cards, newspaper, lager, and tobacco, make the evening pass pleasantly for the frequenters, and there are rarely any disturbances.

But it is getting late. The shops are closing; the butcher is closed; the corner grocery-man has supplied the last customer with her pound of sugar or peck of potatoes; the circulating library has dispensed its last copy of such thrilling romances as "The Fiend Codfish, or the Frantic Fisherman" to the last literary tyro for Sunday reading; passengers grow few and far between in the streets; the mirth grows fast and furious in drinking places of the lower order and it is time for decent people to be in bed. Lights twinkle from sleeping-rooms alike in the shanties along North 3d street and the palatial residences of South 9th. The clock strikes midnight; the policeman's sharp metallic rap on the pavement sounds in Items' ears, and carefully closing the blue umbrella he seeks his virtuous domicile. Another week has closed.

But the startling news?—the murders, the outrages and the other favorite pabulum of the reporters "about town"—did Items succeed in obtaining anything astounding, after his protracted jaunt? To borrow the language of the "shields" at the Station House, there was "nary thing." Items is about to emigrate.

HARVEY SCOTT DISSECTS
THE SKEPTIC INGERSOLL

Harvey W. Scott served as editor of the Portland *Oregonian* for 45 years, from 1865 to 1910. During that time, he was the leading journalist in the Pacific Northwest, and generally he is recognized as one of the most forceful, intellectual, and influential editorial writers that American journalism has produced. Although writing on the various topics of the day, he was especially respected for his editorials on the more enduring ones of literature, history, religion, ethics, and morality. Perhaps no daily editorial writer has been recognized as more authoritative in such areas requiring deep thought.

Scott's prestige arose from a combination of wide reading, mature and critical thinking, and a clear, powerful writing style. His views were especially respected in the field of religion. Reverent but tolerant, he applied an inquisitive mind to examining the nature of religion and its role in the life of mankind. Although a member of the Congregational Church, he did not adhere closely to a particular dogma. Instead, he reasoned that a belief in a Supreme Being was one of the deepest, most universal human characteristics. His reasoning and his writing style are demonstrated in the following editorial dissecting the methods used by the skeptic Robert Ingersoll.

INGERSOLL'S DISREGARD
OF THE UNIVERSAL RELIGIOUS SPIRIT
(Harvey W. Scott; Portland *Oregonian*; April 22, 1870)

Robert G. Ingersoll, better known as "Colonel Bob Ingersoll," continues at intervals his lectures on theological subjects in different parts of the country; and now and then a member of the

clergy takes a hand at answering him. Usually there is plenty of
dogmatism on both sides. Ingersoll attacks with sneers and is repelled with denunciation. On one side is contemptuous, unfair
and exaggerated treatment of the subject, and on the other epi-
thetical abuse. Ingersoll has power, undoubtedly, but it lies
mainly in his tricks of words. When he talks on theological subjects he always takes care to state the position he attacks,
whether it be found in the works of the Bible or in scholastic theology, in a way that makes it both absurd and ridiculous. Smart
parody, clever travesty, or grosser burlesque, with occasional use
of the lighter weapons of satire and wit, give a popular flavor to
an address, and the orator carries off large honors.

Undoubtedly, a great part of the power for which Ingersoll is
noted is in his very remarkable oratory. He is not a great thinker,
but he is a great speaker. Those who remember when—until then
an almost unknown Western lawyer—he took the platform, amid
the buzzing of the great assembly that filled the Cincinnati Exposition Hall, and nominated James G. Blaine for President, will
never forget what a revelation of oratory and influence it was.
Without having any phonographic statistics to go by, we should
judge that Ingersoll speaks at least one-third faster than other
first-class orators of the country. The words, clear, distinct and
perfectly enunciated, come forth like a torrent. It is as if he had so
much to say that he must haste to get it all out, lest the hourglass
should cut him short before he is done. The effect of this is to im-
part some portion of his own enthusiasm to his audience. The
torrent, if they give themselves up to it, takes away their understanding. This is peculiarly the case when he delivers one of those
singular cumulative sentences with which his orations or lectures abound. It is hard to describe one of these artful combina-
tions of words in which one phrase is tacked on to another, then
another and another, until the whole is ended off with a stroke of
assertion or wit that resounds through the audience like the crack
of a whip.

An example may, perhaps, give the idea:—

> For thousands of years men have been disputing about tri-
> fles, they have argued about sacrifices and altars, about cir-
> cumcision and concision, about the cleanness and unclean-
> ness of meats, about initiations and renunciations, about
> ablutions and baptisms, about the person of the Deity and the
> substance of the Trinity, about original sin and the origin of
> evil, about consubstantiation and substitution, about the sup-
> per in one kind or in both kinds, about justification by faith,
> the damnation of infants, the location of hell.

This, delivered with increasing intensity and rapidity, inevitably has the effect on the audience of making them, at least
for the moment, believe that men have actually been occupying

themselves, for the last few thousand years, with trifles, and are only now about to awaken to really important things at the trumpet call of Apostle Ingersoll. Only the cooler heads reflect that there is nothing in all this dogmatism. But, as Johnson said of Junius, he who attacks received opinions shall never want an audience. Ingersoll, and such as he, are at once the product of and a rebound from a hard, speculative, and in many respects unreasonable theology, which belongs rather to former generations than to the present one.

THE NEW YORK *TIMES* TAMES THE TAMMANY TIGER

By 1870 "Boss" William Tweed's Tammany Ring had captured political power in New York City. Through its control of government offices, it ravaged the municipal treasury, stealing as much as $200 million. Tweed and his cohorts expected to grow richer and richer as they stayed longer in office. Their tenure was ensured by gangs of hoodlums who intimidated voters and who cast votes repeatedly under various *noms de plume*, by city account books locked away from public view, by advertising contracts let to newspapers, by special favors and threats of increased taxation to businessmen, and by little gifts here and there to all classes of voters. So confident was Tweed of his invulnerability that he once retorted to charges of impropriety, "What are you going to do about it?"

And there was hardly anything anyone could do or was willing to try—except for the cartoonist Thomas Nast and the New York *Times*. Although Nast's cartoons gained acclaim, it was really the *Times* that presented to the citizens of New York City the hard evidence of malfeasance. The *Times'* campaign provides a model of the problems and persistence demanded of a successful crusade against entrenched interests, and of the difficulties in overcoming apathy and fear and replacing them with public indignation.

The campaign began in September 1870 when Louis Jennings, the *Times'* editor-in-chief, asked editorially how Tweed had gone from poverty to wealth in a matter of five years. The editorial suggested, without offering evidence, that corruption, financial abuse, and swindle were the answer. With a surplus of emotion but a shortage of facts, the *Times'* campaign continued in that vein over the next 10 months.

The Tammany response outwardly was calm, and its members claimed that the *Times'* animus was explained by the city's refusal to pay an advertising bill. Most other newspapers in the city, which received large municipal advertising accounts, criticized the *Times'* intemperate attack. Big advertisers withdrew from the *Times*, and the city challenged the newspaper's title to the land on which its office building sat. After a cursory examination of the city's account books, an audit committee—composed of some of the city's most prominent businessmen—proclaimed that the city's financial affairs were all "administered in a correct and faithful manner." With the *Times'* charges discredited, the Tweed ring swept the city elections a few days later. The newspaper's crusade might have died except for a traffic accident.

In January 1871 the city auditor died when his sleigh overturned on an icy New York street. The ring, in a sloppy mistake, appointed as his replacement an accountant who was working secretly for one of Tweed's political opponents. They copied some of the incriminating records from the city's books and then—after obtaining $20,000 in blackmail money from Tweed to keep the information secret—turned the records over to the *Times*.

When Tweed discovered that the newspaper had the information, he offered publisher George Jones $5 million not to publish it. On July 8, however, the *Times* ran its first installment, a four-column news story detailing the frauds in the rental of city armories. Accompanying the story was an editorial (reprinted below) assailing the ring members as a "gang of burglars." In the following weeks, additional accounts from the ledger books were reprinted daily. Each issue of the paper brought stronger demands from the pubic that ring members be prosecuted. Eventually they were turned out of office, most fled, and Tweed died in jail. The *Times'* campaign still provides the classic model of an editorial crusade against government corruption.

THE RING AND THE CITY ARMORIES
(Louis Jennings; New York *Times*; July 8, 1871)

We lay before our readers this morning a chapter of Municipal rascality which, in any other city but New York, would bring down upon the heads of its authors such a storm of public indignation as would force them to a speedy accountability before the bar of a Criminal Court, or compel them to take refuge in flight and perpetual exile. Here, however, it will, doubtless, be laughed at by some as a good joke, and an evidence of "smartness" on the part of our City officials, be discredited by others as unworthy of belief, and be denounced by the mass of our citizens as an "outrage," but, like other outrages of the same character, to be quietly submitted to because of the supposed impossibility of obtaining redress. Nevertheless, we trust that all our readers will give the article a careful perusal, and that the facts it contains will be treasured up as a part of the accumulated mass of official corruption which is being piled up against the Tammany Ring, and which is destined, at no distant day, to descend like an avalanche upon their heads and crush them beneath its weight.

The source from which the facts and figures relative to the

renting of armories in this City have been obtained, are of the most reliable character, and a large portion of the statements can easily be verified by any citizen who chooses to take a little personal trouble. If there is a single mistake in any of the statements or figures contained in the article, we shall be most happy to publish the correction, provided Mr. Connolly, or any other official concerned will send it to us duly verified. The TIMES has been often charged by those whose interest it is to belittle its exposures of the frauds of the Ring, with making random charges unsupported by facts and specifications. This charge comes with a bad grace from men whose master-stroke of policy for the last three years has been the concealment of all their official transactions from the public eye. These men are in the position of a gang of burglars, who, having stolen all your silver-ware and jewelry and placed them under lock and key, turn around and challenge you to identify your property. In the case of ordinary burglars, you could summon the Courts to your assistance, arrest the thieves, break open the locks and get a sight of your stolen goods. But the Tammany Ring are a law unto themselves; they are the Government; they control the machinery of justice, and own a large share of the Judges. Hence they defy your efforts to detect their villainy, and laugh at the idea of restitution. But, notwithstanding all these drawbacks and difficulties, the TIMES has succeeded in exposing many frauds upon the City Treasury, and has furnished better vouchers for its bills of indictment than Controller Connolly has furnished for the bills he has drawn on our tax-payers. We apprehend that no one will complain of a lack of facts and specifications in the article to which we now call the reader's attention; and that not even the TRIBUNE, or any other of the eighteen daily and weekly papers that have been gagged by Ring patronage, will be able to find an excuse for ignoring the startling record presented elsewhere, on the ground that it is not sufficiently definite.

MASTERS OF THE EDITORIAL

E.L. GODKIN:
MASTER OF THE ANALYTICAL ESSAY

Edwin Lawrence Godkin, at the New York *Evening Post* and, more importantly, the *Nation*, became America's master of the serious editorial essay in the late 19th century. Utilizing logic and clarity—with subtly placed and often cutting ridicule, humor, and irony—he became known, as the editor Oswald Garrison Villard declared, "the greatest of our editorial writers." He combined, as no other writer has, a critical intellect with the ability to express his ideas clearly and forcefully. He kept an intellectual distance from the mainstream of American thought. This assured a detached, analytical viewpoint that enabled him to discern the questions of the moment and examine the dogmas of the day. His writings influenced the nation's educated, sophisticated class as few ever did. Coupled with a disdain for the uneducated masses, however, his approach limited his audience and virtually eliminated the largest groups of Americans from his readership.

Born October 2, 1831, in England, Godkin lived a protected and privileged early life. His father was a controversial writer for Irish newspapers; and, at an early age, the son also felt the itch to write. He served as editor, in fact, of his grade school's newspaper. After graduating from Queen's College, he entered the professional world as a special correspondent for the London *Daily News* and a contributor to the New York *Times*.

When the owners of the *Nation*, formed in 1865 by a joint stock company, began their search for a new editor, they were looking for a staunch abolitionist who would support the Radical stance already put into place. Godkin, contacted after an exhaustive search, was able to provide capital and agreed to abide by editorial guidelines. In 1866, he became editor and part owner. Once he was at the helm, however, the *Nation's* supporters realized it would not be the leading publication fighting for equal rights for blacks. Godkin outwardly supported the Radical cause, but he never shielded certain Radical politicians from criticism. In fact, in the years to come, he was also wobbly when it came to the subject of black suffrage.

The *Nation* appealed to Godkin because of its intellectual and literary bent; and, while there, he often wrote derisive letters to other New York newspapers, criticizing their sensational tactics. The *Herald, Tribune,* and *Sun* were never free from his criticism. Of their faults, he wrote, "It is their unutterable silliness and vulgarity.... Childish hilarity, irreverence, and we may add, childish inventiveness are their leading characteristics."

Although Godkin was sometimes criticized for his conservative ways and his unabashed preference for the educated and elite, his writing skill and talent were beyond argument. His trademark writing style leaves a lasting impression on readers even today. His editorials were characteristically serious and intellectual. The New York *Evening Post's* historian Allan Nevins said, "The prevailing tone of his writings has been well said to be that 'of an accomplished gentleman conversing with a set of intimates at his club.'"

Godkin presented his ideas in an always concise, clear, logical manner. The main characteristic of his editorials was well-organized argument or explanation with a flare for humor or invective. Villard described his writing this way: "Not even those familiar with his style by contact with its daily expression can run over his editorials...without a sense of amazement at their clarity and logic, and their ability to interest at all times, at the way in which he dissected the statement he proposed to attack with the skill of a great surgeon in laying bare the seat of a disease before actually beginning to operate.... [K]nowledge, logic, and power added fact after fact and argument after argument, until the column editorial was complete. 'Never write without conveying information or expressing an opinion with reasons,' was his injunction to a youthful writer."

Nevins added that Godkin's writing "was incisive, graphic, and pithy. But at all times it was simple, without the least straining for effect. He indulged in no rhetoric, he did not excel in epigram, as did [Charles] Dana [at the New York *Sun*], and he had no desire to be brilliant in the sense of merely clever."

His writing was at its best when he attacked an institution or a person. He never backed away from criticizing individuals. His sharp pen punctured many a public character, for he believed that attacks on evils should be as personal as possible. If political corruption, for example, were to be criticized, the most effective technique was to show the corruption in terms of one politician.

In dissecting issues, he could mix force with ridicule, logic with sarcasm, clarity with irony, humor with common sense. Rollo Ogden, an associate of Godkin's, explained that "in verbal or written expression, Mr. Godkin's humour had a great range and variety. He was remarkable for unexpected turns of phrase.... He fell naturally into comic exaggeration, and abounded in original epithet."

Irony was his trademark device; and, as with his other tools, he used it subtly. For his readers, he would present a topic against a background that exposed its ironies. Of Godkin's ability to present essays with a touch of lightness, Nevins said, "The humor was always spontaneous, and could be either genial or scorching. He had a remarkable faculty for humorous imagery.... Godkin was a master of that two-edged editorial weapon, irony, which in clumsy hands may mortally wound the user."

In the pages of his newspaper, he did little to ameliorate his disdain for the common man, America's nouveau riche, the materialism springing up in America, or the press which appealed to these interests. Americans, Godkin thought, were typically uncivilized. Their worship of wealth led to shallow standards, lowered ethics and tastes, crass materialism, and cheap millionaires, and was one of the basic dangers of democratic government.

Godkin believed the spokesman for these values was the press, and he denounced a journalism that would appeal to the base attitudes of the masses. Reform of American journalism was one of his major interests. The function of a paper, he believed, was not to cater to the masses but to take a consistently hard, critical view of important current issues.

Godkin also made a practice of denouncing woman's suffrage, labor reformers, immigration, and evangelical clergymen. His distaste for the common and the uncivil was unconcealed. Although he espoused theories of government beneficial to the common man, he had no real understanding of or sympathy for the poor, the farmers, the working class, or others sharing the rougher aspects of American life. He argued against anything that was destroying the traditional standards.

He did not, however, always write in opposition to "causes." Early in his career, in fact, he adopted the reform of civil service as his own pet crusade. In the pages of the *Nation*, he wrote powerfully and decisively on the issue. Ogden praised his ardor, saying that he "labored for [reform] through organization and correspondence and political appeal."

Under Godkin's editorship, the *Nation's* circulation never totaled more than 10,000, but its subscribers included librarians, leaders in education, clergymen, lawyers, historians, authors, and other editors. His readers were said to have passed Godkin's opinions to the whole population. Yet even Godkin's sophisticated readers sometimes rebelled against him because of his acid writing, his critical outlook, and his plainly limited sympathies with the common people.

The *Nation* became the weekly edition of the New York *Evening Post* in 1881; and in 1883 Godkin became the *Evening Post's* editor after an interesting turn of events. While he and the newspaper's liberal editor-in-chief, Carl Schurz, were in a heated battle over a railway telegraphers' strike (with Godkin attacking the workers), Schurz took a two-week vacation. Godkin used the editorial page to herald his strong opinions and declared himself editor.

Although Godkin was recognized as a great mind, the general public viewed him as somewhat snobbish and brusque. "Impulsive" and "intolerant" were two other words often used to characterize him. Those close to him—other intelligent, cultivated men of the world—painted, however, quite a different picture of their friend. They described him as friendly, genial, and charming.

Today, Godkin's writing stands on its own. At the *Nation*, he combined a critical intellect with the ability to express his ideas clearly and forcefully. To his writing, he also skillfully added touches of subtle humor and irony. His essays shaped the judgments of his contemporaries, and they are as fresh today as they were on publication day.

•The following editorial, written during the Franco-Prussian War of 1870-1871, analyzes the underlying reasons for the failure of peace efforts by outsiders. The problem, Godkin argued, lay in human nature.

PEACE
(*The Nation*)

The horrors of war are just now making a deeper impression than ever on the popular mind, owing to the close contact with the battle-field and the hospital into which the railroad and the telegraph and the newspaper have brought the public of all civilized countries. Wars are fought out now, so to speak, under every man's and woman's eyes; and, what is perhaps of nearly as much importance, the growth of commerce and manufactures, and the increased complication of the social machine, render the smallest derangement of it anywhere a concern and trouble to all nations. The consequence is that the desire for peace was never so deep as it is now, and the eagerness of all good people to find out some other means of deciding international disputes than mutual killing never so intense.

And yet the unconsciousness of the true nature and difficulties of the problem they are trying to solve, which is displayed by most of those who make the advocacy of peace their special work, is very discouraging. We are far from believing that the incessant and direct appeals to the public conscience on the subject of war are not likely in the long run to produce some effect; but it is very difficult to resist the conclusion that the efforts of the special advocates of peace have thus far helped to spread and strengthen the impression that there is no adequate substitute for the sword as an arbiter between nations, or, in other words, to harden the popular heart on the subject of military slaughter. It is certain that, during the last fifty years, the period in which peace societies have been at work, armies have been growing steadily larger, the means of destruction have been multiplying, and wars have been as frequent and as bloody as ever before; and, what is worse, the popular heart goes into war as it has never done in past ages.

The great reason why the more earnest enemies of war have not made more progress toward doing away with it, has been that, from the very outset of their labors down to the present moment, they have devoted themselves mainly to depicting its horrors and to denouncing its cruelty. In other words, they almost invariably approach it from a side with which nations actually engaged in it are just as familiar as anybody, but which has for the moment assumed in their eyes a secondary importance. The peace advocates are constantly talking of the guilt of killing, while the combatants only think, and will only think, of the nobleness of dying. To the peace advocates the soldier is always a man going to slaughter his neighbors; to his countrymen he is a man going to lose his life for their sake—that is, to perform the loftiest act of devotion of which a human being is capable. It is not wonderful, then, that the usual effect of appeals for peace made by neutrals is to produce mingled exasperation and amusement among the belligerents. To the great majority of Europeans our civil war was a shocking spectacle, and the persistence of the North in carrying it on a sad proof of ferocity and lust of dominion. To the great majority of those engaged in carrying it on the struggle was a holy one, in which it was a blessing to perish. Probably nothing ever fell more cruelly on human ears than the taunts and execrations which American wives and mothers heard from the other side of the ocean, heaped on the husbands and sons whom they had sent to the battle-field, never thinking at all of their slaying, but thinking solely of their being slain; and very glad indeed that, if death had to come, it should come in such a cause. If we go either to France or Germany today, we shall find a precisely similar state of feeling. If the accounts we hear be true—and we know of no reason to doubt them—there is no more question in the German and French mind that French and German soldiers are doing their highest duty in fighting, than there was in the most patriotic Northern or Southern home during our war; and we may guess, therefore, how a German or French mother, the light of whose life had gone out at Gravelotte or Orleans, and who hugs her sorrow as a great gift of God, would receive an address from New York on the general wickedness and folly of her sacrifice.

The fact is—and it is one of the most suggestive facts we know of—that the very growth of the public conscience has helped to make peace somewhat more difficult, war vastly more terrible. When war was the game of kings and soldiers, the nations went into it in a half-hearted way, and sincerely loathed it; now that war is literally an outburst of popular feeling, the friend of peace finds most of his logic powerless. There is little use in reasoning with a man who is ready to die on the folly or wickedness of dying. When a nation has worked itself up to the point of believing that there are objects within its reach for which life were well surrendered, it has reached a region in which the wise saws and modern instances of the philosopher or lawyer cannot touch it, and in which pictures of the misery of war only help to make the martyr's crown seem more glorious.

Therefore, we doubt whether the work of peace is well done by those who, amidst the heat and fury of actual hostilities, dwell upon the folly and cruelty of them, and appeal to the combatants to stop fighting, on the ground that fighting involves suffering and loss of life, and the destruction of property. The principal effect of this on "the average man" has been to produce the impression that the friends of peace are ninnies, and to make him smile over the earnestness with which everybody looks on his own wars as holy and inevitable, and his neighbors' wars as unnecessary and wicked. Any practical movement to put an end to war must begin far away from the battle-field and its horrors. It must take up and deal with the various influences, social and political, which create and perpetuate the state of mind which makes people ready to fight. Preaching up peace and preaching down war generally are very like general homilies in praise of virtue and denunciation of vice. Everybody agrees with them, but nobody is ever ready to admit their applicability to his particular case. War is, in our time, essentially the people's work. Its guilt is theirs, as its losses and sufferings are theirs. All attempts to saddle emperors, kings, and nobles with the responsibility of it may as well be given up from this time forward....

•The following editorial epitomizes Godkin's philosophy about the shortcomings of popular society and his approach to writing. Analyzing the superficiality of contemporary culture, he first presents the problem and then explains its causes through use of an illustration.

CHROMO-CIVILIZATION
(The Nation)

The last "statement," it is reasonable to hope, has been made in the Beecher-Tilton case previous to the trial at law, and it is safe to say that it has left the public mind in as unsettled a state as ever before. People do not know what to believe, but they do not want to hear any more newspaper discussion by the principal actors. We are not going to attempt any analysis or summing-up of the case at present. It will be time enough to do that after the dramatis personae have undergone an examination in court, but we would again warn our readers against looking for any decisive result from the legal trial. The expectations on this point which some of the newspapers and a good many lawyers are encouraging are in the highest degree extravagant. The truth is that only a very small portion of the stuff contained in the various "statements" can, under the rules of evidence, be laid before the jury—not, we venture to assert, more than would fill half a newspaper column in all. What will be laid before the jury is, in the main, "questions of veracity" between three or four persons whose credit is already greatly shaken, or, in other words, the very kind of questions on which juries are most likely to disagree, even when the jurymen are entirely unprejudiced. In the present case they are sure to be prejudiced, and are sure to be governed, consciously or unconsciously, in reaching their conclusions by agencies wholly foreign to the matter in hand, and are thus very likely to disagree. There are very few men whose opinions about Mr. Beecher's guilt or innocence are not influenced by their own religious and political beliefs, or by their social antecedents or surroundings. A curious and somewhat instructive illustration of the way in which a man's fate in such cases as this may be affected by considerations having no sort of relation to the facts, is afforded by the attitude of the Western press toward the chief actors in the present scandal. It may be said, roughly, that while the press east of the Alleghenies has inclined in Beecher's favor, the newspapers west of them have gone somewhat savagely and persistently against him, and have treated Tilton as a martyr. The cause of such a divergence of views, considering that both Tilton and Beecher are Eastern men, is of course somewhat obscure, but we have no doubt that it is due to a vague feeling prevalent in the West that Tilton's cause is the democratic one—that is, the cause of the poor, friendless man against the rich and successful one—a feeling somewhat like that which in England enlisted the working-classes in London on the side of the Tichborne claimant, in defiance of all reason and evidence, as a poor devil fighting a hard battle with the high and mighty. One of the reporters of a Western paper which has made important contributions to the literature of the scandal, recently accounted for his support of Tilton by declaring that in standing by him he was "fighting the battle of the Bohemians against Capital." Another Western paper, in analyzing the causes of the position taken by the leading New York papers on Beecher's side, ascribed it to the social relations of the editors with him, believing that they met him frequently at dinners and breakfasts, and found him a jovial companion. All this would be laughable enough if it did not show the amount of covert peril—peril against which no precautions can be taken—to which every prominent man's character is exposed. The moment he gets into a scrape of any kind he finds a host of persons whose enmity he never suspected clamoring to have him thrown to the beasts "on general grounds"—that is, in virtue of certain tests adopted by themselves, judged by which, apart from the facts of any particular accusation, a man of his kind is unquestionably a bad fellow. The accusation, in short, furnishes the occasion for destroying him, not necessarily the reason for it.

In Europe there are already abundant signs that the scandal will be considered a symptomatic phenomenon—that is, a phenomenon illustrative of the moral condition of American society generally; for it must not be overlooked that, putting aside altogether the question of Beecher's guilt or innocence, the "statements" furnish sociological revelations of a most singular and instructive kind. The witnesses, in telling their story, although their minds are wholly occupied with the proof or disproof of certain propositions, describe ways of living, standards of right and wrong, traits of manners, codes of propriety, religious and social ideas, which, taken together, form social pictures of great interest and value. Now, if these were really pictures of American society in general, as some European observers are disposed to conclude, we do not hesitate to say that the prospects of the Anglo-Saxon race on this continent would be somewhat gloomy. But we believe we only express the sentiment of all parts of the country when we say that the state of things in Brooklyn revealed by the charges and countercharges has filled the best part of the American people with nearly as much amazement as if an unknown tribe worshipping strange gods had been suddenly discovered on Brooklyn Heights. In fact, the actors in the scandal have the air of persons who are living, not *more majorum*, by rules with which they are familiar, but like half-civilized people who have got hold of a code which they do not understand, and the phrases of which they use without being able to adapt their conduct to it.

We have not space at our command to illustrate this as fully as we could wish, even if the patience of our readers would permit of it, but we can perhaps illustrate sufficiently within a very short compass. We have already spoken of the Oriental extravagance of the language used in the scandal, which might pass in Persia or Central Arabia, where wild hyperbole is permitted by the genius of the language, and where people are accustomed to it in conversation, understand it perfectly, and make unconscious allowance for it. Displayed here in the United States, in a mercantile community, and in a tongue characterized by directness and simplicity, it makes the actors almost entirely incomprehensible to people outside their own set, as is shown by the attempts made to explain and understand the letters in the case. Most of the critics, both the friendly and hostile, are compelled to treat them as written in a sort of dialect which has to be read with the aid of commentary, glosses, and parallels, and accompanied, like the study of Homer or the Reg-Veda, by a careful examination of the surroundings of the writers, the conditions of their birth and education, the usages of the circle in which they live, and the social and religious influences by which they have been moulded, and so on. Their almost entire want of any sense of necessary connection between facts and written statements has been strikingly revealed by Moulton's production of various drafts or outlines of cards, reports, and letters which the actors proposed from time to time to get up and publish for the purpose of settling their troubles and warding off exposure by imposing on the public. No savages could have acted with a more simple-minded unconsciousness of truth. Moulton, according to his own story, helped Beecher to publish a lying card; got Tilton to procure from his wife a lying letter; and Tilton concocted a lying report for the committee, in which he made them express the highest admiration for himself, his adulterous wife, and her paramour. Here we have a bit of the machinery of high civilization—a committee, with its investigation and report, used, or attempted to be used, with just the kind of savage directness with which a Bongo would use it, when once he came to understand it, and found he could make it serve some end, and with just as little reference to the moral aspect of the transaction.

Take, again, Tilton's account of the motives which governed him in his treatment of his wife and of Beecher. He is evidently aware that there are two codes regulating a man's conduct under such circumstances—one the Christian code and the other the conventional code of honor, or as he calls it, "club-house morality"; but it soon became clear that he had no distinct conception of their difference. Having been brought up under the Christian code, and taught, doubtless, to regard the term "gentleman" as a name for a heartless epicurean, he started off by forgiving both Beecher and his wife, or, as the lawyers say, condoning their offence; and he speaks scornfully of the religious ignorance of the committee in assuming in their report that there was any offence for which a Christian was not bound to accept an apology as a sufficient atonement. The club-house code would, however, have prescribed the infliction of vengeance on Beecher by exposing him. Accordingly, Tilton mixes the two codes up in the most absurd way. Having, as a Christian, forgiven Beecher, he began, thirty days after the discovery of the offence, to expose him as a "gentleman," and kept forgiving and exposing him continuously through the whole four years, the *eclat* of such a relation to Beecher having evidently an irresistible temptation for him. Finally, when Dr. Bacon called him a "dog," he threw aside the Christian *role* altogether and began assailing his enemy with truly heathen virulence and vigor. A more curious blending of two conceptions of duty is not often seen, and it was doubtless due to the fact that no system of training or culture had made any impression on the man or gone more than skin deep. His interview with Beecher, too, by appointment, at his own house, for the purpose of ascertaining by a comparison of dates and reference to his wife's diary the probable paternity of her youngest child, which he describes with the utmost simplicity, is, we venture to say, an incident absolutely without precedent, and one which may safely be pronounced foreign to our civilization. Whether it really occurred, or Tilton invented it, it makes him a problem in social philosophy of considerable interest.

Moulton's story, too, furnishes several puzzles of the same kind. That an English-speaking Protestant married couple in easy circumstances and of fair education, and belonging to a religious circle, should not only be aware that their pastor was a libertine and should be keeping it a secret for him, but should make his adulteries the subject of conversation with him in the family circle, is hardly capable of explanation by reference to any known and acknowledged tendency of our society. But perhaps the most striking thing in Moulton's role is that while he appears on the scene as a gentleman or "man of the world," who does for honor's sake what the other actors do from fear of God, his whole course is a kind of caricature of what a gentleman under like circumstances would really do. For instance, he accepts Beecher's confidence, which may have been unavoidable, and betrays it by telling various people, from time to time, of the several incidents of Beecher's trouble, which is something of which a weak or loose-tongued person—vain of the task in which he was engaged, as it seemed to him, *i.e.*, of keeping the peace between two great men—might readily be guilty. But he tells the public of it in perfect unconsciousness that there was anything discreditable in it, as he does of his participation in the writing of lying letters and cards, and his passing money over from the adulterer to pacify the injured husband. In fact, he carries, according to his own account, his services to Beecher to a point at which it is very difficult to distinguish them from those of a pander, maintaining at the same time relations of the most disgusting confidence with Mrs. Tilton. Finally, too, when greatly perplexed as to his course, he goes publicly and with *eclat* for advice to a lawyer, with whom no gentleman, in the proper sense of the term, could maintain intimate personal relation or safely consult on a question of honor. The moral insensibility shown in his visit to General Butler is one of the strange parts of the affairs.

We have, of course, only indicated in the briefest way some of the things which may be regarded as symptomatic of strange mental and moral conditions in the circle in which the affair has occurred. The explanation of them in any way that would generally be considered satisfactory would be a difficult task. The influences which bring about a certain state of manners at any given time or place are always numerous and generally obscure, but we think something of this sort may be safely offered in consideration of the late "goings on" in Brooklyn.

In the first place, the newspapers and other cheap periodicals, and the lyceum lectures and small colleges, have diffused through the community a kind of smattering of all sorts of knowledge, a taste for reading and for "art"—that is, a desire to see and own pictures—which, taken together, pass with a large body of slenderly equipped persons as "culture," and give them an unprecedented self-confidence in dealing with all the problems of life, and raise them in their own minds to a plane on which they see nothing higher, greater, or better than themselves. Now, culture, in the only correct and safe sense of the term, is the result of a process of discipline, both mental and moral. It is not a thing that can be picked up, or that can be got by doing what one pleases. It cannot be acquired by desultory reading, for instance, or travelling in Europe. It comes of the protracted exercise of the faculties for given ends, under restraints of some kind, whether imposed by one's self or other people. In fact, it might not improperly be called the art of doing easily what you don't like to do. It is the breaking-in of the powers to the service of the will; and a man who has got it is not simply a person who knows a good deal, for he may know very little, but a man who has obtained an accurate estimate of his own capacity, and of that of his fellows and predecessors, who is aware of the nature and extent of his relations to the world about him, and who is at the same time capable of using his powers to the best advantage. In short, the man of culture is the man who has formed his ideals through labor and self-denial. To be real, therefore, culture ought to affect a man's whole character and not merely store his memory with facts. Let us add, too, that it may be got in various ways, through home influences as well as through schools or colleges; through living in a highly organized society, making imperious demands on one's time and faculties, as well as through the restraints of a severe course of study. A good deal of it was obtained from the old Calvinistic theology, against which in the days of its predominance, the most bumptious youth hit his head at an early period of his career, and was reduced to thoughtfulness and self-examination, and forced to walk in ways that were not always to his liking.

If all this be true, the mischievous effects of the pseudo-culture of which we have spoken above may be readily estimated. A society of ignoramuses who know they are ignoramuses might lead a tolerably happy and useful existence, but a society of ignoramuses each of whom thinks he is a Solon would be an approach to Bedlam let loose, and something analogous to this may really be seen to-day in some parts of this country. A large body of persons has arisen, under the influence of the common schools, magazines, newspapers, and the rapid acquisition of wealth, who are not only engaged in enjoying themselves after their fashion, but who firmly believe that they have reached, in the matter of social, mental, and moral culture, all that is attainable or desirable by anybody, and who, therefore, tackle all the problems of the day—men's, women's, and children's rights and duties, marriage, education, suffrage, life, death, and immortality—with supreme indifference to what anybody else thinks or has ever thought, and have their own trumpery prophets, prophetesses, heroes and heroines, poets, orators, scholars and philosophers, whom they worship with a kind of barbaric fervor. The result is a kind of mental and moral chaos, in which many of the fundamental rules of living, which have been worked out painfully by thousands of years of bitter human experience, seem in imminent risk of disappearing totally.

Now, if we said that a specimen of this society had been unearthed in Brooklyn by the recent exposures, we should, doubtless to many people, seem to say a very hard thing, and yet this, with the allowances and reservations which have of course to be made for all attempts to describe anything so vague and fleeting as a social state, is what we do mean to say. That Mr. Beecher's preaching, falling on such a mass of disorder, should not have had a more purifying and organizing effect, is due, we think, to the absence from it of anything in the smallest degree disciplinary, either in the shape of systematic theology, with its tests and standards, or of a social code, with its pains and penalties. What he has most encouraged, if we may judge by some of the fruits, is vague aspiration and lachrymose sensibility. The ability to dare and do, the readiness to ask one's due which comes of readiness to render their due to others, the profound consciousness of the need of sound habits to brace and fortify morals, which are the only true foundation and support of a healthy civilization, are things which he either has not preached or which his preaching has only stifled.

•Godkin's disdain for "chromo-civilization" and for the popular press is nowhere more evident than in the following editorial. The immediate objects of his attack are sensational newspapers and Jim Fisk, an itinerant peddler's son who made millions through speculation, stock manipulation, and bribery and then indulged freely in strong drink, good food, and loose women, taking pleasure in unrestrained public display. In 1870, when Fisk was named colonel in New York's National Guard, full-dress parades became the order of the day. Godkin pointed to coverage of him as a prime example of the faults of the press as it appealed to the shallowest interests of the public. The episodes Godkin addresses in this editorial are the participation of Fisk's regiment in a Boston parade and his action during a New York riot. The following text omits a long exposition about the nature of notoriety following the editorial's first paragraph.

NOTORIETY
(*The Nation*; July 20, 1871)

We are only saying what nearly everybody has either said or thought, when we say that by no means the least marked of the effects of modern society produced by the newspaper press has been the increase and diffusion of the love for publicity through all classes and conditions. This it has accomplished by putting publicity within nearly everybody's reach. The love of fame is of course a passion as old as the race, but it differs essentially from the love of notoriety in this, that fame rests on respect and admiration, in greater or less degree, while notoriety rests simply on the lowest order of curiosity....

Take the case of Fisk. This man came to New York a few years ago, a smart, impudent, and ignorant pedlar, without morals or manners, and with a good deal of animal spirits, and in search of two things—physical enjoyment and notoriety. The physical enjoyment he might have had with a little money, but notoriety he could only get with the help of the newspapers, and this help they gave him to his heart's content. He went incontinently to work to do strange, indecent, and outrageous things, and they went to work to chronicle them and denounce him for them. This was natural enough when he first showed himself on the scene as a swindler and blackguard, but when it was discovered that he was really indifferent to public opinion, that he had no shame and no sensibility, and really enjoyed his bad reputation and liked to be thought lewd and smart and knavish, the press at once began to treat him as a curious phenomenon, and laugh over him, chronicle his movements, record his jokes, give him pet names, and devote an amount of time to the consideration of him as an entertainment simply, which proved the best advertisement any charlatan ever had, and gratified his dearest ambition. To be "in the paper" every day, to be thought wicked by respectable people, to be rt by brokers and drygoods-men and railroad men, of all things most desires. The treatment he received, all his speculations. It advertised his theatre, his and his railroads; it made the box in which he sat, and the carriage in which he rode with his strumpets, the objects on which all eyes were fixed. His fame, in short, filled the continent, and has now filled the civilized world. At last, too, the jocose treatment of him resulted in making him look less disreputable than he was at the beginning; from laughing over him a good deal, people got to thinking him "not such a bad fellow after all"; and, finally, we came to see business suspended at mid-day in the principal thoroughfare of the commercial capital of the country, whose courts and legislature he had corrupted, in order to see him ride down as elected Colonel at the head of a regiment nine hundred strong, composed of respectable young Americans. As colonel of this regiment, he, the other day, asked for a municipal invitation for himself and it from the city of Boston, and, amongst other things, expressed a desire to have "divine service" celebrated for his benefit on Boston Common. The newspapers, thereupon, took this up, and discussed it, and joked over it, showed the absurdity of it in article after article, and paragraph after paragraph, as if Fisk was really trying to play the hypocrite, and was trying to pass himself off as a religious man, the fact being that he was merely gratifying a showman's love of making a sensation, and by the newspaper exposures of him as an impudent dog got all he wanted, and probably far more than he looked for.

The last instance of the way in which the press allows itself to nurture this evil growth is the most flagrant and startling of all. Most certainly the late riot was, to any right-minded man, a very shocking and very solemn occurrence. The slaughter of nearly fifty persons and the wounding of two hundred others by the fire of soldiers in the streets of a great city in a time of profound peace is something by which nobody could well help being deeply impressed, even if it were the result of an ordinary riot raised by plunderers or brawlers. But, considering that the riot was an outbreak of savage bigotry and lawlessness on the part of a very considerable portion of the population of the city, and a portion, too, which exercises a powerful influence on the government of the city and State, it must be admitted that it furnished food for a great deal of painful reflection. Heaven knows, too, it furnished plenty of serious topics for editorial treatment. There is hardly a single interest of the city, political or social, which the mental and moral condition of this ferocious and brutal Catholic rabble does not touch at some point or other. It seems scarcely credible under the circumstances, and yet it is strictly true, that while the dead were still lying unburied, and everybody was filled with horror and indignation, and was trying to form a rational judgment about the cause and probable consequences of the tragedy, the point which most of our leading morning papers, and amongst the evening papers even the Post, treated as apparently second in order of importance, was the manner in which James Fisk, jun., bore himself in the fray. Did, or did he not, stand his ground? Did he fly, or, if so, was he disguised? If disguised, what was the disguise? Was he really hurt, or was it all a sham? Whither did he fly, and where is he now, and what does he think of the whole thing?— were questions which editors and reporters discussed, some gravely, and some jocosely, but all elaborately and at length. It having been finally ascertained that Fisk really was borne from the field disabled, and did really make a hasty escape through fear of the mob, we were treated to whole columns of banter and reprobation of him as a humbug and pretender, and a person wanting in military courage, as if there was something amazingly ludicrous or shockingly disgraceful in this wretched charlatan's unwillingness to expose his body in an honest cause; and as if his career had been of a kind to lead people to expect him to face bullets without flinching, and as if, too—and this is the best or worst of it—he was particular about his reputation for bravery, and would be overwhelmed with shame and mortification at having people believe that he showed the white feather. The whole thing might, perhaps, pass as a very poor joke, if it were not that it is joking of this kind which keeps Fisk and the like of him afloat, and which is likely to produce scores of his successors. We cannot make Fisk a personage of importance, and fill everybody's mind every morning with his doings and sayings, without making Fisk's career an object of secret admiration to thousands, and making thousands in their inmost hearts determine to imitate him. The newspapers ought to remember that, while for some offenders against public decency and security denunciation may be a proper and effective punishment, the only way of reaching others is not to mention them.

•The following editorial, dissecting people's sensitivity to criticism of their use of language, demonstrates Godkin's ability to analyze a commonplace but perhaps overlooked issue with a wry sense of humor.

THE ODIUM PHILOLOGICUM
(The Nation)

Our readers and those of The Galaxy are familiar with the controversy between Dr. Fitz-edward Hall and Mr. Grant White [See The Nation, November, 1873]. When one comes to inquire what it was all about, and why Mr. White was led to consider Dr. Hall a "yahoo of literature," and "a man born without a sense of decency," one finds himself engaged in an investigation of great difficulty, but of considerable interest. The controversy between these two gentlemen by no means brings up the problem for the first time. That verbal criticism, such as Mr. White has been producing for some time back, is sure to end, sooner or later, in one or more savage quarrels, is one of the most familiar facts of the literary life of our day. Indeed, so far as our observation has gone, the rule has no exceptions. Whenever we see a gentleman, no matter how great his accomplishments or sweet his temper, announcing that he is about to write articles or deliver lectures on "Words and their Uses," or on the "English of Every-day Life," or on "Familiar Faults of Conversation," or "Newspaper English," or any cognate theme, we feel all but certain that we shall soon see him engaged in an encounter with another laborer in the same field, in which all dignity will be laid aside, and in which, figuratively speaking, clothes, hair, and features will suffer terribly, and out of which, unless he is very lucky, he will issue with the gravest imputations resting on his character in every relation of life.

Now why is it that attempts to get one's fellowmen to talk correctly, to frame their sentences in accordance with good usage, and take their words from the best authors, have this tendency to arouse some of the worst passions of our nature, and predispose even eminent philologists—men of dainty language, and soft manners, and lofty aims—to assail each other in the rough vernacular of the fishmarket and the forecastle? A careless observer will be apt to say that it is an ordinary result of disputation; that when men differ or argue on any subject they are apt to get angry and indulge in "personalities." But this is not true. Lawyers, for instance, live by controversy, and their controversies touch interests of the gravest and most delicate character—such as fortune and reputation; and yet the spectacle of two lawyers abusing each other in cold blood, in print, is almost unknown. Currency and banking are, at certain seasons, subjects of absorbing interest, and, for the last seventy years, the discussions over them have been numerous and voluminous almost beyond example, and yet we remember no case in which a bullionist called a paper-money man bad names, or in which a friend of free banking accused a restrictionist of defrauding the poor or defacing tombstones. Politics, too, home and foreign, is a fertile source of difference of opinion; and yet gross abuse, on paper, of each other, by political disputants, discussing abstract questions having no present relation to power or pay, are very rare indeed....

The true source of the *odium philologicum* is, we think, to be found in the fact that a man's speech is apt to be, or to be considered, an indication of the manner in which he has been bred, and of the character of the company he keeps. Criticism of his mode of using words, or his pronunciation, or the manner in which he compounds his sentences, almost inevitably takes the character of an attack on his birth, parentage, education, and social position; or, in other words, on everything which he feels most sensitive about or holds most dear. If you say that his pronunciation is bad, or that his language is slangy or ill-chosen, you insinuate that when he lived at home with his papa and mamma he was surrounded by bad models, or, in plain English, that his parents were vulgar or ignorant people; when you say that he writes bad grammar, or is guilty of glaring solecisms, or displays want of etymological knowledge, you insinuate that his education was neglected, or that he has not associated with correct speakers. Usually, too, you do all this in the most provoking way by selecting passages from his writings on which he probably prided himself, and separating them totally from the thought of which he was full when he produced them, and then examining them mechanically, as if they were algebraic signs, which he used without knowing what they meant or where they would bring him out. Nobody stands this process very long with equanimity, because nobody can be subjected to it without being presented to the public somewhat in the light of an ignorant, careless, and pretentious donkey. Nor will it do to cite your examples from deceased authors. You cannot do so without assailing some form of expression which an eager, listening enemy is himself in the habit of using, and is waiting for you to take up, and through which he hopes to bring you to shame.

No man, moreover, can perform the process without taking on airs which rouse his victim to madness, because he assumes a position not only of grammatical, but, as we have said, of social superiority. He says plainly enough, no matter how polite or scientific he may try to seem, "I was better born and bred than you, and acquired these correct turns of expression, of which you know nothing, from cultivated relatives"; or, "I live in cultivated circles, and am consequently familiar with the best usage, which you, poor fellow! are not. I am therefore able to decide this matter without argument or citations, and your best course is to take my corrections in silence or with thankfulness." It is easy to understand how all interest in orthography, etymology, syntax, and prosody speedily disappears in a controversy of this sort, and how the disputants begin to burn with mutual dislike, and how each longs to inflict pain and anguish on his opponent, and make him, no matter by what means, an object of popular pity and contempt, and make his parts of speech odious and ridiculous. The influence of all good men ought to be directed either to repressing verbal criticism, or restricting indulgence in it to the family circle or to schools and colleges.

MASTERS OF THE EDITORIAL

LAFCADIO HEARN:
MASTER WORD PAINTER

Many journalists and critics have argued that there can be no harmony between journalistic writing and literary excellence. Lafcadio Hearn dispelled that premise. His writings, fused with imagination, proved that a journalist could also be a master painter of word pictures.

Because he lived the last half of his life in Japan, where he gained legendary fame as an exotic writer about things peculiarly Japanese, literary critics of the West have approached him only halfheartedly, and journalism historians have virtually ignored him. His work for Cincinnati's *Enquirer* and *Commercial* and New Orleans' *Item* and *Times-Democrat*, however, established him as the most popular editorial writer in both regions. Some 60 books of his fiction and translations of foreign literary works have been published, and selections from his editorials and other journalistic writing have been collected in three book-length anthologies.

Throughout his personal life and professional career, Hearn was known to most contemporaries as an odd, socially shy—yet talented—individual. From the beginning, "unique" was the word most characteristic of his personality and lifestyle. Born in 1850 on an Ionian island formerly called Leucadia (thus his name) of a womanizing Anglo-Irish officer in the British army and his Greek wife, Hearn was soon deserted and sent to live in Ireland with an overbearing aunt. When he was 18, she sent him to live in the United States.

Eventually arriving in Cincinnati, penniless and without anyone to turn to, Hearn for some time lived off odd jobs, slept on vacant lots or in discarded boxes, and generally did little better than starve. Motivated by an insatiable desire to write, however, the neurotically shy young man finally got up just sufficient nerve to submit a free-lance article to the editor of the Cincinnati *Enquirer*, the famed Col. John Cockerill. So impressed was Cockerill, he hired Hearn as a space-rate contributor and later made him a reporter. His five years of work at the *Enquirer* and then the *Commercial* were characteristic of the typical reporter of those days. His writing on the sensational aspects of crime stood out, however, gaining him a reputation as the city's foremost and most graphic writer on the police beat.

Tiring of his predictable, routine job, he decided to journey south—to a region of the country during a period of tentative progress and attachment to its war-torn past. His first months in New Orleans were trying, and he again found himself living from hand to mouth, sleeping in parks, alone, often hungry, at one time desperate to the point of contemplating suicide. But with the city's newest paper, the *Item*, looking for an assistant editor, the frail, shabby would-be writer finally landed a job.

At the *Item* he began to develop his characteristic writing style. His fascination with the exotic and romantic emerged, and he became aware of his new environment in a highly sensitive way. He was required to work only from 10 in the morning until shortly after noon, thus allowing him ample time for independent writing and compensating him for his meager salary of $10 a week. Along with rewriting stories from out-of-town papers and writing an article or two on foreign affairs or literature, each day he wrote an editorial. Although he also served as translator, book reviewer, columnist, and dramatic critic, he worked at a leisurely pace. Combined with the languor of Southern culture, it gave him a chance to discover himself.

His popular column, which he appropriately titled "The Fantastics," was imaginary in scope. He described it as "my impressions of the strange life of New Orleans." He also began to delve into unique topics, some of which were science and Far East cultures. His tastes, which had appeared to be a fascination with the loathsome and morbid in Cincinnati, now began to be refined. The dreadful still attracted him if it were ghostly enough or eerie, but he began to write more about the exotic and the romantic and to draw on his impressions of the tropical dreamy life of New Orleans. "When he would write one of his own little fanciful things," the *Item's* publisher said, "out of his own head—dreams—he was always dreaming—why, then he would work like mad. And people always noticed those little things of his, somehow, for they were truly lovely, wonderful." He often felt lacking in knowledge and technical precision. So he made up for the shortcoming through imagination. He wanted to escape from the "intensely vulgar and detestably commonplace thing" he called American journalism.

His "odd" writings, uncharacteristic of that day's journalism, were his favorite, but he did not concentrate on them to the exclusion of everything else. A versatile assistant editor, he wrote, along with his "Fantastics," news articles, dramatic reviews, and editorials. Although fascinated with the imaginative, he settled easily into normal topics of the editorial page—child labor, machine politics, police inefficiency, government corruption, sanitation needs, civic improvement, white slavery—and the *Item* nestled naturally in its position of community reformer. He got to know the people of the city, the local tragedy, the street drama, the life in its secret corners—and with readers he shared it all in shimmering vignettes.

In 1880, the New Orleans *Times* (founded in 1863) and *Democrat* (founded in 1875) merged; and the new editor, Page Baker, enticed Hearn to join the staff as literary editor. At the *Times-Democrat*, Hearn's role became more specific. He was to provide translations of news and literature from foreign journals and contribute an occasional editorial. Each Sunday he penned "The Foreign Press," his translations of French and Spanish stories, novel excerpts, and articles. The feature was popular with readers. Circulation went up, and the *Times-Democrat* became one of the South's leading newspapers. This more precise role, as well as Baker's understanding and fostering of his new writer's personality, eccentricities, and talent, made the *Times-Democrat* years Hearn's golden age as a journalist. Baker recognized that Hearn's sensitive ego was easily bruised by copywriters' attempts to delete sentences, paragraphs, and odd punctuation. He therefore instructed the paper's typesetters never to alter Hearn's copy.

His interest in writing was kindled anew, and Hearn devoted even more effort to burnishing his style and exploring the realms of imagination, the possibilities and impossibilities of science, the range of human experience, and questions touching on everything from medicine, to sociology, to biology, to pseudo-science. With more time at his disposal, he began to prune his words and polish his phrases to a luster. One of the problems with journalism, he believed, was that editorial writers were given inadequate time to work with their compositions. "No man," he asserted, "can write a really good article every day. If he attempts to do so he weakens his power." Hasty phrases, redundancies, and commonplace usage were the result. At the *Item*—and more obviously at the *Times-Democrat*—he developed a distinctive writing style. Passion and imagination ruled his writing. "My sketches," he said, "although suggested by fact, are moulded and coloured by imagination alone." Later, he declared, "Passion directs the witchery of the pen."

Hearn was a master wordsmith. He paid minute attention to the appearance and sound of words. He worked to achieve a meticulous artistry in word detail. He called it "the magic of words." Perhaps no other American editorial writer has achieved the luminosity, texture, and delicacy of phrasing that Hearn mastered. Writing, to him, was a sensory experience. He filled his pieces, therefore, with sights, sounds, and smells. The writer, Hearn said, must help readers "see the colour of words, the tints of words, the secret ghostly motions of words; hear the whispering of words, the rustling of the procession of letters, the dream-flutes and dream-drums which are thinly and weirdly played by words, the weeping, the raging and racketing and rioting of words; sense the phosphorescing of words, the fragrance of words, the noisesomeness of words, the tenderness or hardness, the dryness or juiciness of words."

One explanation of Hearn's acute awareness of sensory details was the loss of his left eye during a childhood game and severe myopia in the remaining one. Sometimes he admitted that his problems were a blessing in disguise, for they required him to be completely alert with his remaining senses. Thus, he missed nothing of the sounds, smells, tastes, and textures of a scene.

Hearn's writing was not, however, perfect. Although he possessed a vast store of abstruse and varied knowledge on a myriad of subjects, his ideas often were founded on wide reading and his imaginative powers rather than systematic study. Thus, at times his insight was far-fetched and superficial.

American journalism, in Hearn's view, sorely lacked in writing quality and writer's freedom. In the 1880 editorial "French Journalism" he celebrated France's treatment of writers and her general excellence in newspapers. In France, he said, reporters were paid well and weren't expected to produce columns or articles every day. His own practice was to spend whatever time he needed to create a polished composition. "I write a rough sketch," he said, "and labour and labour it over and over again." A French newspaper, he concluded, is "not only a newspaper but a wonderful piece of literary work."

Independent writing projects (several books and magazine articles) prodded him from many directions, and he resigned from the *Times-Democrat* in May 1887. If the truth be told, however, he left because he was, once again, tired of his surroundings. His imagination, as well as his fascination with things foreign, sent him abroad. By the time he left, he had gained a considerable reputation as a Southern literary figure, and his work was read throughout the United States. After he ventured to Martinique, then Japan, however, his words were of little interest to Americans.

The last of his life was spent in Japan; and, after his death, he was argued over and criticized for his unique style. Only in recent years have critics begun to recognize him once again for what he really was—a writer who reconciled the *journalistic* and the *literary*.

•Hearn was both a romantic and a dabbler in science. In the following editorial, he called on the new theory of biological evolution to help try to explain the romantic's wanderlust that comes with springtime.

SPRING FEVER FANCIES
(New Orleans *Item*; March 16, 1879)

Together with the languor and dreaminess begotten by the spring's fragrance and its tepid winds, there comes to many, year after year, in whatever climate or country, but especially perhaps in our own, that vague longing for other lands and strange places—that thirst for the solitude of unfamiliar lands, so romantically termed by Curtis the Camel-Spirit.

Imagination, in this age, has developed this strange feeling to a remarkable degree; and the most imaginative are those most cursed, or blessed, perhaps, by its influence.

Yet it may seem curious that at no other period of the year is the feeling so potent as at this time. It is not winter that inspires dreams of brighter and deeper skies, of whiter moons and larger stars, of sunsets more golden and winds more witchingly fragrant, of feathery-crested palms and strange poisonous flowers that slumber by day and open their pale hearts only to the tropical moon.

In winter the fancy is at least restrained by the local boundaries of familiar places. It hibernates in a species of psychological torpor. The call of daily duty, the strong necessity for active exertion, the hope inspired by present success, occupy the mind with material images and numb the fancy. The stream of Romance is bound up also in the rime of frost, however shadowy the frost-crystals.

Then the spring comes with its burst of roses, its magical perfumes, its genial warmth;—faint mists float up, like phantom Icari vainly struggling toward the sun;—and all the long-pent-up vapors of fancy float upward with them. The heart feels heavy with a vague and mysterious sadness, the walls of the city seem constraining barriers, the wild clouds seem pregnant with omens, and the winds, pure as the heaven of amethyst, seem to bear the dreamer ghostly kisses from lands 'where it is always afternoon.'

It is a homesickness, yet without memories of home; a thirst for freedom, yet there is no sense of imprisonment; a sort of world-weariness too vague for physical analysis. It is as though one might wish to wander through blue deeps of eternity to reach a rosy paradise in some far-sparkling world. Ideas of preexistence, wild theories of metempsychoses and avatars throng upon one at such times.

Of what is this strange sickness born? Have philosophers written of such things or are such things unknown to the arid reasoner though familiar to the heart of the poet?

Darwinism does not teach us yet whether some remote and antediluvian relationship may be found between man and the bird; yet one is almost tempted to fancy that man's spring fever of unrest might have had its origin in the palpitation of a bird's heart. The spring cometh; and the voice of the turtle is heard in the land. The wild birds fly north in the spring; southward in the autumn; happier than we, they may fearlessly gratify the Unspeakable Unrest.

Perhaps our Aryan ancestors, wandering in ages dimly prehistoric—traversing strange lands with their horn-bows at their backs—seeking softer climes and richer lands, may have bequeathed to us from forgotten years this feverish unrest of spring, this vague and undefinable longing for far-away lands.

•As with many of his other editorials, "The Burning of the

Dead" exhibits Hearn's fascination with science, fantasy, and the morbid. It addresses the problem of what to do with the increasing numbers of corpses that are a natural result of larger populations in modern industrialized nations.

THE BURNING OF THE DEAD
(New Orleans *Times-Democrat*, March 30, 1884)

The strong feeling in favor of cremation both at home and abroad is a sign of the times. It is true that this feeling is by no means that of the great majority as yet; but it is the feeling of a very intelligent and imposing minority which has the power to make converts rapidly in multitude. The mind of the nineteenth century is undergoing a reaction in favor of ancient funeral rites and pagan common sense. Is this because we are growing skeptical—because the old superstitions and the Folklore of the Dead are rapidly passing away? Certainly the feeling against cremation is most strong where superstitions do most survive. But the vanishing away of certain dark forms of belief, and the tendency of the times to abandon old customs and old ideas, are themselves due to those vast economical changes which have already modified the face of the world, and broken down barriers between nations. The skepticism of the period is a cause, perhaps—but only a subordinate cause, for the open advocacy of cremation. The great primal cause is the enormous industrial progress of the period, enabling countries to maintain populations ten times larger than could have found support some centuries ago. The world's markets are becoming more colossal than was ever Babylon or Egyptian Thebes; cities of a hundred thousand people spring up every few decades in the midst of what were previously wildernesses; and towns of insignificant size receive sudden nourishment from railroads and swell to metropolitan proportions. In many American cities population doubles itself at astonishingly brief intervals; and the intervening lands are cultivated to their utmost extent by a rapidly increasing race of sturdy farmers. In Europe the increase of population is slower by far, but it is nevertheless astounding when compared with the populousness of the sixteenth and seventeenth centuries. A generation ago London had barely three millions of inhabitants; she has now almost five millions. All the great capitals are becoming more populous. Science and invention have enabled the human race to multiply extraordinarily. But with the increase of life there is the inevitable increase of disease; and the work of Death is becoming so gigantic that the living can scarcely find place for his harvests. Cemeteries are too quickly filled;—the city grows out to them and around them and beyond them; the expenses of extramural burial increase continuously; the earth is overfed with corpses until she can no longer digest them, and the air of each metropolis becomes heavy with odors of dissolution. Inhumation can no longer meet the demands of hygiene;—Science has taken the alarm, and seeks to summon Fire to the assistance of earth. Fire, the All-Producer, as personified in the sun—(*Surya*, 'The Begetter')—is also the All-Purifier. Fire, not earth, shall devour the dead in centuries to come as in centuries that have passed away. Cremation will become at last, not a choice, but a necessity. It may first be established as optional; it will then become obligatory. These are the declarations and predictions of its advocates.

Elsewhere we publish extracts from an excellent article upon that subject, which appeared in the Paris *Figaro*. The author, who is a devout Roman Catholic, admirably points out the absence of any potent religious argument against the incineration of the dead, while he also dwells upon the horrors of slow decomposition and the involuntary yet inevitable condemnation of thousands to a *living burial*. But there is also a poetical side to the sinister question, which might be dilated upon—the swift restoration of the substances of being to their primal source of light and air—the remelting of the body into the pure and luminous elements which formed them. The body soars with the rising of the flame which enwraps it, soars toward that blue to which all eyes turn at times with an indefinite longing—as though there were something of the bird in every human heart.

'The earth,' poetically sang a Vedic poet, 'receives the dead even as a mother wraps the fold of her robe about the weary child who sinks to slumber in her arms.' The thought seems beautiful, but the words are untrue. For the earth is a cannibal;—she devours her children as hideously but infinitely more slowly than the python devours his prey—so hideously that only the bravest soldiers of Science have ever dared to peer into the processes of her digestion—as did Orfila. Perhaps it would be well if certain sentimental opponents of cremation should behold that indescribable treatise of his upon Juridical Exhumation with its frightful colored plates, whose horrors surpass the most loathsome conceptions of madness and the most appalling monstrosities of nightmare. One glance at these secrets of the tomb were enough to convert the bitterest anti-cremationist! And how slow the decay! Sometimes in five years the earth has not consumed its food. Poets may write touching pantheistic madrigals concerning the ultimate blending of all flesh with that 'Universal Paste formed of the shapes that God melts down'; but has the poet ever dared to raise the coffin-lid and observe the ghastly transmutation for an instant? Could even the philosopher dare so much;—for the breath of the tomb is fatal. Death permits only the high-priests of science to study that ghastly chemistry and live! Surely the noblest works of God are wrought in fire;—in flame were born all the hosts of heaven, and of flame is the visible soul of stars;—fire is the creative force of Nature; and to fire alone rightfully belongs the task of redissolving that which it first warmed and shaped into life. Modern respect for the dead is really superficial: it stops at the surface of graves and at the entrances of vaults. To abandon the body of a friend, a child, a woman beloved, to worms and to all the frightful fermentations of the tomb, seems, when we reflect upon it, barbarous—hideous! Even the Parsee Towers of Silence, with their vultures and birds of carrion hovering in spiral flight, contain naught so frightful as do our fairest sepulchres;—better surely abandon the dead unto the birds of heaven than to the worms of earth. Death was not a nightmare to antique civilizations; it became so only when the funeral pyres had ceased to flame, and the funeral urns had ceased to be. There was nothing sinister, nothing awful about the tombs of the Greek or Roman dead—only the graceful vases containing the 'pinch of scentless and delicate dust' gathered from the pyre—'the dust of the soul's own butterfly-wings,' as it has been so daintily termed.

The crematories of the future will do the work better than the pyres of the ancients—much more perfectly, and much more cheaply. Incineration, if not complete, also has its horrors;—excepting a corpse in decomposition, there is nothing so goblin-like and appalling as a half-burned body. The antique process was slow, and in the intervals of feeding the fire there must have been ghastly sights. But in the strong, clear flame of the crematory—retort horror cannot endure an instant. There will be no room for such a spectacle as that described by one witness of the burning of Shelley's remains.

The desire for cremation is a sign of progress, a token of a healthier tendency of mind. Yet, it must be confessed, even cremation, as now advocated in its most scientific form, does not wholly satisfy human feeling in regard to the disposal of the dead. There are strange doubts—obscure as any Egyptian prayer—anxieties and fears.... If it be true that one person in every 5000 is buried alive, might not one in every 5000 also be burned alive? Where is the guarantee, since there is no assurance of death before visible decomposition sets in? Again, who knows precisely when all thought and sensation dies within the most secret chambers of the brain? When must the last spark of being fade out into utter darkness? Only a ghost might know; but the dead have no voice—even in dreams. The assurances of science do not wholly reassure; for science has scarcely yet begun to comprehend the deeper secrets of physiology and the mysteries of life. Some day revelations might be made too terrible to think of—revelations of consciousness resurrected momentarily in the midst of the material dissolution—strange flaring-up of sensations, of fancies and memories long forgotten—weird vitality of remembrances rekindled by the touch of destruction, by the combustion of death—just as characters of invisible ink are made visible by the approach of flame. Electricity alone—that holiest form of fire—may furnish ultimately some satisfactory means of answering all fearful doubt, when it shall become possible to dissolve a body instantaneously—as water is decomposed by the galvanic battery.

•Hearn was especially alert to sensory perception and appealed to the senses in many of his editorials. The following editorial makes special use of the sense of hearing, describing the sounds made by wind blowing past electrical wires. He wrote the editorial as a result of his wanderings around New Orleans seeking to understand electricity. He would go out alone at night along the streets where new electric lines were being strung and listen to the sounds the wind made in them.

THE ROAR OF A GREAT CITY
(New Orleans *Times-Democrat*; November 30, 1884)

When Hogarth painted his story of "The Enraged Musician," whose music was drowned in the thousand cries and noises that surrounded him; when Chambers described "The Roar of a Great City," the blending of a thousand noises, it was of the city of the past they told. Since then this roar has been growing louder and louder, until now, miles away, even before you see the smoky coronet that surrounds the modern city, you can hear a wild growl like that of some enraged beast. Neither Hogarth nor Chambers dreamed of the fierce whistle of the steamboat and locomotive, of the rattle of engine and machinery, of the cannonade as a cotton float flies over the granite pavement, of the stunning noise of the New York Elevated Railroad. All these have come of late years.

The electric light, the telephone and telegraph wires have added new music to our city. When the winds blow at night one can hear a somber, melancholy music high up in the air—as mysterious as that of Ariel himself or the undiscovered music of the Pascagoula. If you want to hear it in perfection, go some of these windy nights we have lately enjoyed to Delord or Dryades, or some of the streets in the neighborhood of the electric light works, where the wires are numerous and the houses low, and where there is a clean sweep for the wind from the New Basin to the river. There the music becomes wild and grand indeed. The storm whistling and shrieking around some sharp corner never equalled it. Above, around, in every direction can be heard this music, sighing, mourning like the tree-tops, with a buzzing metallic sound that almost drowns your conversation—it is like the last wail of a dying man, or the shriek of the angel of death as he clasps his victim to him.

If such it is to-day, what have we to hope for in the future? If the city is already a monstrous spider web, a great Æolian harp, what is its destiny with several new telegraph and telephone companies, and thousands of new poles, and millions of new wires promised us? If this aerial music increases, this shrieking and wailing and moaning will reach such a pitch that we will greet the rattle of the floats and tinkle of the street cars as tending to drown this new noise, and welcome the roar of the city as likely to muffle its meaning.

•Although Hearn was fascinated with the morbid, in the following editorial he criticized people who appeared to romanticize over criminals. The editorial demonstrates his ability to analyze the fundamental features of common human behavior.

THE FASCINATION OF CRIME
(New Orleans *Times-Democrat*, July 27, 1887)

That crime and criminals exercise a strong fascination upon a certain class of people is an undeniable fact. Our exchanges give an abundant proof of this, in their accounts of the attentions lavished on men who have been imprisoned for the committal of atrocious deeds. A wife-murderer who, perhaps, slaughtered his victim with pitiless ferocity, is almost buried under a load of floral tributes from sentimental persons. We read of a negro who, with the aid of an accomplice, had killed an old woman for the purpose of robbery: his cell was filled with offerings of fruit, pound-cake and candy, though whether as a reward of merit, or as a consolation, we are not told. It is stated that he seemed 'contented and happy'—small blame to him! Doubtless, to his ignorant mind, soothed by these influences, the vision of the gallows had vanished into the dimness of improbability. Had he pursued the straight and narrow path of virtue, he would have toiled and sorrowed and gone down to the grave, 'unwept, unhonored and unsung.'

Going a step farther, it is not an uncommon thing for these sentimentalists to wish to link their destinies with that of the criminal. The mere fact that a man has been imprisoned seems to add some mysterious charm to his personality: witness the struggles of a handsome young woman to marry Spies. This peculiarity, however, is not confined to any nationality. When the Count de Molen, after brutally maltreating his wife, and trying to shoot her and his father-in-law, was sentenced to ten years' hard labor, a Roumanian girl was moved to offer him her heart and hand. In the case of Pranzini, it was announced that he received at least fifty impassioned love-letters, many addressing him as 'Unhappy persecuted one.' One of the fair scribes promised to follow him to New Caledonia, and marry him. Perhaps it may add a pang to the punishment of malefactors to have it supposed that they would be willing to ally themselves with such feeble-minded creatures.

But it is not only members of the fair sex who are fond of making pets of jail-birds. In several instances, women arrested for poisoning their husbands have received numerous offers of marriage; apparently on the strength of their evil notoriety. The motives which may actuate such proceedings form an interesting problem. It may be that the adventurous spirit cherishes the vague theory of the familiar superstition that lightning never strikes twice in the same place, and that, by marrying a woman who has disposed of one husband, he secures immunity forever from the poisoned bowl. Or, perhaps, it is a love of excitement and a desire to avoid the ordinary stagnation of domestic peace and happiness.

Even petit larceny is not without its charms, as is proven by the career of Hannah Sykes, a girl who has figured frequently in the police courts. There was a period when she was one of the loudest shouters of the Salvation Army, but was afterward arrested for stealing a dress. On her way to the station, she attempted to escape by leaping from a bridge. When her case came up, Thomas Gray, a New Yorker, asked permission to marry her, although he had never seen her before; so, after he had paid her fine, they were made man and wife. Being questioned with regard to his motives, Mr. Gray replied that he thought she would make a lively wife. No doubt she will.

MASTERS OF THE EDITORIAL

CHARLES DANA AND THE NEW YORK *SUN*: MASTERS OF THE 'CASUAL ESSAY'

Upon hearing of Charles Dana's purchase of the New York *Sun* in 1868, the newspaper's founder, Benjamin Day, declared that the new editor-in-chief would "make a newspaper of it." With the help of the profession's brightest editorial writers, Dana made an international name for himself, his staff, and his newspaper. Today, Dana's *Sun* is remembered in particular for its sparkling writing and always interesting topics. Much of its reputation rested on the talent of the group of editorial writers known collectively as the "Casual Essayists."

Dana himself proclaimed that a newspaper's duty is to give its readers interesting writing. "The invariable law of the newspaper," he explained, "is to be interesting. Suppose you tell all the truths of science in a way that bores the reader. What is the good? The truths don't stay in the mind and nobody thinks any better of you because you have told them the truth tediously." When Dana and his partners—stockholders with him in previous publishing ventures—bought the *Sun*, it had a circulation of 43,000. It immediately gained on its competition and, by 1876, had achieved its highest numbers at 131,000. The secret of the newspaper's salability lay in Dana's own cardinal rule: "Be interesting."

Under Dana the paper developed a bright and interesting writing style probably never matched by any other American newspaper. The first issue of the *Sun* after Dana took over described his approach to journalism. The *Sun*, he wrote, "will study condensation, clearness, and point and will endeavor to present its daily photograph of the whole world's doings in the most luminous and lively manner." Dana has been credited with inventing the human-interest story, and one of journalism's best-known adages belongs to a *Sun* city editor. "When a dog bites a man," John Bogart told a young reporter, "that is not news; but when a man bites a dog, that is news."

The *Sun's* approach to news writing was just as interesting as the subjects it chose to report. Dana himself described the newspaper's style in such terms as *terse, clear, vivid,* and *forceful.* The 1885 editorial "Our Office Cat" described his approach. The *Sun* created the cat after the paper lost a telegraphed message of a speech by President Chester Arthur. Wondering how the *Sun* might explain to readers why it had not reported on the event, Willard Bartlett, an assistant editor, casually suggested the explanation that "the office cat ate it." Dana immediately liked the idea and composed a brief paragraph revealing the cat. Soon the cat began to show up frequently. When editors of the *Sun,* known for its detestation of verbosity and tedium, wished to omit coverage of some event such as congressional debates, they explained simply that "the office cat ate the information." In the editorial describing the cat, Dana wrote, "When a piece of stale news or a long-winded, prosy article comes into the office, his remarkable sense of smell instantly detects it, and it is impossible to keep it from him."

This quality of writing, while used for news, was even more noticeable on the editorial page. Dana's belief in clarity, vividness, and condensation was evident in all editorials, political and otherwise. Although the political editorials suffered from Dana's enigmatic shifts between idealism and cynicism, they were presented boldly and, often, with much humor and biting sarcasm. One of the most famous political labels to come from the *Sun's* editorial pages was "His Fraudulency, Mr. Hayes," referring to President Rutherford B. Hayes, who had won the presidency in the disputed election of 1876.

Sober editorials may appropriately occupy the leading place on the editorial page. But there is a spot also for the interesting, the entertaining, the conversational, even the whimsical. Indeed, a majority of those editorials that impressed contemporary readers and that have been retained by the mind of man were those that did not address grave public questions.

The *Sun's* most popular editorials were its "Casual Essays." They were reprinted by other newspapers and later collected in an anthology. With varied titles like "Pie, Ice Cream and Civilization," "The Oldest Living Graduate," "The Split Infinitive," and "The Subject of Kissing," these light editorials spoke on fads, social manners, and language with an incisiveness and whimsy rarely seen at the time or since. The *Sun's* "Casual Essayists" excelled at both writing with a light touch and taking high-toned humor to the absurd.

The *Sun's* editorial offices became a haven for promising

writers and, eventually, home to the most talented. Dana surrounded himself with editorial writers who fit his ideal—men with broad educations, who drew on the picturesque and the interesting.

Yet, once he hired them, Dana encouraged his writers to develop their own natural style. He always fostered individuality. Commenting in 1875 on certain critics, he declared, "They measure our journalistic production by an English standard which lays it down as its first and most imperative rule that editorial writing shall be free from the characteristics of the writer. This is ruinous to good writing and damaging to the sincerity of writers.... Men with actual capacity of certain sorts for acceptable writing have been frightened off from doing natural and vigorous work by certain newspaper... doctrinaires who are in distress if... the temper and blood of the writer actually show in his work."

Despite the individuality of style, writer anonymity was the rule at the *Sun.* It was broken only once, in 1906 with the revelation that the recently deceased Francis P. Church had authored the perennial favorite "Is There a Santa Claus?" Readers will never know the identity of specific editorials' authors, but the *Sun's* tradition of writing talent is obvious when viewing the editorials as a whole.

Among the best of the *Sun's* editorial writers were Church, Mayo Williamson Hazeltine, Edward Kingsbury, William O. Bartlett, and Fitz-Henry Warren. Although fitting into Dana's broad definition of the "ideal writer," these men (as well as the numerous others) varied greatly in individual style.

Readers of Church discovered a writer who cared little for politics, but loved people. He began his career at his father's religious paper, the New York *Chronicle,* and edited *The Galaxy,* a literary journal of his own creation, before moving to the *Sun.* There, he developed a polished style characterized by simplicity of words, conversational tone, and human-interest appeal.

Hazeltine was, first and foremost, a scholar. Educated at Harvard and Oxford, he spent his entire journalistic career with the *Sun.* Also a literary critic and a principal writer on foreign politics, he wrote in a style that brought sophistication and intelligence to the *Sun's* pages. By providing decent salaries, Dana had been able to attract such educated, capable writers to the *Sun's* staff. After Dana's death in 1897, Hazeltine wrote that "he raised [newspapermen's] vocation to a level with the legal and medical professions as regards the scale of remuneration."

Later a Pulitzer Prize winner for the New York *Times,* Kingsbury revealed in his work for the *Sun* his sense of humor, his appreciation for literature, and his belief in original ideas and phrases. He was noted also for knowledge of New England customs, folklore, and idioms, and of political figures and their vulnerabilities. He probably was the author of one of the *Sun's* most celebrated editorials, "The Oldest Living Graduate."

Bartlett was not a journalist by profession; he wrote his articles from his law office, directly below the *Sun's*. His talent lay in political editorial writing. His forcible, straightforward style—no useless words or phrases—made the *Sun* a topic of both admiration and derision. He penned the famous 1878 editorial slogan "No King! No Clown! To Rule this Town" that the *Sun* used against New York City's corrupt political machine.

Warren had worked with Dana before, as a writer for Horace Greeley's New York *Tribune*, and had penned the disastrous cry "Forward to Richmond!" (often mistakenly attributed to Dana) which resulted in the Union army's ill-prepared attack and subsequent defeat at the first Battle of Bull Run in 1861. It read:

THE NATION'S WAR-CRY
Forward to Richmond! Forward to Richmond! The Rebel Congress must not be allowed to meet there on the 20th of July! BY THAT DATE THE PLACE MUST BE HELD BY THE NATIONAL ARMY!

His editorials—making free use of figures of speech, evocative quotations, and historical allusions—were the most literary at the *Sun*.

All of these writers followed the wise counsel of Dana and, yet, wrote with their own individual styles. His ability to recognize and encourage talented writers made the *Sun* the strongest staffed newspaper of its time.

As the *Sun* celebrated its 50th birthday in 1883, editor Edward Mitchell attributed its success to its "outspoken expressions of honest opinion... the substitution of the absolute standard of real interest to human beings... bright and enjoyable writing." Following Dana's death, Joseph Pulitzer, who replaced Dana as America's leading newspaper figure, called the *Sun* "the most piquant, entertaining newspaper in the world."

•Here is the editorial in which Dana described the *Sun's* office cat. It is a good description also of Dana's approach to newspaper writing.

OUR OFFICE CAT
(Charles Dana; New York *Sun*; January 12, 1885)

The universal interest which this accomplished animal has excited throughout the country is a striking refutation that genius is not honored in its own day and generation. Perhaps no other living critic has attained the popularity and vogue now enjoyed by our cat. For years he worked in silence, unknown, perhaps, beyond the limits of the office. He is a sort of Rosicrucian cat, and his motto has been "to know all and to keep himself unknown." But he could not escape the glory his efforts deserved, and a few mornings ago he woke up, like Byron, to find himself famous.

We are glad to announce that he hasn't been puffed up by the enthusiastic praise which comes to him from all sources. He is the same industrious, conscientious, sharp-eyed, and sharp-toothed censor of copy that he has always been, nor should we have known that he is conscious of the admiration he excites among his esteemed contemporaries of the press had we not observed him in the act of dilacerating a copy of the Graphic containing an alleged portrait of him.

It was impossible not to sympathize with his evident indignation. The Graphic's portrait did foul injustice to his majestic and intellectual features. Besides, it represented him as having a bandage over one eye, as if he had been involved in controversy and had had his eye mashed. Now, aside from the fact that he needs both eyes to discharge his literary duties properly, he is able to whip his weight in office cats, and his fine, large eyes have never been shrouded in black, and we don't believe they ever will be. He is a soldier as well as a scholar.

We have received many requests to give a detailed account of the personal habits and peculiarities of this feline Aristarchus. Indeed, we have been requested to prepare a full biographical sketch to appear in the next edition of "Homes of American Authors." At some future day we may satisfy public curiosity with the details of his literary methods. But genius such as his defies analysis, and the privacy of a celebrity ought not to be rudely invaded.

It is not out of place, however, to indicate a few traits which illustrate his extraordinary faculty of literary decomposition, so to speak. His favorite food is a tariff discussion. When a big speech, full of wind and statistics, comes within his reach, he pounces upon it immediately and digests the figures at his leisure. During the discussion of the Morrison Bill he used to feed steadily on tariff speeches for eight hours a day, and yet his appetite remained unimpaired.

When a piece of stale news or a long-winded, prosy article comes into the office, his remarkable sense of smell instantly detects it, and it is impossible to keep it from him. He always assists with great interest at the opening of the office mail, and he files several hundred letters a day in his interior department. The favorite diversion of the office-boys is to make him jump for twelve-column articles on the restoration of the American merchant marine.

He takes a keen delight in hunting for essays on civil-service reform, and will play with them, if he has time, for hours. They are so pretty that he hates to kill them, but duty is duty. Clumsy and awkward English he springs at with indescribable quickness and ferocity; but he won't eat it. He simply tears it up. He can't stand everything.

We don't pretend he is perfect. We admit that he has an uncontrollable appetite for the Congressional Record. We have to keep this peculiar publication out of his reach. He will sit for hours and watch with burning eyes the iron safe in which we are obliged to shut up the Record for safe-keeping. Once in a while we let him have a number or two. He becomes uneasy without it. It is his cat-nip.

With the exception of this pardonable excess he is a blameless beast. He mouses out all the stupid stuff and nonsense that finds its way into the office and goes for it tooth and claw. He is the biggest copyholder in the world. And he never gets tired. His health is good, and we have not deemed it necessary to take out a policy on any one of his valuable lives.

Many of our esteemed contemporaries are furnishing their offices with cats, but they can never hope to have the equal of the *Sun's* venerable polyphage. He is a cat of genius.

•Following is the best-known of any editorial ever published in any newspaper. It was written by Francis Church, who, one acquaintance said, had all the literary gifts, "the tender fancy, the sympathetic understanding of human nature, the humor, now wistful, now joyous, the unsurpassed delicacy of touch." Church was assigned the job of writing an editorial in response to a letter from eight-year-old Virginia O'Hanlon, and he took it on only reluctantly. Within a short time, however, he produced the editorial that brought him journalistic immortality.

IS THERE A SANTA CLAUS?
(Francis P. Church; New York *Sun*; September 21, 1897)

We take pleasure in answering at once and thus prominently the communication below, expressing at the same time our great gratification that its faithful author is numbered among the friends of The Sun.

Dear Editor: I am eight years old. Some of my little friends say there is no Santa Claus. Papa says "if you see it in The Sun it's so." Please tell me the truth, is there a Santa Claus?
Virginia O'Hanlon.

Virginia, your little friends are wrong. They have been affected by the skepticism of a skeptical age. They do not believe except they see. They think that nothing can be which is not comprehended by their little minds. All minds, Virginia, whether they be men's or children's, are little. In this great universe of ours man is a mere insect, an ant, in his intellect, as compared with the boundless world about him, as measured by the intelligence capable of grasping the whole of truth and knowledge.

Yes, Virginia, there is a Santa Claus. He exists as certainly as love and generosity and devotion exist, and you know that they abound and give to our life its highest beauty and joy. Alas! how dreary would be the world if there were no Santa Claus. It would be as dreary as if there were no Virginias. There would be no childish faith then, no poetry, no romance, to make tolerable this existence. The eternal light with which childhood fills the world would be extinguished.

Not believe in Santa Claus! You might as well not believe in fairies! You might get your papa to hire men to watch in all the chimneys on Christmas Eve to catch Santa Claus, but even if they did not see Santa Claus coming down, what would that prove? Nobody sees Santa Claus, but that is no sign that there is no Santa Claus. The most real things in the world are those that neither children nor men can see. Did you ever see fairies dancing on the lawn? Of course not, but that's no proof that they are not there. Nobody can conceive or imagine all the wonders there are unseen and unseeable in the world.

You may tear apart the baby's rattle and see what makes the noise inside, but there is a veil covering the unseen world which not the strongest men that ever lived could tear apart. Only fancy, poetry, love, romance can push aside that curtain and view and picture the supernal beauty and glory behind. Is it all real? Ah, Virginia, in all this world there is nothing else real and abiding.

No Santa Claus! Thank God! he lives and he lives forever. A thousand years from now, Virginia, nay, ten times ten thousand years from now, he will continue to make glad the heart of childhood.

•Next to "Is There a Santa Claus?" the following editorial was the most popular of the *Sun's* casual essays. Internal evidence indicates that its author was Edward Kingsbury. Edward Mitchell, the *Sun's* editor, said of him: "For a third of a century Kingsbury was a prime factor in making the paper's editorial page what it was said by the kind-hearted to be. He had most of the talents except that of self-promotion. He caught speedily the inherited characteristics, and added to these the rich qualities of a personality almost unique for exquisite humor, fine wit, broad literary appreciation, and originality of idea and phrase."

THE OLDEST LIVING GRADUATE
(New York *Sun*; January 30, 1901)

The King has no solitary preeminence in never dying. He shares his mortal immortality with another potentate and great public character, the Oldest Graduate. There is always an Oldest Graduate; and always there are heirs waiting for the succession. Mr. BENJAMIN D. SILLIMAN, distinguished and fortunate in so many other regards, was also for some time the Oldest Living Graduate of Yale; and now that honor belongs to Judge Cutler of '29, who lives in Waterbury, where they make the watches. May these be wound up for many a day before he yields his crown to the heir apparent. At 93 the Oldest Living Graduate is or should be but a boy. After waiting seventy odd years for his title, he will be in no hurry to give it up. He should enjoy it to the full, be merciful in his reminiscences, and look with an indulgent pity on the lads of 90 and 91 who want his job.

For, flower unloved of Amaryllis though it be, this honor is greatly prized. The survivor in this Tontine has beaten all his contemporaries at college. He can say to Time, as BERANGER said:

"Old Postilion, hold-up, hold up;
Let us drink a stirrup cup."

It is too much for this glory to go to a man otherwise famous, as Mr. Silliman was or as HORACE BINNEY was. The latter, an illustrious lawyer whose fame is perhaps as dim now as that of most great lawyers who have not held high political office, was graduated at Harvard in 1797, if we remember well, and he was the oldest living Harvard man for some time before be was cut off in '95. An Oldest Living Graduate who has no other fame than that is to be preferred. Such was JOSEPH HEAD of Harvard, of 1804. He lived in some little town. With his bent form, his VAN WINKLE beard, his long staff, he looked what he was as he marched among the younger generations in the yard on Commencement Day, "the oldest living grad-oo-ate," as he pronounced it after the fashion of his rural youth. Good old JOSEPH HEAD, if that was his name! One thinks with kindness of him, and all his predecessors; and of his successors in the procession.

In every college from A to Z something of affection attaches to the college elder and leader of the line. Of ordinary distinction the graduate may grow tired, be it his or that of a classmate. Of the class of 1825 at Bowdoin, of 1829 at Harvard, of 1853 at Yale, it has been possible to hear too much. At Brunswick, 1875, Mr. BLAINE happily expressed the weariness which the constant celebration of the celebrated brings. "I am glad to hear," he said, "that those members of the class of 1825 who are illustrious on earth are happy in heaven."

The graduate whose ambition it is to become the Oldest Living Graduate scorns all loud and easier fames. In seclusion and with perfect modesty of spirit, he sets before himself early the high goal. He accepts philosophically all detriments which Fate and Fortune send. "I am no longer young," he says to himself, "but why should I wish to be? Everybody who stays in the game must get old and how few can become the Oldest Living Graduate? I am not handsome, witty, eloquent, or even popular. I don't have to be, in my business, which is that of living to be the O.L.G. My classmate, HOOKER HAYNES, has made most of the money there is in the world. My classmate, BRATTLE HOLLYOKE, has married most of the rest. I don't need money in my business. BYLES is a Bishop,

DWIGHT is a Senator. BILL TRUMBULL is a Trust. I haven't any office. I don't direct anything. I have little property and less hair. But I think I can outlive every man in my class and I mean to do it. Let them last into the nineties if they can. I'll take an even hundred, and one to carry, if necessary."

The young chaps just out of college may not know this harmless ambition at first. They are too young—confound 'em! We remember hearing GEORGE BANCROFT, 60 years after his graduation, imparting the fact to a freshman. The freshman gaped and gasped in wonder. How was it possible for a man to have been graduated 60 years ago. If NEBUCHADNEZZAR had come into the room and tried to sell a book on vegetarianism, that freshman could not have been more surprised. But youth's the stuff will not endure. It doesn't take the truly wise graduate long to find the most reasonable object of desire. He nourishes the gentle vision in his heart. He sees himself a well-preserved ancient of 98, with a face like a BALDWIN apple and still tolerable legs. His gold-headed cane is less a staff than a part of his make-up; 'tis a representative of the monumental pomp of age. He wears, for effect, a tall hat of the fashion of 50 years before. He prides himself on the cut of his frock coat. His surviving hair is soft and white. A perfect gentleman of the old school. "Young gentlemen," says the Oldest Living Graduate, "I ascribe my remarkable health and long life to the fact that for seventy-five years I have never smoked nor drank." "Boys," he says, to a few striplings of 90-odd assembled around the punch bowl, "I attribute my good health and looks to the fact that for eighty years I have taken a nip of good stuff regularly every day. But I never overdid it as you do."

We once knew an Oldest Living Graduate who would walk on the railroad track, although he was nearly a hundred and deaf as a post. This is encouraging for beginners, as it seems to show that the O.L.G. is born, not made by training. Only a very few years ago there happened to live in the same town the Oldest Living Graduate and the next-to-oldest living graduate. They were great cronies and as lively as crickets. But each watched the distressingly robust health of the other with some alarm. "WILLIAM is looking a leetle peaked," JOHN would say; "he oughtn't be out in the cold so much at his age." And both lived in health to the very edge of the hundred. The man who will devote himself with a single mind to becoming the Oldest Living Graduate deserves to be happy.

•The *Sun's* casual essays discoursed on a multitude of lighter topics of the day, and one of the favorites was food. The following editorial exhibits the essayists' slapstick humor at its best.

THE TRIUMPH OF HASH
(New York *Sun*; March 25, 1903)

The Hull House Woman's Club of Chicago has said and done

many things for the benefit of many sciences and the world; but we are especially grateful to it for its recent utterance on hash. Domestic economy is an exhaustible subject, and even the smallest contribution to it should be accepted with thanks. Thus, a Hull House economist tells us that old cravats should be made into sofa pillows. It may be that everything can be made into sofa pillows, a fact that explains, in part, the universality of those articles. As the proverb says, you cannot see the lounge for the pillows. We can't live by sofa pillows alone, but there is an analogy, perhaps an esoteric relation, between sofa pillows and hash, as everything can be and has been made into hash. Hash is as general as the casing air and almost as vital. Hull House avers that hash is the cheapest thing for human nature's daily food, sound and kind as diet, hygienic, strengthening; in short, infinite riches in a little room. And Hull House speaks the truth.

But not the whole truth. Who can give to hash the multifarious praise or justice its myriad-sided virtues merit? Hash is the fifth element. Hash is the quintessence of all the aliments. Hash is the perpetual tertium quid, the almagest of the table, the grand secret of the alchemy of the kitchen. It is the true democratic, liberal, all-containing, composite, miscellaneous dish. Not even sociology can compare with it in extent of table of contents. Hash is a masterpiece of creative art. It is capable of all the flavors and fragrances, melodies and symphonies. Let Scotchmen sing its brother, haggis. We stick to hash and shall stick until our hash is settled. Hash is the one and only all-pervading, self-governing, independent, free and equal American dish. There is strength in the very name of it, that comes down like a chopping knife on the chopping tray. Antonio Perez, a Portuguese-Maltese cat of Provincetown, Mass., will rush madly to the kitchen if you merely say "hash!" and is sometimes deceived by the similar sound, the assonance, of a sneeze. Is there any old boy within the sound of our voice who has forgotten the merry song of the chopping knife when the mince-meat was prepared and alligated in the kitchen? What is mince-meat but hash a little sublimated and decorated?

What is the real native American word for a waiter? "Hash-slinger," a word of power, guiltless of servile connotation, having something of whirlwind and passion. The "hash-slinger" has his shirt sleeves rolled up. He walks defiantly, with the port of a sovereign. He slings the hash at you scornfully. For "hash" has assumed all its rights. It takes all other foods in its all-embracing arms. It is the generic name of food. All food is "hash." The eating house, the restaurant, the lordliest lobster-palace, is but a "hash-house." Democracy drips from that chunky and admirable word "hash." Hash! Millions eat it, joyfully, happily, suspiciously, according to the thermometer of their livers and their confidence in the cook. WALT WHITMAN should have written a paean of hash. Hash cheered the insides of pioneers. Hash marched or sailed in prairie schooners to the Pacific. Hash made the bone and muscle and brain of innumerable Americans. Hash, composed of everything, entered into the composition of all our men of energy. Mad ANTHONY WAYNE, ISRAEL PUTNAM, ANDREW JACKSON, GEORGE ROGERS CLARK, ate hash. Good hash makes a good man. Difficult, perverse, dangerous hash can be digested and survived only by men predestinate to distinction and of dauntless stomachs. Hash kills off the weaklings and fits the fittest for their careers. Hash is a duty when it is not a pleasure. Never forget that, with the highest respect to NOAH JOHNSON, hash is the food of heroes.

There is a certain corn-beef hash with poached eggs which is the highest hash-mark of the century; the perihelion, the apotheosis of hash. All hash is profitable either to the maker or to the consumer or to both. Cheap snobs who turn up their noses at honest friend Hash will be suitably cut up and browned for their sin in a region where frying "on the grid" is a specialty.

Once more we thank the Hull House Woman's Club for its appreciation of a great American institution.

MASTERS OF THE EDITORIAL

JOSEPH PULITZER AND THE NEW YORK *WORLD*: MASTERS OF THE EDITORIAL CRUSADE

When Joseph Pulitzer wanted society to change, he did everything he could to change it. Countless crusades filled the pages of the New York *World* after Pulitzer purchased the newspaper in 1883. His vision of the newspaper as "an institution which should always fight for progress and reform... never tolerate injustice or corruption... [and] always remain devoted to the public welfare" has had a lasting impact on American journalism.

With his death in 1911, he left behind a fortune—both materially and professionally. He had become a millionaire with his hugely successful St. Louis *Post-Dispatch* and New York *World*, and he had almost single-handedly reinvented American journalism. It was largely owing to his influence that the crusade became a standard part of newspaper practices.

Pulitzer was born in Budapest, Hungary, on April 10, 1847, the son of educated and prosperous parents. From the time he was a young boy, he dreamed of being a soldier. His rejection by the Hungarian, French, and English army sent him to the United States, where he was finally accepted into the Union army during the Civil War. He joined the ranks of boy-soldiers and served diligently in the New York Cavalry. After the war, he began to search for work and, knowing little English, had a hard time finding a job. Told as a joke that St. Louis was an ideal place to learn English, he moved there, not realizing that St. Louis had one of the largest German-speaking populations in the nation. After many odd jobs, he finally found his niche, however, as a reporter for the German *Westliche Post.*

He became a prodigious writer, working long hours and contributing several columns to every issue of the newspaper. Politics became one of his favorite topics, and he soon became known in St. Louis and throughout Missouri as a leader of liberal Republican thought. He even was elected to the Missouri legislature for a term (despite the fact that, at the age of 22, he was legally too young to serve). He found, however, that his talent was in writing about politicians, not in dealing with them personally.

In 1878, he purchased the foundering St. Louis *Dispatch.* He took over its run-down offices, dilapidated machinery, low circulation, mediocre reputation, and—most importantly—its wire-service franchise. Within two years, it had, as a result of Pulitzer's energetic news policy and zealous advocacy of reform, the highest circulation in the city. Profits likewise soared, and Pulitzer began looking around for larger fields.

The method by which he gained readers was one that he would follow a few years later with the New York *World.* He preached and practiced anti-big-business liberalism. He converted from liberal Republicanism to Democratic ideology, but he claimed to be nonpartisan, a claim that was true in the sense that he did not officially tie his newspaper to the Democratic party. Although he himself was known for his political views, he determined that his newspaper would serve the people in an unselfish way. Attacking social injustices from all directions, he considered himself society's watchdog. He attacked selfish industrialists and their control of government, trying to enlighten readers to poverty and bad working conditions. When he purchased the *Dispatch,* he proclaimed that it would be "the organ of truth... will advocate principles and ideas rather than prejudices and partisanship."

While heralding reform, he attempted to build up circulation among working-class readers with sensational tactics. The *Dispatch's,* and later the *World's,* columns were filled with news of drunken brawls, prostitution rings, and gambling houses. Large, eye-catching headlines and bold illustrations shouted the news. His trademark style of sensational features was extremely popular and pulled in thousands of sales dollars. When criticized for his sensational news tactics, he would reply that his purpose was mainly to attract readers to the news columns in the expectation that they also would read the editorial pages.

While Pulitzer was slowly building an empire in Missouri, in New York City the newspaper scene was a crowded, confused one. The large *Evening Post, Sun, Tribune,* and *World* all wrestled for the city's readership, with other smaller publications pulling segments of the population to themselves. In fact, Joseph's brother Albert owned the *Morning Journal*, one of the less traditional newspapers. It was especially known for its sensationalism.

Supposedly on his way to Europe for a vacation with his family, Pulitzer stopped in the city and surveyed the situation. He talked with his brother and met with the other successful editors (men like Charles Dana, Whitelaw Reid, and James Gordon Bennett Jr.). Then, before almost anyone realized it, he purchased the *World* from the industrialist Jay Gould for a high $340,000. He never went to Europe. Within two years of his purchase, Pulitzer had led the *World* to the forefront of New York journalism. It quickly gained the highest circulation in the city.

With his new newspaper, Pulitzer put a plan into action very similar to the one he had used with the *Dispatch*. He filled the *World* with sensational material, while also fighting for civil and social reform. His aim, he said, was to reach the uneducated and struggling masses of citizens. In celebration of his 60th birthday, he published his views on the *World's* mission. He described the newspaper as "An institution which should always fight for progress and reform; never tolerate injustice or corruption... always remain devoted to the public welfare; never be satisfied with merely printing news." On another occasion—this time, the *World's* 30th birthday—he rallied his readers to the liberal causes he and his publication supported. He declared: "The struggle for liberty is mainly a struggle against the abuses of authority.... Issues change, but principles remain eternal, and there is no truce in the battle for human rights." Following Pulitzer's death, Frank Cobb, the *World's* editor said, "His passionate jealousy of the editorial integrity and independence of the *World* knew no bounds."

Cobb's eulogy bears quoting because of what it reveals about the reasons for the *World's* editorial success. Pulitzer, he wrote, regarded "a newspaper not as private property but as public property... independent of everything except public interest—independent even of its own proprietor when occasion required.... His aim was to make a newspaper that... would hold itself beyond every form of influence except that of the public welfare....

"Although he was the owner of *The World*... he was in no sense a newspaper publisher. Practically all his knowledge of counting-room affairs was second-hand. He once told me... that in all the years of his journalistic career he never spent an hour at any one time in the business office. Nothing connected with *The World* appealed to him less than its income and profits.... Its prosperity was a means, never an end.... To him journalism was never a business; it was the most powerful and responsible profession in which any man could engage." Cobb's views are instructive for an understanding not only of Pulitzer but also of one of the reasons no newspaper since has exercised an editorial leadership even faintly resembling that of the *World*.

Over the years, Pulitzer's crusades were many and varied. Among others, he attacked prostitution, promoted insurance reform, opposed industrial monopolies, and took a vigorous part in numerous political campaigns. One of his earliest and most successful crusades was one to save the Statue of Liberty. One can see in it the techniques that Pulitzer employed. Liberty was one of Pulitzer's chief lifetime concerns; and in 1885, it offered him an ideal opportunity to increase the public prominence of his paper. In the early 1870s the French had begun their project to donate a gift to the United States to symbolize the unity between the two nations. They collected one million or so francs and commissioned the creation of the statue. The American government set aside space on Bedloe Island, and in 1877 a committee was appointed to raise funds for the base. A concrete foundation was laid, but by 1883, when the statue was ready to be shipped, $100,000 still was needed to build a pedestal for it.

The Statue of Liberty appealed directly to Pulitzer's strongest feelings. An immigrant himself, he remembered his own arrival in America and his sense that it was truly the land of opportunity. On March 16, 1885, he kicked off his own campaign to raise money for the pedestal. First, he decided that the *World's* resources would be devoted constantly to the campaign. In this campaign as in others, Pulitzer served as manager and orchestrator rather than as journalist. He directed his editors and editorial writers to give special attention to it. Although he would suggest ideas and techniques, he left the actual job of writing news and editorials to his staff.

In the Statue of Liberty campaign, the *World* appealed directly to the ordinary citizens of New York and the nation. After providing the background on the efforts of the French to give a gift properly symbolizing the love of liberty shared with Americans, the inaugural editorial in the campaign proposed a plan for the "whole people of America" to contribute the money for the pedestal. Rather than relying on American millionaires—since the statue was not a gift from French millionaires—the editorial encouraged everyone to give something, no matter how little. That editorial was the beginning of a massive crusade. Donations poured in from across the country. Eventually, the full $100,000 that was needed was raised; and the nation, the *World* proudly declared, was "saved from disgrace."

To achieve the success he desired at the *World*, Pulitzer surrounded himself with outstanding editors, reporters, and columnists. Considering the editorial page to be the heart of the newspaper, he assigned his best employees to work there. As a result, the *World's* editorial office was staffed by some of the most exceptional individuals in American journalism for several decades at the end of the 19th and beginning of the 20th centuries. Most of the editorial writers published anonymously, but among them was Frank Cobb, who was serving as editor-in–chief at the time of

Pulitzer's death and who symbolized the unswerving dedication to reform and liberalism that the *World* stood for. Today, Cobb is remembered as one of history's greatest editorial writers. He is spotlighted later in this anthology.

A letter Pulitzer wrote in 1910 revealed his theories on excellence in journalistic writing. In it, he highlighted four rules by which newspapers should live: (1) concentrate on "what is original, distinctive, dramatic, romantic, thrilling, unique, curious, quaint, humorous, odd, apt to be talked about...," (2) discover "what is the one distinctive feature, fight, crusade, public service or big exclusive" and then present one "striking feature each issue... prepared before, with nothing left to chance," (3) discover the "difference between a paper made for the million, for the masses, and a paper made for the classes.... I would not make a paper that only the judges of the Supreme Court and their class would read," and (4) stress "accuracy, accuracy, accuracy. Also terseness, intelligent, not stupid, condensation.... No picture or illustration unless it is first class both in idea and execution." The Pulitzer Prizes, which were established through an endowment from Pulitzer, today recognize such principles of journalism and are the most prestigious awards in the field.

The *World* became the yardstick by which other newspapers were measured. Pulitzer's dedication to social reform and to the common masses of people was studied and his method of presenting circulation-building news was imitated. In editorial writing, he and the *World's* staff of writers provided the model for how crusading should be done.

•In 1884, on the eve of the presidential election, the *World* published an editorial that had a direct effect on enough votes to sway the election outcome away from Republican James Blaine and to Democrat Grover Cleveland. The subject was a dinner that rich industrialists held in Blaine's honor. While Republican and other Democratic newspapers treated the dinner as a good promotional event for Blaine, the *World* alone recognized how it could be used to paint Blaine as the partner of the industrialists and the enemy of working people.

SHALL JAY GOULD RULE THE COUNTRY?
(New York *World*; October 30, 1884)

The mask is off and Blaineism stands revealed in its true colors.

Up to the present time, we have heard from Blaine and his organs nothing but expressions of affection for the workingmen of the country and eulogies upon the Republican party as their "protector."

This sort of campaigning has not produced promising results. The election is close at hand. New York, the pivotal state, is conceded to be certain for Cleveland by 60,000 majority.

Broken down and despairing, Blaine hastens back to New York, throws the "People's Friend" role aside and appeals to the enemies of the Republic to save him.

Money, Money, Money! to overthrow the honest will of the people and to enable him to steal from them the Presidency by bribery and fraud, is his prayer.

He calls around him the railroad grabbers and speculators, the favored bankers who have enjoyed the profits of syndicates, the representatives of the most grasping monopolies in the country, and his cry to them is the cry of the horse-leech: "Give! give! give!"

Read the list of the Blaine banqueters who are to fill his pockets with money to corrupt the ballot-box. Are they the friends of the workingmen? What humbug! Are they in sympathy with labor? What fraud! Are they not mostly railroad kings, Wall Street millionaires, greedy monopolists, lobbyists, and speculators, who have grown wealthy on public grants, legislation and special privileges?

Let the people answer when they read the names!

Do the people believe that the Jay Goulds, Sages, Fields and others who banqueted at Delmonico's last night poured a corruption fund into Blaine's pocket without a consideration? Do they not know that these selfish Money Kings took for their security a mortgage on the Administration, as they took a mortgage on the Supreme Court bench four years ago?

It was a Feast of Fraud. It meant danger to the Republic. Unless rebuked by the people it will mean death to the liberties of the people. Death to real protection of Labor from the insolent tyranny of Capital. Death to the Republic itself eventually!

Shall Jay Gould rule this country? Shall he own the President? Is not his power too dangerous already?

•Here is the editorial that kicked off the *World's* campaign to raise money for the Statue of Liberty pedestal.

AN APPEAL
(New York *World*; March 16, 1885)

Money must be raised to complete the pedestal for the Bartholdi statue. It would be an irrevocable disgrace to New York City and the American Republic to have France send us this splendid gift without our having provided even so much as a landing place for it.

Nearly ten years ago the French people set about making the Bartholdi statue. It was to be a gift emblematical of our attainment of the first century of independence. It was also the seal of a more serviceable gift they made to us in 1776, when, but for their timely aid, the ragged sufferers of Valley Forge would have been disbanded and the colonies would have continued a part of the British dominion. Can we fail to respond to the spirit that actuated this generous testimonial?

The statue is now completed and ready to be brought to our shores in a vessel especially commissioned for the purpose by the French Government. Congress, by a refusal to appropriate the necessary money to complete preparations for its proper reception and erection, has thrown the responsibility back to the American people.

There is but one thing that can be done. We must raise the money.

The *World* is the people's paper, and it now appeals to the people to come forward and raise this money. The $250,000 that the making of the statue cost was paid in by the masses of the French people—by the workingmen, the tradesmen, the shop girls, the artisans—by all, irrespective of class or condition. Let us respond in like manner. Let us not wait for the millionaires to give this money. It is not a gift from the millionaires of France to the millionaires of America but a gift of the whole people of France to the whole people of America.

Take this appeal to yourself personally. It is meant for every reader of the *World.* Give something, however little. Send it to us. We will receive it and see that it is properly applied. We will also publish the name of every giver, however small the sum given.

Let us hear from the people. Send in your suggestions. We will consider them all. If we all go to work together with a firm resolve and a patriotic will we can raise the needed money before the French vessel bearing the Bartholdi statue shall have passed the unsightly mass on Bedloe's Island that is now but a humiliating evidence of our indifference and ingratitude.

•The following editorial provides a good example of a simple, direct, yet forceful technique of writing that the *World* employed.

A QUESTION
(New York *World*; January 9, 1887)

The Interstate Commerce bill is opposed
　　By Jay Gould;
　　By C. P. Huntington;
　　By the Western cattle rings;
　　By Philip D. Armour;
　　By stock jobbers, large and small;
　　By corporations generally;
　　By Leland Stanford, the millionaire and corporation Senator.
It is favored by
　　The Western farmers;
　　The Eastern merchants;
　　The boards of trade and transportation;

Anti-monopolists in general;
The people.
Ought the Interstate Commerce bill become law or suffer defeat?

•The following editorial provides an example of the "parallel column" technique that the *World* was fond of using as a means of highlighting its opponents' contradictions.

"THRIFTY MERCHANT—PRODIGAL SON"
(New York *World*; July 1895)

Philadelphia, July 27—The trouble among the employees of ex-Postmaster General Wanamaker over the low wages and petty tyranny of the floor bosses is serious. Since the publication of the employees' grievances and their steps to organize for self-protection, detectives have been employed in Wanamaker's store to find out the employees who have joined the union. The new labor league, which numbers over one thousand, threatens to go out in a body if any of their number is discharged. The league, the Retail Employees' Protective Association, claim they are paid but $4 a week, and are subjected to petty and unnecessary fines for trivial faults. The delegates from the different leagues have formed a mutual protection agreement with the Knights of Labor, and at a meeting of District Union No. 1120 K. of L., a resolution was passed pledging moral and financial support to the employees in their efforts to obtain more liberal wages and conditions of labor. It is common knowledge that the Wanamaker employees below a certain grade have fewer privileges and have to bear greater exactions than employees of any other drygoods firm.

Paris, July 27—All Paris is talking of the prodigal extravagance of Rodman Wanamaker, the young son of ex-Postmaster General Wanamaker, of Philadelphia, who spent $20,000 this week on a single dinner for 22 guests. Even in this city of sumptuous dining it is doubtful whether so much money was ever squandered on a single feast. It was given in the Pavilion d'Armenonville, a famous restaurant in the Bois de Boulogne. Twenty-two of the finest equipages called at the same moment at the residences of the guests and brought them to the banquet hall. The decorations were marvelous. Luminous fountains planted upon great blocks of ice kept the air cool. It was not one dinner but 22 independent dinners, separately served, one to each guest. Each guest had before him a whole leg of mutton, a whole salmon, truffled fowl, a basket of peaches, and a double magnum of champagne, besides bottles of wine of sacred vintage and fabulous cost. After the banquet costly jewelry was distributed to the guests, among whom were a number of young titled Frenchmen. Paris newspapers speak of the banquet as magnificent, but in bad taste.

•In 1908 President Theodore Roosevelt began criminal libel proceedings against Pulitzer and the *World* over their charges that $40 million involved in the United States' acquisition of land for the Panama Canal had been paid illegally to a syndicate. The *World* claimed that Roosevelt had deliberately lied about the money. In the following editorial, Pulitzer and Frank Cobb responded to Roosevelt's libel threat by declaring that he could not intimidate the *World* or Pulitzer into dropping their efforts to get Congress to investigate the Canal land payment. Roosevelt did succeed in getting Pulitzer indicted, but the courts threw out the charges.

LESE-MAJESTY
(New York *World*; December 16, 1908)

Mr. Roosevelt is mistaken. He cannot muzzle *The World*.

While no amount of billingsgate on his part can alter our determination to treat him with judicial impartiality and scrupulous fairness, we repeat what we have already said—that the Congress of the United States should make a thorough investigation of the whole Panama transaction, that the truth may be known to the American people.

It is a most extraordinary circumstance that Mr. Roosevelt himself did not demand such an inquiry. All his protestations of outraged virtue, all his torrents of imprecation and denunciation, end with the amazing assertion that "there is nothing whatever, in which this Government is interested, to investigate about this transaction."

The World fully appreciates the compliment paid to it by Mr. Roosevelt in making it the subject of a special message to the Congress of the United States. In the whole history of American Government no other President has ever paid such a tribute to the power and influence of a fearless, independent newspaper.

The World likewise appreciates the importance and significance of the President's statement when he declares to Congress that the proprietor of *The World* should be "prosecuted for libel by the Governmental authorities," and that "the Attorney General had under consideration the form under which the proceedings against Mr. Pulitzer shall be brought."

This is the first time a President ever asserted the doctrine of lese-majesty, or proposed, in the absence of specific legislation, the criminal prosecution by the Government of citizens who criticized the conduct of the Government or the conduct of individuals who may have had business dealings with the Government. Neither the King of Great Britain nor the German Emperor would venture to arrogate such power to himself. Yet Mr. Roosevelt proposes to use all the power of the greatest government on earth to cripple the freedom of the press on the pretext that the Government itself has been libeled—and he is the Government.

We are aware that for many years Mr. Roosevelt has been savagely displeased with the editorial conduct of *The World*. It is true that we have criticized him sharply and frankly whenever we believed the public interest required, just as we have heartily commended and supported him whenever we believed the public interest would thereby be advanced. Mr. Roosevelt's attack on *The World* can be explained only on the theory that he believes he can muzzle the paper, and our recent impeachment of his veracity seems to have been the last straw that broke his autocratic back.

Mr. Roosevelt's lamentable habit of inaccurate statement makes it impossible to accept either his judgments or his conclusions. In his message he does not state correctly even so simple a matter as the pretended causes of his grievance.

He says, for example, that *The World* asserted that there was "corruption by or on behalf of the Government of the United States." No such charge was made.

He says that "among those persons who, it was alleged, made 'huge profits' were Mr. Charles P. Taft, a brother of Mr. William H. Taft, then candidate for the Presidency, and Mr. Douglas Robinson, my brother-in-law." No such charge was made.

If *The World* has libeled anybody we hope it will be punished, but we do not intend to be intimidated by Mr. Roosevelt's threats, or by Mr. Roosevelt's denunciation, or by Mr. Roosevelt's power.

Mr. Roosevelt's seething indignation about *The World's* "libel upon the United States Government" is an exquisite indictment indeed, coming as it does from a President who less than a week ago officially insinuated in his message that the congress of the United States was composed of scoundrels who amended an appropriation bill because "Congressmen did not themselves wish to be investigated by Secret Service Men."

No other living man ever so grossly libeled the United States as does the President who besmirches Congress, bulldozes judges, assails the integrity of courts, slanders private citizens, and who has shown himself the most reckless, unscrupulous demagogue whom the American people ever trusted with great power and authority.

We say this not in anger but in sincere sorrow. *The World* has immeasurably more respect for the office of President of the United States than Theodore Roosevelt has ever shown during the years in which he has maintained a reign of terror and vilified the honor and honesty of both public officials and private citizens who opposed his policies or thwarted him in his purposes.

So far as *The World* is concerned, its proprietor may go to jail, if Mr. Roosevelt succeeds, as he threatens; but even in jail *The World* will not cease to be a fearless champion of free speech, a free press and a free people.

It cannot be muzzled.

The Professional Era, 1900-Present

With the beginning of the 20th century, two trends of paramount importance to editorial writing could be seen taking shape. The first and more important was the growth of newspapers as big business. The second—which seemed to some people to be a counterpoising force but which in reality was an outgrowth of the first—was the professionalization of journalism.

Attending the growth of newspapers as business enterprises was—and continues to be—an emphasis on profit as the primary motive of newspaper owners. Even while the preeminent editors such as Charles Dana, E. L. Godkin, and Joseph Pulitzer practiced their art in the late 1800s, huge new forces were closing in on journalism. The changes had begun with the penny press. When partisanship ceased to be the primary purpose of the newspaper, a means of economic support was cut from under the editorial writer. Even while the great personal editors were at the height of their glory in the 1800s, the news and business departments were becoming the real supporters of their papers. Here and there throughout the latter part of the 19th century a shining name in journalism stands out, but the motive of profit—sustained by the concepts of readership through news and of business efficiency—was already taking over the newspaper profession. By the 20th century it dominated.

For those looking for dates, we might name 1896 as the conspicuous year of the victory of business over expression as the prime purpose of journalism. That was the year Pulitzer, in the name of financial health for his *World*, was swept fully into the circulation war with William Randolph Hearst. Responsible expression gave way to frenzied sensationalism. But even more important in the history of journalism's change to big business was Adolph Ochs' assumption in 1896 of the management of the foundering New York *Times*. Reacting against the sensationalism and boisterous editorial policies of Pulitzer and Hearst, Ochs revitalized the *Times* on the basis of thorough news coverage, objectivity, sound business practices, and a strong financial base. In these, the *Times* became the model for America's 20th-century newspapers.

The potential benefits of such an approach to the newspaper profession are obvious. Partisanship is reduced, readers are given the unbiased information necessary to make well-founded decisions, newspapers can afford to hire qualified personnel, financially stable newspapers can resist efforts by advertisers to influence editorial policy, and so forth.

On the other hand, as ideas of business efficiency took over, competition was reduced, newspaper content became standardized, chain ownership multiplied, the corporate structure of papers became commonplace, the value of newspapers increased, and the newspaper became in most cases primarily a business investment. These changes had several effects on editorials.

As news received greater emphasis, the eminence of the editorial faded. The editorial was replaced by the news report as the heart of the paper. The direct persuasive impact of editorials may have suffered consequently. Illustrating the changed attitude about the nature of newspaper influence, the chain publisher E. W. Scripps declared frankly, "Our headlines are our editorials."

Because the editorial page came to be viewed as secondary, little importance or money was placed in it. On most papers, the page came to be understaffed; editorial writers had inadequate time to devote to the writing of editorials; and the general quality of editorials suffered. As a counterpoint to those trends, it should be pointed out that many, mostly larger newspapers continued to place considerable emphasis on the editorial page, allotting it substantial resources and staff members. The professional concerns of individual writers and of writers' organizations also provided evidence of a widespread commitment to editorial writing. The professional activities of many writers would indicate that in some ways editorial writing today exhibits more talent and commitment than at any time in the past.

Despite such healthy signs in the field, however, the tone and tenor of the editorial changed under the influence of corporate journalism and professional attitudes. Editorials became less passionate and more reasoned.

One could point to a number of reasons for the change, but one factor was the disappearance of competing papers. When partisan competition and vigorous expression were the rule, newspapers attempted to appeal to limited groups of readers. When profit emerged as a paper's motive, newspapers attempted to broaden their appeal by presenting both sides of issues and even-tempered opinion. When a city's one newspaper was its only one, and the paper's readership was composed of liberals and conservatives, Republicans and Democrats, poor and rich, the newspaper ownership found it incumbent to be circumspect in its editorial comment. Pulitzer Prize winner W.W. Waymack in 1942 pointed out this principle: "Both the economic pressure (what constitutes 'good business') and a fair recognition of social obligation reinforce the principle of news objectivity, divorced from editorial bias. They also dictate less of passion and more of reason in editorials."

In some regards, this attitude must be respected. When most

cities have only one daily, it would be unfortunate if that paper became the opinionated mouthpiece of one faction or cause. Although corporate newspapers have striven to appear nonpartisan, some have, on the other hand, tended to adhere to the conservative line and stands that are good for business interests. This would appear to be a natural result of the fact that newspaper owners themselves are businessmen. On the other hand, working journalists tend to be ideologically liberal. Being no different from their fellow journalists, many editorial writers have imparted a liberal perspective to their writing.

Editorial writing in the 20th century came to be marked also by a noticeable absence of boldness. Circumspection engendered by business concerns sometimes gave way to timidity. "American journalism," *Editor and Publisher* editorialized in 1937, "... is officed by too many people intent upon balance sheets, and content with a product that holds circulation and causes no complaints from advertisers and articulate readers." At another time, an editor of *Editor and Publisher* told the American Society of Newspaper Editors: "Reader confidence has been impaired because too many newspapers seem, on their face, to be cautious to the point of cowardice, morbidly expedient, slyly illiberal, holding back from any forthright part in the great controversies that are sweeping the country, and many people deduce that they are hogtied by managements in league with special interests."[1]

The business character of newspapers also changed the position and nature of the person who wrote editorials. "Personal editors" disappeared, employees with the function only of writing editorials emerged, and much of the editorial page was given over to syndicated columnists. These changes in personnel duties resulted from changes in the complexity, size, and motives of newspapers. As the size of the newspaper operation grew, the owner no longer was capable of performing all its functions. With increased complexity and operating expenses, owners, concerned about financial health, had to devote their attentions more and more to the business end of their papers. They had little time to write editorials.

Often, the editor was no longer the boss. In the 19th century, a paper's editor had also been its owner. The editorials of the paper were known to be the voice of the editor. Today, the editor often is simply the employee of a corporation and the editorial merely the anonymous, amalgamated voice of an institution. Compare a number of notable newspapers of the last century with those of today. The *Tribune* was considered Greeley's paper; the *Times*, Raymond's; the *Sun*, Dana's; the *Evening Post*, Bryant's and later Godkin's. What major paper today is identified as the voice and property of its editorial writer? How many readers can even name

---

[1] Quoted in Gayle Waldrop, *Editor and Editorial Writer* (New York, 1948), 42.

the editor of the local paper, much less that of the editorial writer?

As the newspaper grew in size, its functions were divided into the hands of departments. Specialization became the rule. The successor to the personal editor was the editorial writer, often multiplied into the editorial staff. Being an employee, the editorial writer did not speak with the authority of ownership. The effect this had on editorial writing was pointed out in the 1930s by Eric Allen, a professor of journalism at the University of Oregon. "Now this subordinate," he wrote, "being a subordinate, and being known to be a subordinate, began to be more or less kicked around. Among his worst critics were his fellow subordinates. The circulation crew wanted him for heaven's sake to lay off editorials that caused opinionated people to stop the paper.

"The advertising crew wanted to know why in God's name did he always pick on the biggest advertiser to excoriate when the woods were so completely filled with other and worse malefactors of great wealth who didn't advertise. The news staff, perhaps the most critical of all, sneered at his sesquipedalian sentences, full of semicolons and with the periods three inches apart. It was largely at the insistence of the skilled and experienced news room that the editorial writer finally succumbed to the rule of literary composition that no editorial should be longer than one's pencil and that as the pencil wears shorter the editorials get better. Also the news staff advised the editorial staff to be catholic in its choice of subject matter, to write in simple language, to remember that the readers of the paper included women and children and many humble people, and that even the most intellectual human being had many interests close at home that were stronger than even his interests in the high and the ultimate.

"It was all very discouraging."[2]

The opinion function today often falls not on a staff writer but on an outsider, the syndicated columnist. Columnists frequently provide owners with better, more informed writing at a cheaper price than can editorial writers. Because columnists are not anonymous, the public can more often identify them than a newspaper's anonymous editorial writer. They may even be thought of as filling, in some fashion, the void left by the demise of the personal editor—except, of course, that they are distant, not local, voices.

Liberal critics charged that the views of editorial writers shifted with whatever opinion their employers ordered or thought would increase circulation for the corporate newspaper. They could point to Arthur Brisbane, chief editorial writer for the Hearst newspapers for more than 30 years, for proof. Even though he popularized the editorial page, his published views could

---

[2]Eric W. Allen, "Economic Changes and Editorial Influence," *Journalism Quarterly* 8 (Fall 1931): 352.

change from issue to issue depending on the political and social ideological peregrinations of his boss. The late Pulitzer Prize winning editor of the Richmond (Va.) *Times-Dispatch*, Virginius Dabney, writing in 1945, summed up what he saw as the effect that the newspaper's evolution into big business had had on the ideology of editorial writing. "Today," he said, "newspapers are Big Business and they are run in that tradition. The publisher, who often knows little about the editorial side of the operation, usually is one of the leading business men in his community, and his editorial page, under normal circumstances, strongly reflects that point of view. Sometimes he gives his editor a free hand, but far oftener he does not. He looks upon the paper primarily as a 'property,' rather than as an instrument for public service. There are brilliant and honorable exceptions to these generalizations, but an American editor was disconcertingly close to the mark when he spoke not long ago of 'the blinker-wearing stupidity of publishers as a class—men with the vision of soap manufacturers and the souls of oysters because almost all of them come from the counting room....'

"The fact that the average American publisher is not only conservative, but frequently reactionary, and the further fact that he often imposes his views upon his editor, is the greatest single reason why the American editorial page has declined so sharply in influence. Instead of letting trained newspapermen conduct the paper, an art and mystery about which many publishers know little or nothing, they insist upon inflicting their prejudices and predilections upon the entire staff. It is in the realm of editorial policy that this interference produces its most appalling results. The publisher who is imbued with blind preconceptions concerning social and economic questions, preconceptions which stem from no particular study, but merely from the fact that he associates almost entirely with people entertaining similar notions, is hardly the sort of person to formulate an editorial policy which is fair to all classes in the community."[3]

The state of editorial writing today is not as politically bleak as Virginius Dabney painted it almost five decades ago. The influence that the business character of newspapers has exerted on editorial writing has been balanced by the professionalization of the field. Conservative editorial pages are balanced by liberal ones, and today the standardization of journalism ideology now poses a greater threat to open inquiry than political ideology does. Personal editors did not vanish in the 20th century, and at no other time in history have there been more polished editorial writers than today. William Allen White, owner and editor of the Emporia (Kan.) *Gazette* from 1895 to 1944, and Henry Watterson, part-owner and editor of the Louisville (Ky.) *Courier-Journal* from 1868 to 1921, are outstanding examples of editorial writers who

---

[3]Virginius Dabney, *Saturday Review of Literature* (February 24, 1945).

spoke with the power of ownership. Frank Cobb and Walter Lippmann, both editors of the New York *World*, wrote with a force and depth seldom matched. Perhaps no editorial writer ever matched the Portland *Oregonian's* Ben Hur Lampman's mastery of language. More recently, Ralph McGill and Eugene Patterson of the Atlanta *Constitution* proved that editors of a major newspaper need not be anonymous editorial writers. Despite subjugating himself to Hearst, Arthur Brisbane showed that even an employed writer could gain fame in the editorial field.

Editorial writing today also has substantial talent practicing the craft. Paul Greenberg of the Pine Bluff (Ark.) *Commercial* and James Kilpatrick, who went from editorial writing in Richmond, Virginia, to become a nationally syndicated columnist, are prime examples. In reading the winning editorials in such national contests as those sponsored by the American Society of Newspaper Editors and the Pulitzer Prizes, one cannot help but admire the work of many of today's editorial writers. While it is true that even some contest winners are stupendously dull, even superficial, and that most newspapers' editorials are considerably less interesting than readers' letters to their editors, it nevertheless is true that there is a substantial group of editorial writers who do a fine job. They recognize the weaknesses of the field, and they work hard at their own writing. They have their own organization, the National Conference of Editorial Writers, which does not hesitate to illuminate the problems in the field and sponsors a number of activities aimed at improving the craft. Among the entire body of working journalists today, no group is more critical of its own work or more committed to quality.

MASTERS OF THE EDITORIAL

HENRY WATTERSON: MASTER OF PERSONAL JOURNALISM

Close to the end of his career, Louisville *Courier-Journal* editor Henry Watterson declared that "it is not all-important that an editorial page attract attention. If it is honest and represents the paper with respectable soundness of judgment, that is all that is really needed. I doubt if a widely known editor has any pecuniary value to a newspaper."

Those words may have been the most misleading of his career, for he himself symbolized the incredible stature that a good editor can attain with the public. Watterson embodied "personal journalism," for his grand writing style made him known throughout the nation and his editorials affected public consciousness as few have ever done.

Watterson discovered a love for writing at an early age. His father, Harvey Watterson, edited the Washington *Union*. Soon, his son was following in his footsteps. At 18, Henry had, to his surprise, a group of poems accepted for publication in *Harper's Magazine*. After doing free-lance (or "hack") work for such cosmopolitan newspapers as the New York *Times* and *Tribune*, he came into his own as editor in 1862 of the Chattanooga *Daily Rebel*. Six years later, he moved to the newspaper where he remained for the rest of his career.

At the *Courier-Journal*, Watterson perfected an extravagant editorial style that had been evident, but unpolished, in his previous career. His opinions became ramrod straight, and his writing style became grandiose, rhythmic, and powerful.

Soon, readers no longer stated "The *Courier-Journal* said," but "Henry Watterson said." This unequivocal link between editor and publication is the mark of what is known as personal journalism. In his day, newspapers were seeing the last of the great personal journalists. He, along with Horace Greeley, Henry Raymond, and Charles Dana, embodied the spirit of their own newspapers. Watterson, however, would live to see the arrival of corporations in the newspaperman's world, and he lamented it. "Newspapers," he said, "are more and more becoming like the railroads and the banks, pure corporate affairs. Less and less does the individual writer cut any real figure."

Watterson's influence on public opinion was widespread. At a time when politics was on every citizen's mind—before, during, and after the Civil War—the editor's opinion of politicians and policies attracted multitudes of readers. He coined an astounding number of phrases that attained national vogue. Here is a sampling from his comments on presidential elections:

• The "star-eyed Goddess of Reform" (expressing Watterson's interest in a lower tariff in the 1884 presidential election).

• "If we go [to New York] for a nominee, we shall walk through a slaughter-house to an open grave" (opposing Grover Cleveland as the Democrats' 1892 presidential nominee).

• "No compromise with dishonor" (expressing his support for William McKinley in the 1896 campaign).

• "A Mess of Pottage and a Man of Straw" (opposing William Howard Taft in the 1908 election).

• "The Kaiser candidate" (opposing Charles Evans Hughes in the 1916 election).

Political editorial writing held an especially strong grip on Watterson. The bulk of his editorials were political in nature, beginning in the 1860s with reflections on the Civil War and ending in 1918 with critiques of worldwide politics. When not writing of battles or political campaigns, he ventured into the realm of political personalities. The two presidents he found most interesting—Abraham Lincoln and Theodore Roosevelt—were his favorite subjects. He held Lincoln in high regard, believing that the President could bring restoration to the war-torn nation. Watterson, a Southerner, had always, in fact, been a strong advocate of progress in the South. Of Lincoln, he wrote: "There was, in his habitual kindness, a most unfailing and a very firm note." Of Roosevelt, the editor's sentiment was quite different. Watterson referred to him flippantly as "the Man on Horseback" and more viciously as "as sweet a gentleman as ever scuttled a ship or cut a throat."

Despite his long series of popular sayings, he was never more pleased than with the sulfurous phrase he hurled at German rulers with the 1914 war in Europe only a month old: "To Hell with the Hohenzollerns and the Hapsburgs." The phrase (actually the last sentence in a brief editorial) soon achieved widespread popularity, became a standard part of the *Courier-Journal*'s masthead, and was repeated by Watterson in numerous later editorials. It also became the war cry, of politicians and private citizens alike, against the German government.

Watterson often went on the speaking circuit and was admired for his oratory skills. He never, however, attempted to take his fiery political stances beyond the speaking lectern or the writing desk. Although more than a few individuals tried to promote him as a presidential contender, he always refused. Unlike Greeley, who died shortly after his devastating loss in the 1872 presidential election, Watterson never wanted to sit in the politician's chair. His power lay in the ability to write and speak and, perhaps, sway public opinion on who *should* sit in that chair.

Watterson gained national recognition for many of his editorials. He received the 1918 Pulitzer Prize for two of them, "Vae Victus" and "War Has Its Compensations," written to celebrate America's entry into World War I on April 6, 1917. Judges praised the editorials for their aim of "arousing the American people to their international duty and... convincing a section of the country by tradition hostile to universal military service of the wisdom and necessity of its establishment." Of all the celebrated editorials he penned, however, the most widely read was one written in the anger that followed the sinking of the ship *Lusitania*. In the editorial, "The Heart of Christ—The Sword of The Lord and Gideon," were combined his grand writing style, prophetic power, and leadership of public opinion. Only two days before the *Lusitania* went down, sunk by a German torpedo with the loss of 1,198 lives, he had asked, following the sinking of a tanker, "Suppose... it had been the Lusitania...what then?" This foresight revealed his almost uncanny understanding of the world around him.

Long before the sinking of the British steamliner, Watterson's style had been flowery, long, flowing, and metrical. His best writing, however, was done during the era of World War I, when he had come out of semi-retirement, when his rich experience and wide knowledge of the world had replaced his early lack of stylistic and intellectual discipline. In the later years, his writing, although full-blown as ever, displayed a vitality and versatility perhaps unmatched by that of any other editorial writer. On serious issues he wrote with a vigor of expression that smashed opposing sides. Although he also could be an engaging conversationalist on casual editorial topics, he was at his best when attacking.

His writing style was marked by a number of features, the most prominent being intensity of feeling, forcefulness of language, alliteration, meter, rhythm, parallelism, simile, and metaphor. His frequent use of historical and literary allusions is illustrated by the title of the *Lusitania* editorial. The biblical phrase "the sword of the Lord and Gideon" (Judges 7:18) serves aptly as the title of an editorial calling for retribution in war.

From the building where he wrote such emotion-stirring editorials, Watterson ran an efficient and always interesting newspaper operation. Although not imposing, he struck a commanding figure. His flowing white mustache and mane of hair made him appear fatherly, yet powerful—and helped account for his Kentucky nickname of "Colonel." His squinting eyes, the result of a childhood accident that left him blind in the right eye, created the image of an aging man who found it hard to read his own powerful words. His failing eyesight, in fact, was cause for one of the office's favorite topics—the editor-in-chief's illegible handwriting. His habit of capitalizing words for emphasis was another result of his "handicap."

With writers, he always encouraged new talent. As long as editorials were accurate and a credit to his newspaper, they would run next to his. Every issue of the *Courier-Journal* contained a full editorial page, often filling five columns with staff-written opinions.

After his retirement in 1918, his name remained on the masthead as Editor Emeritus and he continued to write editorials for two years. He ended his 50-year association with the newspaper when he could not resign himself to its support of the League of Nations. In his final editorial, he wrote of the League controversy: "I want to warn the people against mischief. I would give them the benefit of long and varied experience." This was a fitting end to a journalism career characterized by broad knowledge of the world and concern for his nation.

Watterson died three years later. Many attempted to describe his success and glorify his life. His own words, however, spoke louder than any others. In 1918, after hearing that he had been awarded the Pulitzer Prize, the aging editor laughed, "The gander-legged boys in the City Editor's room will find out that the old man is a promising journalist."

•Written near the beginning of Watterson's career, the following editorial demonstrates his descriptive and bold language.

KENTUCKY

(Louisville *Courier-Journal*; December 25, 1868)

A little after mid-day on the 25th of December, 1778, a group of ten or a dozen pioneers in buckskin knee-breeches and linsey-woolsey hunting-shirts gathered around a log heap in front of a cabin, which, from a high cliff, overlooked the frozen bed and snowy banks of the Kentucky River. It was very bleak and cold. The sun had not shone out since the second day of the month. The streams were everywhere choked with ice. The very springs were inaccessible, and game was scarce and powder scarcer still. Foremost among the little knot of woodsmen were Daniel Boone and James Harrod; and they had met, as they declared, to offer up their prayers to God on behalf of the "brave men and patriots" who were "fighting the battles of freedom beyond the mountains." They knelt down and prayed accordingly; they sang a hymn; they adopted what they called a resolution; and then, having affirmed devotion to the cause of the colonies against the Crown, they dispersed, each going his several ways, but all inspired by the same good purpose and free-born spirit.

In those days there were negro slaves in Massachusetts. There were none in Kentucky. But the laws of commerce and of climate had their way. The Massachusetts slaveholders found that negro labor was not profitable among them. They, therefore, sold their slaves into the South and invested the money in that which was profitable. No one blames them. They did what they thought was best and what they had undoubted right to do. The times were not so "civilized" nor so "progressive" as they have since become. Doubtless if Massachusetts had the matter to reconsider and go over again, she would free all of her slaves, vote each family a homestead, build for each a snug cottage and, having comfortably stowed the poor dears away in cosy homes, kindle for each a blazing fire, put a kettle on it and thrust into the kettle a Christmas turkey, amid whose steaming odors the songs of Whittier and of freedom would ascend to heaven!

Time sped on. There was a deal of trouble for many and many a year; and wars with the savages; and wars with Britain; and wars with Mexico, and tariff wars and what not. But the country went on growing and prospering until it was so big and prosperous that it forgot its early vows and its early struggles and its early lessons. More's the pity! It forgot them all, and it fell together by the ears and no man can say that it did not demonstrate to the full its boasted fighting capacity. Somebody, however, had to get the better of the shindy; and the muscle and the numbers were with the North, and the North came out winner. It won not only the practical item which it contended for, but in the scuffle it got several trifles which it had not at first expected; so that, the arms of the combatants being laid aside, the spectacle that was presented to the world was curious to see—slavery gone; secession abandoned; the Union in condition for immediate restoration; and peace hovering, like a goddess crowned with olive-leaves, about the threshold of every home in the land.

We do not propose to review what followed. Kentucky was not one of the seceding States. She stood true to the principles which were enunciated in those memorable resolutions at which it is common to hear men sneer. Whatever may be said of those resolutions, they embody a just and true spirit, and mean nothing which is base, or sordid, or narrow, or slavish, or mean. Kentucky's head was with the Union and her heart was with the South; for it is the nature of a generous and manly people to sympathize with the weak in its struggles with the strong. The war closed. Kentucky alone of the free States that were left in the Union was true to herself and to the professions with which the war was begun. She proscribed no one. She gave welcome to all. Today she is prosperous, peaceful, happy. The laws are better enforced in Kentucky than in Indiana. There is less crime in Kentucky than in Ohio. Tennessee is poor. Missouri is poor. Both are the victims of despotic power running roughshod over the liberties and disregarding the private rights of the people. In Kentucky there is no partisan militia. In Kentucky there are no franchise laws. In Kentucky there are no threats of confiscation. Public opinion is the only arbiter of public questions, and every man is allowed to hold office who obtains votes enough. As in Massachusetts, public opinion is very much one way. There the people are Republicans for the most part; vote the Republican ticket; decline to vote for Democratic candidates or Democratic measures and are, we dare say, conscientious. Here it is exactly reversed. We are, for the most part, Democrats; we vote the Democratic ticket; we decline to vote for Republican candidates and measures; we are perfectly honest and think we have a right, as free citizens of a free republic, to decide for ourselves.

For so doing and so thinking we are denounced as traitors to our country and a despotism is sought to be placed over us by those who claim that we ought to be forced to vote for Republican candidates and Republican measures, and who declare that if we do not, we are guilty of rebellion and should be punished therefore.

This was not the spirit of Boone and his companions, who prayed God to bless Massachusetts on Christmas day, 1778. It was not the spirit of the Kentuckians who fought the battles of the country from King's Mountain to the City of Mexico. It is a newborn spirit; the spirit of rapine and war, not of liberty and peace. That the people of Kentucky should regard it with detestation is reasonable and natural. That they should cling the more tenaciously to their original fastening as the pressure from without becomes more violent is also reasonable and natural. But they are not intolerant or inhospitable, but kind, generous, peaceful, enterprising, progressive; faithful to the past; liberal with the present; hopeful of the future. The snows of nearly a hundred years have come and gone since the Christmas of 1778. Many a change has come also over the land. The canebrakes are all gone. The old pioneers are all gone. Their graves are deep-sunken under the ploughshare, and are hid beneath the clover blooms. But the hardy manhood; the warm, impulsive love of freedom; the honest hatred of persecution; the keen sympathy with the weak and suffering, all these noble sentiments that honored the lives of the fathers remain and are illustrated by the children in the unanimity with which they resist the despotism, and we may divide on a thousand issues; but as long as it continues we are one in opposing it as unnecessary, tyrannical, and cruel.

•Few writers have been better than Watterson at the editorial profile. The following characterization of President Theodore Roosevelt shows Watterson's swaggering style at its best.

HE OF THE BIG STICK
(Louisville *Courier-Journal*; October 11, 1904)

The Republican organs affect to be mightily amused by the attitude of the *Courier-Journal* toward the pending campaign, the portents of the political situation and the personality of the President.

"You went on about General Grant," they exclaim, "just as you are going on about Theodore Roosevelt; yet none of the things you prophesied came to pass!"

General Grant did not get the Third Term which his friends arranged for him to get and which was foreshadowed by the Force Bill of 1875. That bill was beaten because certain Republicans, with Mr. Blaine at their head, dared not put such power in General Grant's hands. Although the Republicans stole the Presidency two years later it came to them so handicapped that they were obliged to get down from the high horse they had been riding and hedge a little. One of the last acts of General Grant, before he went out of office, was to withdraw the troops from the South. The carpetbag Governments could not stand without troops. So Hayes let the carpetbaggers go.

In 1885 Cleveland came in. The course of party absolutism was arrested. It was again held up by the election of 1892. Although nothing was accomplished by either of the Cleveland Administrations other than a transfer of the patronage from one party to the other, they were beneficent interludes to the single-party idea. They signalized the power of the people to change the political complexion of their Government by the ordinary process of election. They served warning upon the Republicans that they did not own the earth. They were illustrations of the Democratic principle. If the Force Bill had passed? If General Grant had got a Third Term? If there had continued an unbroken line of Republican Presidents? What then?

In the trial of forces immediately before us the people have the opportunity to make a third exhibition of the same kind. If they avail themselves of the opportunity we shall have four years at least of tranquility at home and abroad. We shall take a look at the books, stop the leaks, suspend the autocracy having its source in the White House and resting on a clique of Gray Wolves in the Senate and on the Speaker and his Committee on Rules in the House, revitalize both Parliamentary Government and the Reign of Law, and thus checking the tendencies of absolutism, we shall preserve the even tenor of our way, achieving such practical Reforms as may from time to time seem to be wise and fit.

We need a man in the Chief Magistracy who is a Magistrate, and not a Mountebank. We need a just and sensible man, not a theorizing experimentalist. In every respect Judge Parker realizes the Magistrate. In every respect Theodore Roosevelt embodies the Mountebank.

Immoderate in everything, the Republican organs distort the reasonable plea of conservative men against the retention of such a man as Theodore Roosevelt at the head of affairs into a prediction of crowns and scepters and dungeons and the like, refusing to discuss the issues of the campaign on their merits, or to allow any criticism of their idol. We specify his disregard of the law. "Oh," they say, "you called him a pirate." We trace his sinister character through his writings. "But," they say, "you called him a pirate." We show the dangers of party absolutism, the selfish tyranny of personal ambition, the menace of foreign complication and domestic corruption incident to a dynasty encrusted in power and illustrated by examples, some of them startling in character, and the chorus repeats, "but you called him a pirate."

Because Theodore Roosevelt is a man of good moral character, well-born and well-educated, the men around him, his official servants, and their newspaper organs, assume for him every excellence. They forget that there are other vices than those of drunkenness, lechery and profanity. A man may be a decorous man, yet a mean and brutal man; he may wear the cloak of religion, yet be rapacious, cruel and unclean. Some of the most worthy men in domestic life have shown themselves most grasping and vicious in their relations to the State. May a man not be decent and selfish? May he not be decorous and dangerous?

We judge Mr. Roosevelt by his writing and his official conduct. His writing shows us a self-confident, supercilious iconoclast. The vengeful spirit which led him first to wrong and then to insult an old man like Jefferson Davis shows through every printed page of his voluminous productivity. It is not alone that his judgment is faulty, but that his spirit is niggardly. He claims everything for himself, gives nothing, allows nothing, to anybody else. He assails whole classes as well as individual men. Yet his composition is equally inconsistent and illogical. He began a

Free Trader, to end a High Protectionist. He built himself up as a Civil Service Reformer, to end the most shameless spoilsman. Do these things mean nothing? How can any upright, thoughtful American respect or admire such a man?

But, his conduct in office has been both brutal and reckless. Why do not some of his organs defend his treatment of Miles? Why are they so persistently silent as to his treatment of Dewey and Schley?

The Panama business was a villainy from start to finish. Why do not some of the newspapers which are abusing us defend it? Forty millions taken from the Treasury to be given to a syndicate of Parisian Stock Gamblers. Ten millions more to a group of stool-pigeons on the Isthmus set up by these Stock Gamblers. A solemn treaty trampled under foot. War levied on a weak Nation by Executive order. The whole beastly swindle as transparent as the day; horrible, infamous; and the man who has put this disgrace upon us, can do no wrong!

Yet, this man is working his Presidential campaign from the White House, which he has converted into a Robber Castle, collecting tribute from the great corporations through Cortelyou, his man-of-all-work, having brought them first to subjection through the Detective System of the Department of Commerce.

Nothing so shameful and shameless has ever been known in American politics; but its author—the man who is to get the usufruct—is above all law, is a law unto himself, and can do no wrong.

He must be elected because he is good.

We must let well enough alone.

The people are not saying much. They are just thinking. Maybe, the 9th of November, the man with the "big stick" will wake up to find it but a broken reed.

•Here is the brief editorial that served as a war cry for Americans who favored the United States' joining the Allies against Germany.

TO HELL WITH THE HOHENZOLLERNS AND THE HAPSBURGS
(Louisville *Courier-Journal*; September 3, 1914)

Herman Ridder [a German-American editor] flings Japan at us. Then he adduces Russia. What does he think now of Turkey? How can he reconcile the Kaiser's ostentatious appeal to the Children of Christ and his pretentious partnership with God— "meinself und Gott"—with his calling the hordes of Mahomet to his aid? Will not this unite all Christendom against the unholy combine? May Heaven protect the Vaterland from contamination and give the German people a chance! To Hell with the Hohenzollerns and the Hapsburgs.

•Of all of Watterson's celebrated editorials, the most widely copied was one written in the anger that followed the sinking of the ship *Lusitania*. In it were combined his grand writing style, prophetic power, and the reasons he exercised such a large leadership of public opinion. His query to President Woodrow Wilson of what Wilson meant by the phrase that "strict accountability" would be applied to Germany for such actions soon became insistent and international.

THE HEART OF CHRIST—
THE SWORD OF THE LORD AND GIDEON
(Louisville *Courier-Journal*; May 9, 1915)

That which *The Courier-Journal* has feared—which it has been for weeks forecasting as likely to happen—has come to pass. A great ocean liner, passing peacefully to and from an American port—carrying a harmless ship's company of noncambatant men, women and children, many of them American citizens—has, without chance of escape, or time for prayer, been ruthlessly sent to the bottom of the deep and some thousand, or more, gone to their death, drowned and mangled by the murderous onset of a German submarine. Truly, the nation of the black hand and the bloody heart has got in its work. It has got in its work not upon armed antagonists in fair fight on battle front, but upon the unoffending and the helpless, sailing what has always been and should ever remain to the peaceful and the peaceloving God's free and open sea.

Nothing in the annals of piracy can in wanton and cruel ferocity equal the destruction of the Lusitania.

It seems but yesterday that the Titanic went down. Dire tragedy!—it might have acted even upon the madmen of Berlin as a deterrent—served as an object lesson in pity—made the occasion of some reflection and relenting. But Berlin has lost all the perspectives of civilization. The General Staff knows not the laws of Heaven or earth. The Hohenzollern, infuriate, fears only the loss of his throne and his crown. The Highbrow professors and philosophers of the Prussian Universities, putting Christianity beneath their feet, have taught only the gospel of brutality and hate. With them might alone is right. Woe to him that gets in the way. And, in answer to the wail that went up from the ashes of Louvain—from the stricken of Antwerp and Rheims—to the cry and horror from human nature everywhere, came this answer, not in defense, but in reassertion:

"We have made one fundamental principle clear: for the fault of the individual the community to which he belonged must suffer. The village in which our troops had been shot at by the civilian population was burnt down. If the culprit was not discovered, a few representatives were taken out of the general population and shot, women and children not being touched, except when they were found with weapons in their hands.

"This principle may seem hard and cruel—it has been developed from the customs of modern and ancient war history, and as far as it can be spoken of at all is recognized. It is also justified by the theory of setting an awful example ('abschrecken'). The innocent must suffer with the guilty; and, when the latter cannot be found, they must suffer for the guilty, not because misdeeds have been done, but in order that they may be attempted no longer.

"Every burning down of a village, every shooting of hostages, every decimation of the population of a district whose inhabitants had taken up arms against the approaching troops is far less an act of vengeance than a signal of warning for the country which has not yet been occupied. And about this there can be no doubt; the burning of Battice, Herve, Louvain and Dinant were effective as warning signals.

"Does anybody in the world imagine that the population of Brussels would have allowed us to act as though we were in our own land if they had not trembled for our revenge, and were not trembling still?

"War is no drawing-room game; war is hell-fire. He who sticks his finger into it will burn his hand, his soul and his life. The poor, confused, misled Belgian Nation has been sacrificed to this fate."

As it was in Belgium and France so shall it be in Britain. As it was on the land so shall it be upon the ocean. The earth shall be made terrible and they that go down to the sea in ships shall know the fires of perdition and feel the wrath of Satan.

The decree of Satan went forth from Berlin. The instruments of Satan were forged at Essen. There was but a single Satanic abatement. Satan's Ambassador at Washington—shameless in his infamy, under the Sign Manual of Satan's Embassy, insolent in its disregard of law, or consequences—gave warning that the deed was hatched, that the tools were ready and that those who went upon this English boat, trusting to her convoy and her speed, took their lives in their hands, not recking the Devil's hatred, nor his devices. This was done not to save, but to intimidate; not to warn, but to terrorize.

Shall any just man say that the Count von Bernstorff is not guilty of murder and that his colleague in crime, Dernburg, is not accessory to murder, and that each and every German, or pretended German-American, applauding this fearful butchery is not a murderer at heart?

II

But, comes the query, what are we going to do about it? Are we at the mercy of the insane Hohenzollern, not only through his emissaries sending his odious system of government and debasing theories of castism affecting superiority to our doors, and proclaiming them, but bringing his war of conquest and murder across the line of our transit and travel over the high seas, which are ours to sail as we list without let or hindrance from man, or monarch, from his or from anyone on land or water? Must we as a people sit down like dogs and see our laws defied, our flag flouted and our protests whistled down the wind of this lordling's majestic disdain? Must we as a Nation emulate at once the impotence and the docility of China, and before such proof of the contempt in which we are held by him and his, throw up our hands in entreaty and despair, saying to the insistence of autocracy, to the insolence of vanity, "thy will is law!"?

What could the President have meant when he declared that the Government of the United States would hold the Government of Germany to "a strict accountability" in the event that its war zone pronunciamento resulted in the loss of the life of a single American? How did he intend that his countrymen should understand him when he put forth his supplementary protests? Are we a sovereign, or are we a vassal?

Please God, as all men on earth shall behold, we are a nation; please God, as Europe and all the world shall know, we are Americans.

Too long already have we submitted to the free hand of the foreigner at home and abroad. Months ago should the Pan-German propaganda, issuing from the German Embassy—led by the German Ambassador—erecting in the heart of our country a treasonable organization to support the German foray upon Belgium and France, and control our own domestic politics—have been ended. Bernstorff should have been severely rebuked and warned to proceed at his peril. For less Genet, the Frenchman, and Crampton, the Englishman, had been ordered away. Dernburg should never have got beyond Ellis Island. Harvard should have sent Munsterburg packing. Ridder should have been put under bond. The followers of these among the German-Americans should have been given the option of repeating their oaths of allegiance, with fresh guarantees for good behavior, or of returning to the Fatherland they had fled to escape military service, to fight for their blessed Kaiser directly under his imperial eye and eagles. Bartholdt should have been promptly expelled from Congress and driven back to Hesse, where he came from and belongs. The poor and honest Germans of the United States—those who came here to better their fortunes and escape despotism and castism—those who when they took out their naturalization papers, confessing Republicanism and Democracy, meant it—those who have no interest, part or lot with Kaiserism, who ceased to be Germans and became Americans—should be rescued alike from the teaching and contamination of the newly rich of Germans whose dearest hope is to go "home" and build castles on the Rhine, and from the Highbrow writers and Herr Doctors who worship at the shrine of the Hohenzollern, having learned their lesson from the Highbrows of Heidelberg, Gottingen and Bonn.

Each of these latter is a German, not an American, and, in the event of war, or a state of war, would become a German spy. They have from the first relied upon the "German vote" to see them through. They were even bold enough to try it prematurely at Chicago. In all their newspapers they threaten us. In spite of the President's patience, his equal and exact neutrality, they are already pushing him and saying what they are going to do to him in 1916.

It is of the first importance that they be made to know that they are aliens and do not own the country yet, nor dominate its politics. They must be brought to understand that their enmity, not their friendship, is to be courted. As long as the German-American Alliance pretended to charity and aspired to music it was, where not wholly approved, yet amiably tolerated, but, as a German Colony, planting imperial ideas, as a Know-Nothing Lodge, blacklisting Americans, we will none of it; and the sooner its leaders are made to realize this the better for them and for us.

The Courier-Journal will not go the length of saying that the President should convene the Congress and advise it to declare against these barbarians a State of War. This may yet become necessary. Whilst actual war is not possible—Germany having no fleet we can sweep off the briny deep, nor army near enough to be met face to face and exterminated—yet are we not wholly without reprisal for the murder of our citizens and the destruction of their property. There are many German ships—at least two German men-of-war—in the aggregate worth many millions of dollars, within our reach to make our losses—repudiated by Germany— good, and their owners—robbed by Germany—whole again.

We must not act either in haste or passion. This catastrophe is too real—the flashlight it throws upon the methods and purposes of Germany is too appalling—to leave us in any doubt what awaits us as the bloody and brutal work goes on. Civilization should abjure its neutrality. It should rise as one mighty, God-like force, and, as far as its moral influence and physical appliance can be made to prevail, forbid the riot of hate and debauch of blood that, like a madman, is running amuck among the innocent and the unprotected.

This holy Sabbath every pulpit in America should send a prayer to God in protest; every patriotic Minister of the Gospel of Christ should lift his voice in protest, and, more than all—the Christian President of the United States, a cool and brave man, sprung from a line of heroes and saints—ceasing longer to protest, should act, leaving no doubt in the minds and hearts of any that he is not merely a leader in Christ, but a leader of men and nations, and that he holds aloft the Sword of the Lord and Gideon!

•When the United States declared war on Germany, Watterson wrote "Vae Victis!" and "War Has Its Compensations" within a four-day span. Both editorials were typical of his sonorous, flowery, marching style. The Pulitzer Prize committee, which awarded him the 1918 honor, declared that the editorials "were directed toward arousing the American people to their international duty and toward convincing a section of the country by tradition hostile to universal military service of the wisdom and necessity of its establishment." Reprinted here is one of the two editorials, the rousing call to arms, "Vae Victis!"

VAE VICTIS!
(Louisville *Courier-Journal*; April 7, 1917)

"Rally round the flag, boys" — Uncle Sam's Battlesong;
"Sound the bold anthem! War dogs are howling;
Proud bird of Liberty screams through the air!" — The Hunters of
    Kentucky

It is with solemnity, and a touch of sadness, that we write the familiar words of the old refrain beneath the invocation to the starry banner, the breezy call of hero-breeding bombast quite gone out of them; the glad shout of battle; the clarion note of defiance; because to us, not as to Nick of the Woods, and his homely co-mates of the forest, but rather as to the men of '61, comes this present call to arms.

We may feel with the woman's heart of Rankin of Montana, yet repudiate with manly disdain the sentimental scruples of Kitchin of North Carolina.

There are times when feeling must be sent to the rear; when duty must tow the line; when the aversion brave men have for fighting must yield to the adjuration, "Give me liberty, or give me death!" That time is now upon us.

Unless Patrick Henry was wrong—unless Washington and the men of the Revolution were wrong, that time is upon us. It is a lie to pretend that the world is better than it was; that men are truer, wiser; that war is escapable; that peace may be had for the planning and the asking. The situation which without any act of ours rises before us is as exigent as that which rose before the Colonists in America when a mad English King, claiming to rule without accountability, asserted the right of Kings and sent an army to enforce it. A mad German Emperor, claiming partnership with God, again elevates the standard of right divine and bids the world to worship, or die.

From the beginning the issue was not less ours than of the countries first engaged. Each may have had ends of its own to serve. Nor were these ends precisely alike. At least France—to whom we owe all that we have of sovereignty and freedom—and Belgium, the little David of Nations—fought to resist invasion, wanton, cruel invasion; to avert slavery, savage, pitiless slavery. Yet, whatever the animating purpose—whatever the selfish interests of England and Russia and Italy—the Kaiser scheme of world conquest justified it.

In us it sanctifies it. Why should any American split hairs over the European rights and wrongs involved when he sees before him grim and ghastly the mailed figure of Absolutism with hand uplifted to strike Columbia where these three years she has stood pleading for justice, peace, and mercy? God of the free heart's hope and home forbid!

Each of these three years the German Kaiser was making war upon us. He was making war secretly, through his emissaries in destruction of our industries, secretly through his diplomats plotting not merely foreign but civil war against us, and, as we now know, seeking to foment servile and racial insurrection; then openly upon the high seas levying murder upon our people and visiting all our rights and claims with scorn and insult—with scorn and insult unspeakable—at this moment pretending to flout us with ignominy and contempt. Where would the honest pacifist draw the line?

Surely the time has arrived—many of us think it was long since overdue—for calling the braves to the colors. Nations must e'en take stock on occasion and manhood come to a showdown. It is but a truism to say so.

Fifty years the country has enjoyed surpassing prosperity. This has over-commercialized the character and habits of the people. Twenty-five years the gospel of passivism, with "business is business" for its text, has not only been preached—indiscriminately—oracularly without let or hindrance, but has been richly financed and potentially organized. It has established a party. It has made a cult, justifying itself in a fad it has called Humanity—in many ways a most spurious humanity—and has set this above and against patriotic inclination and duty.

Like a bolt out of the blue flashed the war signal from the very heart of Europe. Across the Atlantic its reverberations rolled to find us divided, neutral, and unprepared. For fifteen years a body of German reservists disguised as citizens have been marching and counter-marching. They grew at length bold enough to rally to the support of a pan-German scheme of conquest and a pro-German propaganda of "kultur," basing its effrontery in the German-American vote, which began its agitation by threatening us with civil war if we dared to go to war with Germany. There followed the assassin sea monsters and the airship campaign of murder.

All the while we looked on with either simpering idiocy or dazed apathy. Serbia? It was no affair of ours. Belgium? Why should we worry? Foodstuffs soaring—war stuffs roaring—everybody making money—the mercenary, the poor of heart, the mean of spirit, the bleak and barren of soul, could still plead the Hypocrisy of Uplift and chortle: "I did not raise my boy to be a soldier." Even the Lusitania did not awaken us to a sense of danger and arouse us from the stupefaction of ignorant and ignoble self-complacency.

First of all on bended knee we should Pray to God to forgive us. Then erect as men, Christian men, soldierly men, to the flag and the fray wherever they lead us—over the ocean—through France to Flanders—across the Low Countries to Koln, Bonn and Koblenz—tumbling the fortress of Ehrenbreitstein into the Rhine as we pass and damming the mouth of the Moselle with the debris of the ruin we make of it—then on, on to Berlin, the Black Horse Cavalry sweeping the Wilhelmstrasse like lava down the mountain side, the Junker and the saber rattler flying before us, the tunes being "Dixie" and "Yankee Doodle," the cry being Commonwealth of the Vaterland—no peace with the Kaiser—no parley with Autocracy, Absolutism and the divine right of Kings—to Hell with the Hapsburg and the Hohenzollern!

MASTERS OF THE EDITORIAL

ARTHUR BRISBANE:
MASTER OF HUMAN-INTEREST EDITORIALS

In 20th-century American journalism, Arthur Brisbane stands perhaps as the most widely read and commercially popular editorial writer. His simply written editorials—on such sensational topics as crime and drunkenness—appealed to the masses. He was also one of the nation's first syndicated columnists; his "Today" column was carried in 1,000 papers nationwide with 30 million readers. As managing editor of William Randolph Hearst's New York *Journal*, he became the nation's highest paid newspaperman, earning up to $260,000 a year.

Brisbane was born in Buffalo, New York, in 1864. His father, a zealous social reformer, instilled in him the need to make a mark on the world. Years later, when he was a successful editor, Brisbane remembered, "My father taught me that if I died without doing something to help the lot of the common people my life would have been a failure and the hottest place in hell would be too good for me."

He lived a comfortable early life and, as a teenager, traveled to Europe to study. He returned in 1883 to New York City and landed a job at Charles Dana's *Sun*. Later, he admitted that he had known "nothing about newspaper work." At only 23, he was promoted to editor of the *Sun's* evening edition. Work followed at Joseph Pulitzer's New York *World*. Then, in 1897, he became editor of Hearst's New York *Journal*, the *World's* chief competitor. He remained there until his death on Christmas Day 1936. Most of his work with the *Sun* and the *World* is forgotten, and the fame of his newspaper career is tied closely to his editorial writing and other work for Hearst.

Sensationalism was the rule at New York dailies; and, although Brisbane privately did not find much appeal in the practice, he quickly discovered that the bold headlines and grisly pictures boosted circulation and brought in high revenues. He even boldly stated that "sensationalism is also the method of heaven," pointing out the yellow color of the sun's rays and of gold. He came to believe that his effectiveness as a writer and editor rested on his ability to mirror the world. If the world was full of divorce, murder, crime, and other assorted scandal, then it was his duty to reflect that. "Newspapers are not dull," he stated. "They are... more or less accurate reflectors."

His advocacy of sensational tactics, however, may also have rested in their ability to make him a rich man. If he did not utilize them, he said, journalism "would bring me an income of only five thousand dollars per year or so. Now I get one hundred thousand, which is much more pleasant." Critics often argued that he was primarily interested in accumulating money and adulation. Although recognizing his popularity, some deplored his simple writing style that allowed for that popularity. Some claimed that his writing was "inocuous," that his editorials were "simple" and "banal," and that "his mental equipment was a jerry-built structure, compounded of odds and ends he had picked up here and there."

Despite any character flaws he might have possessed, Brisbane must be remembered for his incredible popularity. His outspoken nature, his mastery of the human-interest editorial, and his simple writing style endeared him to the masses. He always presented his opinions in a bold, unflinching manner; he enjoyed it when his editorials created conflict. One of his favorite editorial topics was the question of what would be the outcome in a fight between a gorilla and a man. "He certainly knew what would provoke popular discussions," one critic pointed out.

Political issues often presented Brisbane with a subject to support boldly or criticize. He wrote of political figures, World War I, the Depression, and trusts (a favorite topic) with heated words. One of his most outspoken views was presented in an editorial that seemed to advocate the assassination of President William McKinley. Brisbane wrote: "Did not the murder of Lincoln... hasten the era of American good feeling and perhaps prevent the renewal of fighting between brothers?" Soon after, McKinley was shot and the *Journal* denounced. Brisbane apologized and eulogized the dead leader in glowing terms.

His forté, however, was the human-interest story, written in a simple, appealing style. Its subject was commonplace. The writing was never difficult to read. A contemporary author of a textbook on editorial writing called Brisbane "the most brilliant living exponent of [the human-interest] type of editorial." Another contemporary said, "He is, indeed, the leader among the writers of human-interest editorials, and his reputation and influence are the result of this remarkable ability of his to write about his manifold subjects in a way that makes them interesting by showing their bearing upon every day human concerns."

Brisbane's effectiveness resulted primarily from the themes he chose and his style. The themes of his best editorials were significant and universal. Taking generally known facts, he would examine them from a fresh point of view and then present them to the reader in a simple manner. His writing was concise, wasting no words to paint a clear picture. Each phrase and idea served a specific purpose. He used short, punchy sentences and simple words that appealed to universal sympathies. In so doing, he made his editorials understandable to all readers at both an intellectual level and an emotional level. He began the editorial "Too Little and Too Much" this way: "Here is a quotation from a very wise person called Aristotle." That short sentence simplifies the importance of the great philosopher in a way any reader could identify with. All of the editorials included in this anthology illustrate this point equally well.

Brisbane's editorials were universal in their appeal, but still he questioned the capacity of editorials to influence readers. He rhetorically asked, "Why do we talk daily through our newspapers to ten millions of people and yet have not influence to elect a dog catcher?... Simply because we are foolish enough to think that commonplaces passed through our commonplace minds acquire some new value." Despite his dubious attitude, he himself produced a number of editorials of lasting value. He sometimes composed pieces which elicited a strong emotional response and helped the reader for the first time gain an insight into obvious fundamental conditions.

When Brisbane died on Christmas Day 1936, opinions concerning his journalistic career and his personal life were mixed. Hearst papers, naturally, praised him. Others openly criticized him, labeling him "a worshipper of success." The view closest to reality, however, was one expressed by a fellow newspaperman: "The death removes one of the most gifted and contradictory personalities in American journalism."

In his editorial "What Should Be a Man's Object in Life?" Brisbane had stated: "... every man whose life history is worth the telling, did something for the good of other men." Did he, personally, serve other men as he preached in his editorials? That question is arguable. The fact that he was one of the most popular journalists America has ever known is not.

•The following editorial about a Salvation Army worker demonstrates Brisbane's ability to take commonplace scenes and present them vividly using simple language.

A GIRL'S FACE IN THE GASLIGHT
And An Important Part Of The World's Work
(New York *Journal*)

On a corner of Rector street, down near the river, a loud drum was beating. A guitar and a tambourine competed shrilly with the drum's dull booming. Slowly a careless crowd gathered round the Salvation Army workers.

There were bare-headed women, little girls holding little babies in their arms, sailors drunk, and one or two sober, 'longshoremen pleased with the sound of the drum, and a few of the thin, hungry faces that disturb our well-fed happiness.

The man beat his drum, standing erect and proud in his army uniform.

The two thin, nervous young women played on guitar and tambourine with all their force, striving to gather the crowd whom they hoped to make better men and women.

Thirty or forty people gather—glad to accept any noise and excitement in their dull lives.

The music stopped, and a young girl stepped to the centre of the circle.

She was frightened. Her voice was weak at first. Gradually her thin, pale face grew animated.

Her blue eyes dilated. In a dull, routine way, doing her best, earning respectful silence from the night crowd, she told her story:

"I was bad. I tried to be good. But I couldn't do it with my own strength. I asked God to save me. He did save me. He will save you, if you will ask Him."

She spoke with a strong German accent. With all her deep, earnest soul, with all her poor, limited mental force, she longed to help the men and women around. As she spoke she bent her head farther and farther back, until her eyes looked up to the sky. There, with perfect faith, she saw the God whose work she was humbly doing in the muddy streets and flickering gaslight of the riverside.

While she could control her voice and her deep emotion she talked on her one theme—the power of God to help the helpless. But she believed, and she felt what she said. Soon the tears ran over from her upturned eyes, and she could speak no more.

Then a man began—thickset, earnest, with a strong Scotch accent. He talked to the men about him in a rough way that appealed to them.

———

As the crowd stood listening many passed. A few were contemptuous; the majority were indifferent.

If you see these workers you ask perhaps:

"What good do they do?"

That is the question that may be asked of every man that ever lived, and only One can answer it.

The thin, white-faced girl, playing, singing and preaching in the dirty street, does this:

She touches the heart of a half-drunken man. Turning from the saloon door he goes home, and takes to his wife and children as much of his wages as is left, a feeling of repentance, good resolutions.

Her tears are answered by the tears of miserable girls and women who sink back into the shadow as they watch her pure face. Through them she helps to undo the horrible, soul-destroying work of brutal civilization.

Mysteriously, diversely, the work of the world is done.

The storm, endless in its power, washes down the mountaintops to fertilize the valley.

The tiny earthworm works in darkness, crumbling up its little patch of earth to make it fit food for plants.

Each does its work.

The mighty intellect with cyclonic force gives to mankind grand, general views of cosmic grandeur, and introduces to minds prepared the "eternal silences," and the vast serene fields of divine law.

•The following editorial demonstrates Brisbane's apparent concern for a common urban social problem. Especially evident in it is Brisbane's recognition of contradictions that existed in many such situations.

THE "CRIMINAL" CLASS
Did This View Of It Ever Occur To You?
(New York *Journal*)

Much interest just now in criminals.

Much horror aroused by depravity.

Many plans more or less appropriate for making the air pure.

Many good men, politicians, women and bishops, who spent the Summer at the seaside willing now to spend a few days wiping "crime" off the earth.

What is crime? Who are the criminals? Who makes the criminals?

Do criminals viciously and voluntarily arise among us, eager to lead hunted lives, eager to be jailed at intervals, eager to crawl in the dark, dodge policemen, work in stripes and die in shame? Hardly.

Will you kindly and patiently follow the lives, quickly sketched, of a boy and a girl?

The Girl

Born poor, born in hard luck, her father, or mother, or both, victims of long hours, poor fare, bad air and little leisure.

As a baby she struggles against fate and manages to live while three or four little brothers and sisters die and go back to kind earth.

She crawls around the halls of a tenement, a good deal in the way. She is hunted here and chased there.

She is cold in Winter, ill-fed in Summer, never well cared for.

She gets a little so-called education. Ill-dressed and ashamed beside the other children, she is glad to escape the education. No one at home can help her on. No one away from home cares about her.

She grows up white, sickly, like a potato sprouting in a cellar. At the corner of a fine street she sees the carriages passing with other girls in warm furs, or in fine, cool Summer dresses.

With a poor shawl around her and with heels run down she peers in at the restaurant window, to see other women leading lives very different from hers.

Steadily she has impressed upon her the fact, absolutely undeniable, that as the world is organized there is no especial place for her—certainly no comfort for her.

She finds work, perhaps. Hours as long as the daylight.

Ten minutes late—half a day's fine.

At the end of the day aching feet, aching back, system ill-fed, not enough earned to live upon honestly—and that prospect stretches ahead farther than her poor eyes can see.

"What's the charge, officer?"

"Disorderly conduct, Your Honor."

There's the criminal, good men, politicians, women and bishops, that you are hunting so ardently.

The Boy

Same story, practically.

He plays on the tenement staircase—cuffed off the staircase.

He plays ball in the street—cuffed, if caught by the policeman.

He swings on the area railing, trying to exercise his stunted muscles—cuffed again.

In burning July, with shirt and trousers on, he goes swimming in the park fountain—caught and cuffed and handed over to "the society."

A few months in a sort of semi-decent imprisonment, treated in a fashion about equivalent to that endured by the sea turtle turned over on its back in the market.

He escapes to begin the same life once more.

He tries for work.

"What do you know?"

"I don't know anything; nobody ever taught me."

He cannot even endure the discipline of ten hours' daily shovelling—it takes education to instill discipline, if only the education of the early pick and shovel.

He has not been taught anything. He has been turned loose in a city full of temptation. He had no real start to begin with, and no effort was ever made to repair his evil beginning.

———

"What's the charge, officer?"

"Attempted burglary; pleads guilty."

"Three years in prison, since it is his first offence."

In prison he gets an education. They teach him how to be a good burglar and not get caught. Patiently the State boards him, and educates him to be a first-rate criminal.

There's your first-rate criminal, Messrs. Bishops, good men, politicians and benevolent women.

———

Dear bishops, noble women, good men and scheming politicians, listen to this story:

In the South Sea Islands they have for contagious diseases a horror as great as your horror of crime.

A man or woman stricken with a loathsome disease, such as smallpox, is seized, isolated, and the individual sores of the smallpox patient are earnestly scraped with sea shells—until the patient dies. It hurts the patient a good deal—without ever curing, of course—but it relieves the feelings of the outraged good ones who wield the sea shells.

You kind-hearted creatures, hunting "crime" in great cities, are like the South Sea Islanders in their treatment of smallpox.

You ardently wield your reforming sea shells and you scrape very earnestly at the sores so well developed.

———

No desire here to decry your earnest efforts.

But if you ever get tired of scraping with sea shells, try vaccination, or, better still, try to take such care of youth, to give such chances and education to the young, as will save them from the least profitable of all careers—crime.

———

Rich good men, nice bishops, comfortable, benevolent ladies—every man and woman on Blackwell's Island, every wretched creature living near a "red light," would gladly change places with any of you.

Scrape away with your sea shells, but try also to give a few more and a few better chances in youth to those whom you now hunt as criminals in their mature years.

God creates boys and girls, anxious to live decently.

Your social system makes criminals and fills jails.

•Brisbane frequently dealt with fundamental questions of religion and faith. His most common approach was to try to explain abstract ideas in everyday terms. The following editorial provides one of his attempts to deal with the question that philosophers and theologians have debated for ages and to deal with it in terms that an ordinary person could understand.

THE EXISTENCE OF GOD— PARABLE OF THE BLIND KITTENS
(New York *Journal*)

The notion that small things, the petty details of life, such as money getting, marriage questions, etc., are uppermost in the modern human brain is entirely false.

If an editor asks: "Is marriage a failure?" he receives just so many answers, and then the interest dies out.

If he asks: "Should a wife have pin money?" or "What is the easiest way for a woman to earn a living?" he ceases to receive answers after a short time.

But to questions concerning the immortality of the soul, the existence of God, and man's destiny here and hereafter, the answers are endless. Letters on such matters have been received here by thousands. Every day the mail brings new and intelligent contributions to the questions that have kept men praying, thinking, fighting and hoping through the centuries:

"Is there a God, and will my soul live forever?"

———

Very interesting are the expressions of faith which fill a majority of the letters. Interesting also are the letters of doubters, atheists, agnostics and the many intoxicated with a very little knowledge, who have decided to substitute their own wisdom and doubt for the belief of the ages—the belief in God and in personal immortality.

Many think science has discovered that we could get on very well without a God. But science has done just the contrary. And here, if you please, we shall build up a sort of parable:

———

A Man had a box full of motherless blind kittens. He was very kind to them. He put their box on wheels and moved it about to keep it in the sun. He gave them milk at regular intervals. With loving kindness he drove away the dog which growled and scared the little kittens into spitting and backraising.

The kittens trusted the Man, loved him and felt that they needed him. That was the age of faith.

One day a dog got a kitten and tore it to pieces.

The kitten had disobeyed orders and laws. It had crawled away from the box.

Another kitten, with one eye now partly open, got thoughtful and said: "There is no such thing as Man. Or, if there is such a thing, he is a monster to let little Willie get torn up. Don't talk to me about Kitten Willie being a sufferer through his own fault. I say there is no such thing as a Man. We kittens are bosses of the universe and must do our own fighting."

That speaker was the Ingersoll kitten.

A kitten of higher mental class opened both eyes just a little and actually made observations.

Said he: "I am a scientist. I discover that we owe nothing to Man's kindness. We are governed by laws. This box is on wheels. It rolls around in the sunlight of its own volition. True, I do not know who shoves it, but no Man could do it. Further, I discover that there is such a thing as the law of 'milk-passing.' Milk comes this way just so often. Its coming is nature's law. It has always come. It always will come. Good-night, I am going to sleep. But don't talk to me any more about a kind Man. It's all law, and I am certainly great, for I saw the laws first."

That was the Newton kitten, but he lacked the Newton faith.

We have no time to tell what the Darwin kitten said. He was very long-winded.

But this happened. The kittens grew up—such as did not perish through their own fault. They got their eyes fully opened. They saw the Man, recognized him and asked only to be allowed to stay in his house. "Excuse us," they said, "for being such foolish kittens. But you know our eyes were not quite open."

"Don't mention it," said the kind Man. "Go down cellar and help yourselves to mice."

———

That's the end of the parable. We are all blind kittens, and our few attempts at explaining nature's wonders and kindness only get us into deeper and deeper mysteries.

We discover that the earth goes round the sun. But the greatest scientist must admit his inability to tell or guess why it goes. "Give me the initial impulse," he says, "and all the rest is easy."

The blind kittens in their wagon say: "Give our wagon just one shove and we'll explain the rest."

The kitten gets hold of a law of "milk-passing" and substitutes that for man's individual kindness.

The feeble-minded agnostic seizes the law of gravitation and thinks he can discard God with gravity's help.

But the great mind that defined gravity's law was a religious mind—too profound to see anything final in its own feeble power.

Newton was no atheist. None better than he knew the mysterious character of his law. That it has worked from all eternity "directly as the mass and inversely as the square of the distance" he knew and told his fellow-creatures. That is all he knew and all that any man knows about it.

To-day Lord Kelvin, a worthy follower in Newton's steps, is asked to explain why gravity acts. He can only say:

"I accept no theory of gravitation. Present science has no right to attempt to explain gravitation. We know nothing about it. We simply know nothing about it."

Darwin asks, without answering his question: "Who can explain what is the essence of the attraction of gravitation?"

———

To our doubting friends we say: Doubt if you must. But doubt intelligently and doubt first of all your own blind kitten wisdom. Remember that you at least know absolutely nothing. Study and think. Read. But don't let the half-developed wisdom of others choke up your brain and leave you a mere clogged-up doubting machine.

Whatever you do, never interfere with the faith of others. Spread knowledge, spread facts. Keep to yourself the doubts that would disturb others' happiness and do them no good. Tell what you know. Keep quiet about what you guess.

•The following editorial was Brisbane's most popular. Although written around 1900, it was used in the prohibition movement of the 1920s. The author of a 1924 book on editorial writing named it as one of the "great single editorials of the country." The sophisticated reader may find the statement of the moral in the editorial's final two paragraphs as disturbingly obvious. For the average reader, however, an obvious conclusion is more effective than a subtle one. Brisbane recognized that his audience was composed, not of sophisticated readers, but of average ones.

THOSE WHO LAUGH AT A DRUNKEN MAN
(New York *Evening Journal*)

How often have you seen a drunken man stagger along the street!

His clothes are soiled from falling, his face is bruised, his eyes are dull. Sometimes he curses the boys that tease him. Sometimes he tries to smile, in a drunken effort to placate pitiless, childish cruelty.

His body, worn out, can stand no more, and he mumbles that he is going home.

The children persecute him, throw things at him, laugh at him, running ahead of him.

Grown men and women, too, often laugh with the children, nudge each other, and actually find humor in the sight of a human being sunk below the lowest animal.

The sight of a drunken man going home should make every other man and woman sad and sympathetic, and, horrible as the sight is, it should be useful, by inspiring, in those who see it, a determination to avoid and to help others avoid that man's fate.

****

That reeling drunkard is going home.

He is going home to children who are afraid of him, to a wife whose life he has made miserable.

He is going home, taking with him the worst curse in the world—to suffer bitter remorse himself after having inflicted suffering on those whom he should protect.

And as he goes home men and women, knowing what the home-coming means, laugh at him and enjoy the sight.

****

In the old days in the arena it occasionally happened that brothers were set to fight each other. When they refused to fight they were forced to it by red-hot irons applied to their backs.

We have progressed beyond the moral condition of human beings guilty of such brutality as that. But we cannot call ourselves civilized while our imaginations and sympathies are so dull that the reeling drunkard is thought an amusing spectacle.

MASTERS OF THE EDITORIAL

FRANK COBB:
MASTER OF FORCEFUL STYLE

Frank Irving Cobb forged his reputation in an era when corporate ownership of newspapers was making editorial writers little more than office hirelings. At the New York *World*, he presented his opinions with a forcefulness and clearness matched by few other editorial writers in the 20th century. Many contemporaries considered the *World's* editorial page the most influential in the nation and credited it for a renaissance of the newspaper editorial function. When Cobb died in 1923, his employer praised him as a man who "became a power and a personality in the United States, writing editorials he did not sign in a paper he did not own." He was in many respects the first outstanding modern editorial writer.

Born and reared in the raw Midwest, Cobb spent his early life with the people of the country and small towns. He experienced hardships—a grasshopper infestation caused an early family move—and earned an education in the primitive public schools. He developed an affinity for the common man, a trait still obvious years later in his work for a metropolitan newspaper. In 1890, at the age of 21, he was appointed superintendent of the high school at Martin, Michigan. After one year, however, he changed his profession, joining the Grand Rapids *Herald* as a reporter, then correspondent and city editor. Work at the Grand Rapids *Eagle* and Detroit *Evening News* followed. In 1900, he became the Detroit *Free Press's* leading editorial writer.

After making the *World* America's preeminent newspaper in the late 1800s, Joseph Pulitzer was forced by blindness and tortured nerves to give up direct supervision. The paper began to decline. In 1904, therefore, he began a search for a new editor who could revive the paper's editorial strength and stature. William H. Merrill, the chief of the editorial page, was growing old; and his writing lacked the power it once had. The *World's* editorial staff was filled capably by such men as John Heaton, Horatio Seymour, and Ralph Pulitzer (the owner's son), but the elder Pulitzer could look to none of them to succeed him as editor. He wanted a young man who knew history and politics; who had a keen perception and a concise, direct, forceful style; who could write with clarity, brevity, and punch; and who could provide dynamic and persuasive leadership for the liberal causes Pulitzer espoused. In short, he wanted another, younger Joseph Pulitzer. To find the right man, Pulitzer dispatched one of his personal secretaries, Samuel M. Williams, on a nationwide hunt. Journeying from city to city, Williams read the editorials in the local papers. In Detroit, he sensed he was nearing completion of his mission.

Williams recognized real talent in the writing of the *Free Press*. Most editorials he had read in other newspapers were ponderous and uninspired. In Cobb's columns, he discovered a writing style and a political mind very similar to Pulitzer's. But Pulitzer wanted details about Cobb. "What," Pulitzer asked, "has Cobb read in American history, Rhodes, McMaster, Trevelyan, Parkman? What works on the Constitution and constitutional law? Has he read Buckle's History of Civilization?... Search his brain for everything there is in it." After several meetings between Williams and Cobb and more than several communications between Williams and Pulitzer, the hesitant writer was convinced to travel to New York. After meeting with Cobb, Pulitzer proclaimed: "Cobb will do. He knows American history better than anyone I have ever found.... In time, we can make a real editor of him." In the spring of 1904 Cobb, at the age of 34, reported to the *World* as one of its several editorial writers, not knowing that he had been picked to replace the legendary Pulitzer as its chief.

In Cobb, the *World* had acquired a man not only well-versed in American history, but a true scholar in every sense of the word. Aside from keen political and historical perspectives, he had vast knowledge in science, philosophy, music, and literature. Williams described him as a "brilliant conversationalist, an omnivorous reader, a shrewd observer, a forceful talker, and a keen analyzer of men and affairs... the Ideal Editor."

The relationship between Pulitzer and Cobb grew to be one of mutual respect, and the prerogative the owner gave the employee resulted largely from the fact that they shared similar attitudes about what a newspaper should be. They agreed that the prime motivation should be to make a paper a public servant, a fighter for liberal causes in aid of the mass of the people, rather than a corporation with a basic purpose of making profit.

Preeminence for the individual editorial writer usually has rested on a combination of intellect and writing skill. With the knowledge and insight that Pulitzer had recognized in Cobb, the latter combined an admirable writing style, one that was clean, forceful, and interesting. Henry Watterson, editor of the Louisville *Courier-Journal* and a brilliant editorial writer himself, called Cobb "the strongest writer of the New York press since Horace Greeley." Although the authorship of his editorials was anonymous, contemporaries declared that "Cobb's work was signed by his style." He possessed a versatile style. It was said that he "could swing the bludgeon or wield the rapier at will." He might attack deserving targets with brilliant sarcasm or biting irony, but he also could write with a lightness of touch when the subject merited such treatment.

Cobb was one of the first editorial writers whose style was marked by modern conciseness and economy. Hating florid phrases and bombast, he stated his ideas clearly and simply. The results were editorials that reached readers at a simple—though usually very emotional—level. Ralph Pulitzer, in a personal tribute after Cobb's death, put it this way: "Everything he handled became simple in his handling of it. Sometimes he would simplify a bewildering situation or a tangled thought with one easy touch of intuitive analysis. Sometimes he would labor with his might on some cunningly elusive subtlety, and in the end his directness would simplify it into surrender."

To get a point across in a simple manner, Cobb often used the method of repetition, of both the same words or a simple variation of words. It was a rare Cobb editorial in which repetition was not used. Other stylistic devices Cobb used included figures of speech, alliteration, literary and historical allusions, and rhetorical and direct questions. Cobb's editorial columns always caught the reader's eye with an attention-getting title. Headlines such as "The Twilight of the Gods" and "1796 or 1917?" carried readers into the column. He often started his editorials with short, simple sentences and left a powerful, yet questioning punch in the last sentences.

Despite any "literary" quality his editorials might have assumed because of his use of such devices, Cobb always put facts first. He adamantly believed that editorial writing could be both factual and vigorous at the same time. Pulitzer's *World* will always be remembered for its sensational qualities—its bold use of photographs and big headlines. But Cobb never let those practices get in the way of accurate news. He said on more than one occasion that "editors are reporters." In his eyes, there was no need for a schism between factual and interesting writing. He explained: "it is necessary to interest people greatly in order to get a hearing for the things that [Pulitzer] wishes to say."

The "things" he and Pulitzer wanted to say to the public were almost always political. Countless editorials penned by Cobb brought public attention to political corruption and social injustices. He was never afraid to say what he believed. Boldly and unrelentingly he attacked targets. Whether they were corrupt officials or dangerous ideas, he assaulted them directly and vigorously.

His editorials were among the most respected of his time, and his editorial leadership was recognized in a number of causes. The *World's* campaign against corruption by the Equitable Insurance Company in 1905-1907 encouraged reform legislation in New York which served as a model for laws in other states. Its investigation of the construction of the Panama Canal uncovered much corruption and focused public attention on the financial dealings of government officials involved. Cobb was the leading editorial writer voicing the prevailing American attitude of restraint toward entering World War I and wholehearted efforts after entry. He was American journalism's strongest and most consistent supporter of the League of Nations and opponent of tyranny in the aftermath of the war. He was recognized also for his insight into the problems of the United States' constitutional form of government in the 20th century and for his strong advocacy of human freedom.

Fellow journalists admired Cobb not only for his editorial ability, but also for his personal characteristics. He was unassuming, lacking in conceit, honest, and generous. He enjoyed the company of other, less important staff members of the *World* and was a favorite among the staffers in the newsroom. Although he was a dynamic, engaging, and knowledgeable conversationalist, he did not condescend toward anyone of lesser knowledge or station. He was known as a man who had received no special favors but had earned every benefit he had gotten out of life.

Cobb died young, at 54 years of age. His career had been an interesting study in contrasts. Although his editorials were unsigned, they did not reflect the depersonalized, institutionalized voice of a corporation. Instead, they were the statements of an individual in a newspaper that was the manifestation of the individual.

Walter Lippmann, at one time an assistant to Cobb, became editor upon Cobb's death. But neither his intellect nor his temperament was suited to carrying on the paper as a leading popular journal. The *World* itself expired in a merger with the New York *Telegram* in 1931.

•Published during the 1912 presidential campaign, the following editorial demonstrated the impact of Cobb's leadership. Some contemporaries credited it with having persuaded Democrats to give Woodrow Wilson, whom Cobb had supported from early in the campaign, his first presidential nomination. With Wilson in the lead at the Democratic national convention but far short of the votes necessary for the nomination after the 43rd ballot, the deadlocked convention adjourned over Sunday, leaving plenty of time for leaders of political machines to make deals and give the nomination to someone else. In a Monday morning editorial, Cobb warned convention delegates that to do so would leave the party in the clutches of what he called the "money power" and its puppets. Wilson received the nomination on the third ballot taken that morning.

WILSON—NO COMPROMISE
WITH RYAN AND MURPHY
(New York *World*; July 1, 1912)

It is too late to talk compromise at Baltimore.

Ryanism and Murphyism have created an issue that makes the nomination of Woodrow Wilson a matter of Democratic life or death.

To compromise now is for the Democratic National Convention to surrender to Thomas F. Ryan.

To compromise now is for the Democratic National Convention to surrender to August Belmont.

To compromise now is for the Democratic National Convention to surrender to Charles F. Murphy.

To compromise now is for the Democratic National Convention to surrender to Wall Street.

To compromise now is for the Democratic National Convention to surrender to Tammany Hall.

To compromise now is to send a Democratic ticket into the campaign shackled to bossism and plutocracy.

To compromise now is to give Theodore Roosevelt the supreme issue that he needs.

Compromise was possible until the Ryan-Murphy conspiracy was fully revealed and the Tammany boss carried out the terms of his bargain with the Clark managers by throwing New York's ninety votes to Champ Clark. Compromise was possible until Mr. Bryan was compelled by the inexorable logic of events to repudiate Champ Clark's candidacy and vote for Woodrow Wilson. Compromise was possible until it became apparent to every intelligent man that the Ryan-Murphy-Belmont-Hearst coalition had set out to strangle progressive Democracy, destroy Mr. Bryan politically and prevent the nomination of Woodrow Wilson at any cost.

Compromise is no longer possible. There can be no Democratic harmony, there can be no Democratic unity, there can be no Democratic integrity, until the convention overwhelms this shameful alliance between corrupt finance and corrupt politics.

It is the duty of Mr. Bryan to stand fast in his support of Gov. Wilson, and it is the duty of true Democrats to stand fast in their support of Mr. Bryan. Whatever their differences with him in the past, he is fighting today the battle of honest Democracy, he is fighting the battle of the American people, and he is fighting it manfully and magnificently.

The Ryan-Murphy coalition will now accept anybody except Wilson. If the convention yields to the plea for a compromise candidate, it will be a Ryan-Murphy victory.

A thousand Roosevelt orators will be thundering from the stump their denunciation of Democracy's surrender to Wall Street.

The issue that is vital to Roosevelt's campaign for a third term will come to his hand ready made. The Democratic party might as well retire from the contest as to go before the country with the Ryan-Murphy taint upon its ticket.

This is no longer a question of Woodrow Wilson's political strength, great as that is. It is no longer a question of his availability, self-evident as that is. Ryan and Murphy have left honest Democrats no choice. Ryan and Murphy have left honest Democrats no alternative. Ryan and Murphy have made Wilson's nomination the crucial test of the Democratic Party's fitness to live.

As Stephen A. Douglas once said, "There can be no neutrals in this war—only patriots or traitors."

•Cobb wrote the following editorial immediately after the outbreak of World War I.

AN INDICTMENT OF CIVILIZATION
(New York *World*; August 1, 1914)

In Vienna, there is a doddering old man, the offspring of a tainted house, who sits on the throne of the dual empire.

In St. Petersburg, there is a weak, well-meaning neurotic who by the accident of birth happens to be the Czar of All the Russias.

In Berlin there is a brilliant, talented, ambitious manipulator of politics who is German Emperor by grace of the genius of Bismarck, Moltke, and Roon.

Of these three men, only the one in Berlin has more than mediocre abilities; yet the three are permitted to play with the lives of millions of men, with property worth thousands of millions of dollars, with the commerce and industry and prosperity and laws and institutions not merely of empires and kingdoms but of continents. It is left to them to determine whether the world is to witness the most deadly and devastating war of all history.

The thing would be laughable, ridiculous, if it were not so ghastly.

War of itself may be wise or unwise, just or unjust; but that the issue of a world-wide war should rest in the hands of three men—any three men—and that the hundreds of millions who will bear the burden and be affected in every relation of life by the outcome of such a war should passively leave the decision to those three men is an indictment of civilization itself.

Human progress is slow indeed when a whole continent is still ready to fight for anything except the right to life, liberty, and self-government.

•Among editorial writers, Cobb was one of the staunchest but most thoughtful advocates of suffrage for women, seeing it as one instance of the progress of civilization. The following editorial on the subject demonstrates his ability to present a reasoned, forceful argument on such an issue.

WOMAN'S RIGHT TO VOTE
(New York *World;* March 14, 1915)

Whether the Equal Suffrage Amendment to the Constitution of New York is ratified by the voters of the States next fall will depend upon the attitude of women themselves.

If the majority of women earnestly desire the suffrage for themselves and their sex, the amendment will probably be adopted. On this question men voters are sure to be mightily swayed by the opinions of the women members of the family. If the majority of women are antagonistic or indifferent, the amendment will be defeated.

The World has made an effort to arrive at the sentiment, in a general way, of women themselves toward the suffrage. The results may be summarized in this fashion:

1. Among women who express an opinion either way, a very large majority desire the vote.

2. Most of the women to whom opportunity was given to express their sentiments had no opinion either for or against suffrage, and are presumably not yet interested in the issue.

The neutral attitude of the women who are without opinion does not affect the merits of the question, but if they maintain this attitude it will seriously affect the results at the polls.

As to the issue itself, *The World* is frank to admit that it knows of no valid arguments against woman suffrage which do not apply with equal force against manhood suffrage. Government is merely the expression of the political purposes of the community. The community is made up of men and women, all of whom have an equal right to life, liberty and the pursuit of happiness. No adult woman of sound mind is subjected to a guardianship in any of the affairs of life except politics. She may buy and sell, she may sue and be sued, she may own property and convey property—she may do anything that a man may do except vote. In other words, she may do everything except exercise a direct power upon the political institutions to which she is subject. This is a negation of democracy.

From the day of the Magna Charta down to the day of the New

Freedom the genius of republican institutions has steadily sought to broaden the base of the electoral power—to make these institutions more democratic. Originally, only the King had the vote. What the barons won all landholders eventually acquired. The States of the United States finally swept away property qualifications and established manhood suffrage. The Negro was enfranchised, and now comes woman, the last remaining element in the body politic, to demand that a right which cannot be denied to citizens of the United States on account of race, color or previous condition of servitude shall not be denied on account of sex.

The argument that government is based upon force and that women should not be allowed to vote because they are deficient in physical prowess hardly deserves to be taken seriously. Governments hire their force as they hire all their other service. Even when they resort to conscription they pick and choose—and pay. No country in modern times ever did or ever could muster its entire male population into its military establishment. Probably half of the entire German Army today is engaged in duties that are practically civilian. All of war is not fighting in the trenches or goose-stepping to the front. The French women who gather the harvests and the German women who plough the fields perform a military service no less important than that of the men on the firing-line. Without their efforts in providing food the men could not continue the war.

Most of the conventional arguments against woman suffrage are fantastic, but not less so than most of the popular arguments in favor of woman suffrage. All pretense that votes for women will "purify politics" may be dismissed as "clotted nonsense," to use Carlyle's favorite objurgation. Women will not purify politics. They never have done so in States in which they have the vote, and they never will. As a sex, women average no better than men. They are no more honest. They are no more disinterested. They are no more patriotic. Their public ideals are no higher, but rather lower, if anything. As a class they are less wise in general affairs than men because their experience is less wide. The classes that already vote necessarily have a clearer understanding of the functions and limitations of government than the classes that are seeking the vote.

Women suffrage will not reform government in the conventional moral sense, although in the long run it will produce a more representative and responsible government. If we may judge the future by the past, the immediate effect of woman suffrage will be to disorganize government and add to its confusion. That is what has always happened when the franchise was extended. Each new influx of voters submerged the old order, and the former standards of public service deteriorated for the time being, much to the anguish of the Brahmin classes, but not to the permanent injury of society. Enlarging the suffrage does not purify government, but enlarging the suffrage stabilizes and strengthens democracy, and hence the ultimate influence is invariably for the general good. In a democracy the people do not exist for the Government, but the Government exists for the people, and every adult person subject to government may reasonably ask for a voice in ordering the policies of that Government.

For women to demand suffrage on the ground that they are purer and nobler and holier than men is to argue against their own cause. An oligarchy of virtue would be only one degree less oppressive than an oligarchy of vice. Nobody has ever obtained the franchise on the mere pretext that he was pure in heart, and nobody ever will. The franchise is not granted in order that politics may be purified, but in order that the holder of the franchise may the better protect his life, liberty, property and welfare under the Government to which he is responsible as a citizen.

Votes for women will not improve the quality of government, but it will make women more intelligent and more responsible, and hence society as a whole must inevitably benefit. The ballot box is a mighty university. It has proved so in the case of men and it must prove so in the case of women, or the experience of history is false.

Moreover, the political influence already exerted by a few women makes it highly desirable that all women be enfranchised in order to re-establish the balance. Under republican institutions power without responsibility is a grave evil. Women today have great power in government, but no responsibility. Various organizations of women, which probably do not represent 10 per cent of the sex, maintain at times a veritable reign of terror in legislative bodies by pretending to speak in the name of all women. In consequence, half the country is now bedevilled by some form or another of harem government which in no respect is a true expression of public opinion. Legislators who are no better than they ought to be are forever making ridiculous concessions to women agitators on the theory that official sympathy with such moral yearnings is a shrewd method of diverting public suspicion. The statute books are loaded down with foolish laws dictated by a few crusading women and enacted in a spirit of "The ladies—God bless them?" An overwhelming majority of women have had no voice in this legislation, and they disclaim all responsibility for its results. But the statutes remain, the situation grows worse from year to year, and all laws fall more or less into contempt through this legislation bred of fanaticism and hypocrisy.

We know what would probably happen if government were in the hands of women, and Anthony Comstock, Charles Edward Russell and the Anti-Saloon League were accepted as the spokesmen for all the disfranchised males. Yet something of that sort is going on all the time in State capitols in the name of women. The only antidote to the influence of some women upon government is the influence of all women upon government. When all sex limitations upon suffrage have been removed the political power of those women who are obsessed with the idea that government must assume the spiritual characteristics of a communistic prayer meeting will be restricted to their own votes and the votes of those who are actually in sympathy with them.

But if the claim that votes for women will purify politics is sentimental nonsense, the counter-claim that votes for women will wreck the home is equally absurd. Protecting the home is one of the favorite recreations of American Bourbonism. The home is the oldest of human institutions. It is older than government. It protects itself. It is not government that maintains the home, but it is the home that maintains government. It was because of homes that governments were established. An institution that has withstood the vicissitudes of centuries is not likely to collapse because the women of a community spend half an hour in a voting booth on the first Tuesday after the first Monday in November. If the home could survive St. Paul, it can survive the ballot.

Eliminating from the suffrage controversy all of its cant and twaddle, the question is a straight issue of whether all the adult citizens of the state shall be entitled to a vote in making the laws to which all of them are subject, or whether this privilege shall be the exclusive property of half of these citizens who gain their political power by the accident of sex.

Lincoln once said that this Republic was founded on the rule of "root, hog, or die," and women are no less amenable to that principle than are men. The amiable theory that it is man's function to provide and woman's function to be sheltered is a living lie, as millions of women wage-earners can testify. Sometimes man provides and sometimes he doesn't. The woman who is sheltered today may be working in a factory tomorrow to support herself and her children. Hunger knows no sex. Want knows no sex. Necessity knows no sex. Law knows no sex. Property knows no sex. Only the ballot box knows sex.

But the ballot box once knew rank. It once knew land and primogeniture. It once knew income and money and family. All those paraphernalia of privilege have been swept away, and the disability of sex will follow. In the steady sweep of democracy the time will come when the present opposition to woman suffrage will seem as short sighted and senseless as the former opposition to manhood suffrage now seems.

Democracies always move forward. That is their law of self-preservation. If they stand still or retrograde they are lost.

•The following editorial is illustrative of Cobb's concern for the conditions of working Americans and of his use of the stylistic technique of repetition.

THE FORGOTTEN MAN
(New York *World*; September 3, 1922)

Nearly forty years ago Prof. William A. Sumner of Yale prepared a lecture entitled "The Forgotten Man." That lecture has since taken its place among the classic American contributions to political economy.

"The Forgotten Man" was never more timely than it is now, and it would be worth hundreds of millions of dollars to the American people if President Harding and Congress could be persuaded to study it until Sumner's thought had become part of their own mental processes—or if they could learn only this much:

> Wealth comes only from production, and all that the wrangling grabbers, loafers and robbers get to deal with comes from somebody's toil and sacrifice. Who, then, is he who provides it all? Go and find him, and you will have once more before you the Forgotten Man.
>
> You will find him hard at work because he has a great many to support. Nature has done a great deal for him in giving him a fertile soil and an excellent climate, and he wonders why it is that, after all, his scale of comfort is so moderate. He has to get out of the soil enough to pay all his taxes, and that means the cost of all the jobs and the fund for all the plunder. The Forgotten Man is delving away in patient industry, supporting his family, paying his taxes, casting his vote, supporting the church and school, reading his newspaper and cheering for the politician of his admiration, but he is the only one for whom there is no provision in the great scramble and the big divide.
>
> Such is the Forgotten Man. He works, he votes, generally he prays—but he always pays—yes, above all, he pays.

The Forgotten Man was never more completely forgotten than he is now. Congress does not know that he exists. The President suspects that there is such a person, who may turn up at the polls in November, but he is not quite sure.

In the meantime the Forgotten Man has been given over to be plundered. Congress is helping the sugar crowd rob him, the woolen crowd rob him, the cotton manufacturers rob him, the steel crowd rob him, and left him at the mercy of the profiteers in every line of trade.

Mr. Gompers boasts that the Industrial aristocrats of the American Federation of Labor are still within 5 per cent of their war-time wages, but the Forgotten Man has been liquidated until the limit of his capacity has been reached. Yet he must take up the burden again to pay for the cost of the railroad strike and the long row between the executives and the union leaders over seniority. He must pay for the coal strike, with the operators and the miners splitting the unearned increment. Not only must he pay but he must skimp himself on fuel because it has been necessary to exhaust all the reserve stocks of coal in order to enable the trade to fix a price that makes it worth while for the operators and the unions to divide the swag.

It is the Forgotten Man who will ultimately pay for the Soldiers' Bonus, for the ship subsidy and for all the grandiose schemes of Congress, and he will pay for these in odd hours when he is not already busy in paying the cost of the war. In order to encourage him a monopoly tariff is to be imposed on him, to advance the price of everything he uses and give every privileged interest an opportunity to take something more away from him as he goes back and forth to his work.

No lobbies ever represent the Forgotten Man in Washington. He is neither incorporated nor organized. He cannot pass the increased price along, because he is the ultimate consumer as well as the initial producer. His function in the scheme of things is to work and to pay—and to believe what his Representative and his Senator tell him about the glories of the Government.

HARVEY NEWBRANCH URGES TOWNSPEOPLE TO ABIDE BY THE RULE OF LAW

In September 1919 a black man was arrested for the rape of a white woman in Omaha, Nebraska. A mob gathered, broke the man from jail, and lynched him. Harvey Newbranch, editor of the *Evening World-Herald*, chronicled the episode and the rioting that followed. In a passionate editorial, he called on fellow citizens to respect the rule of law. It was the first of numerous editorials on the theme of law-and-order during racial crises to win the Pulitzer Prize. None of the later ones, however, surpassed the quality of Newbranch's work.

While passion burned in the words, the editorial still exhibited a well-defined logic. Newbranch clearly stated the polarity between lawlessness and obedience to the law. A number of themes discussed are worth considering because they are common in later Pulitzer editorials—themes dealing, for example, with the necessity of obedience to law, the injustice of racial prejudice, the shame of rioters as cowards and animals, the blaming of authorities for their failure to uphold the law, and the appeal to civic pride in the good reputation of a town.

LAW AND THE JUNGLE
(Harvey E. Newbranch; Omaha *World-Herald*; Sept. 30, 1919)

There is the rule of the jungle in this world, and there is the rule of law.

Under jungle rule no man's life is safe, no man's wife, no man's mother, sister, children, home, liberty, rights, property. Under the rule of law protection is provided for all these, and provided in proportion as law is efficiently and honestly administered and its power and authority respected and obeyed.

Omaha Sunday was disgraced and humiliated by a monstrous object lesson of what jungle rule means. The lack of efficient government in Omaha, the lack of governmental foresight and sagacity and energy, made the exhibition possible. It was provided by a few hundred hoodlums, most of them mere boys, organized as the wolf-pack is organized, inflamed by the spirit of anarchy and license, of plunder and destruction. Ten thousand or more good citizens, without leadership, without organization, without public authority that had made an effort to organize them for the anticipated emergency, were obliged to stand as onlookers, shamed in their hearts, and witness the hideous orgy of lawlessness. Some of them, to their blighting shame be it said, respectable men with women and children in their homes, let themselves be swept away by the mob spirit. They encouraged if they did not aid the wolf-pack that was conspiring to put down the rule of law in Omaha—that rule which is the sole protection for every man's home and family.

It is over now, thank God!

Omaha henceforth will be as safe for its citizens, and as safe for the visitors within its gates, as any city in the land. Its respectable and law-abiding people, comprising 99 per cent of the population, will see to that. They have already taken the steps to see to it. The first step was taken when the rioting was at its height—taken belatedly, it is true, because they had placed reliance on the public authorities to safeguard the order and good name of Omaha. The blistering disgrace of the riot has aroused them. There will be no more faltering, no more fickleness, no more procrastination, no longer the lack of a firm hand. The military aid that has been called in is only temporary. It serves to insure public order and public safety for the day, for the week. But the strengthening of the police force of the city, its efficient organization under wise and competent leadership, is a policy that public sentiment has inaugurated and that it will sternly enforce. As to that there will be neither equivocation nor delay. Nor will there be any hesitancy or laxness in the organization, and rigid use if need be, of civic guards to keep the streets and homes and public places of Omaha secure.

The citizenship of Omaha will be anxious that the outside world should know what it was that happened and why it happened. Let there be no mistaking the plain facts. The trouble is over now. It was a flare-up that died as quickly as it was born. Omaha is today the same safe and orderly city it has always been. It will be safer, indeed, hereafter, and more orderly, because of the lesson it has so dearly learned. And the flareup was the work—let this fact be emphasized—of a few hundred rioters, some of them incited by an outrageous deed, others of them skulkers in the anarchistic underbrush who urged them on for their own foul purposes of destroying property and paralyzing the arm of the law. If the miserable negro, Brown, had been removed from Omaha in time, as he should have been; if, failing to remove him, the public authorities had taken vigorous measures to prevent the congregation and inflaming of the mob, the riot would never have occurred. An organized and intelligently directed effort in advance would have preserved the good name of Omaha untarnished. It would have prevented the lynching. It would have saved our splendid new courthouse from being offered up in flames, its defense with the mob-victim in it, a costly sacrifice on the altar of law and order. There would have been no thought, even, of the amazing attempt to lynch the mayor of Omaha, bravely and honorably discharging his duty as chief magistrate in resisting the wolf-pack.

It would be impossible to speak too strongly in condemnation of the rioters or in the uncompromising demand for their stern and swift punishment, whoever they be, wherever they can be found. They not only foully murdered a negro they believed to be guilty. They brutally maltreated and attempted to murder other negroes whom they knew to be innocent. They tried to lynch the mayor. They wantonly pillaged stores and destroyed property. They burned the courthouse. In the sheer spirit of anarchy they pulled valuable records from their steel filing cases, saturated them in gasoline, and burned them. They burned police conveyances and cut the fire hose, inviting the destruction by fire of the entire city. Their actions were wholly vile, wholly evil, and malignantly dangerous. There is not a one of them who can be apprehended, and whose guilt can be proved, but should be sent for a long term to the state prison. And toward that end every effort of every good citizen, as well as every effort of the public authorities, from the humblest policeman to the presiding judge on the bench, must be directed. There can be no sentimentalizing, no fearful hesitancy, no condoning the offense of these redhanded criminals. The pitiful bluff they have put up against the majesty of the law, against the inviolability of American institutions, must be called and called fearlessly.

To the law-abiding negroes of Omaha, who, like the law-abiding whites, are the vast majority of their race, it is timely to speak a work of sympathy and support. Any effort on the part of any of them to take the law into their own hands would be as culpable and as certainly disastrous as was the effort of the mob. In the running down and maltreating of unoffending men of their color, merely because they were of that color, they have been done odious wrong. They naturally and properly resent having been confined to their homes, in trembling fear of their lives, while red riot ran the streets of the city. But their duty as good citizens is precisely the same as that of the rest of us, all of us, who have been outraged and shamed as citizens. It is to look to the law for their protection, for their vindication, and to give the law every possible support as it moves in its course. The law is their only shield, as it is the only shield of every white man, no matter how lowly or how great. And it is the duty of all, whites and blacks alike, to uphold especially the might of the law—to insist, if need be, on its full exercise—in protecting every colored citizen of Omaha in his lawful and constitutional rights.

For the first time in many years—and for the last time, let us hope, for many years to come—Omaha has had an experience with lawlessness. We have seen what it is. We have seen how it works. We have felt, however briefly, the fetid breath of anarchy on our cheeks. We have experienced the cold chill of fear which it arouses. We have seen, as in a nightmare, its awful possibilities. We have learned how frail is the barrier which divides civilization from the primal jungle—and we have been given to see clearly what that barrier is.

It is the Law! It is the Might of the Law, wisely and fearlessly administered! It is respect for and obedience to the Law on the part of the members of society!

When these fail us all things fail. When these are lost all will be lost. Should the day ever come when the rule that was in Omaha Sunday night become the dominant rule, the grasses of the jungle would overspread our civilization, its wild denizens, human and brute, would make their foul feast on the ruins, and the God who rules over us would turn His face in sorrow from a world given over to bestiality.

May the lesson of Sunday night sink deep! May we take home to our hearts, there to be cherished and never for a moment forgotten, the words of the revered Lincoln:

Let reverence of the law be breathed by every mother to the lisping babe that prattles on her lap; let it be taught in schools, seminaries and colleges; let it be written in primers, spelling books and almanacs; let it be preached from pulpits and proclaimed in legislative halls and enforced in courts of justice; let it become the political religion of the nation.

Frank O'Brien Explains
The Burial of the 'Unknown Soldier'

One of the most popular winners of the Pulitzer Prize for Editorial Writing was Frank O'Brien's tribute on the occasion of the burial of America's "Unknown Soldier" November 11, 1921, in Arlington Cemetery. Its appeal derived from its nobleness of ideas and the universality of O'Brien's descriptions.

The editorial was more emotional and more "artistic" than standard editorials of today, but despite the emotionalism of the subject the editorial really had a very simple, formal structure. Its lead sentence stated the three meanings of the burial, and the body simply explained each in order. The first two paragraphs were devoted to the burial as a "symbol," the next two to its "mystery," and the final two long paragraphs and summary sentence to the "tribute." Tying all three together was a strong religious motif.

THE UNKNOWN SOLDIER
(Frank M. O'Brien; New York *Herald*; November 11, 1921)

That which takes place today at the National Cemetery in Arlington is a symbol, a mystery and a tribute. It is an entombment only in the physical sense. It is rather the enthronement of Duty and Honor. This man who died for his country is the symbol of these qualities; a far more perfect symbol than any man could be whose name and deeds we knew. He represents more, really, than the unidentified dead, for we cannot separate them spiritually from the war heroes whose names are written on their gravestones. He—this spirit whom we honor—stands for the unselfishness of all.

This, of all monuments to the dead, is lasting and immutable. So long as men revere the finer things of life the tomb of the nameless hero will remain a shrine. Nor, with the shifts of time and mind, can there be a changing of values. No historian shall rise to modify the virtues or the faults of the Soldier. He has an immunity for which kings might pray. The years may bring erosion to the granite but not to the memory of the Unknown.

It is a common weakness of humanity to ask the questions that can never be answered in this life. Probably none to whom the drama of the Unknown Soldier has appealed has not wondered who, in the sunshine of earth, was the protagonist of today's ceremony. A logger from the Penobscot? An orchardist from the Pacific coast? A well driller from Texas? A machinist from Connecticut? A lad who left his hoe to rust among the Missouri corn? A longshoreman from Hell's Kitchen? Perhaps some youth from the tobacco fields, resting again in his own Virginia. All that the army tells of him is that he died in battle. All that the heart tells is that some woman loved him. More than that no man shall learn. In this mystery, as in the riddle of the universe, the wise wonder; but they would [sic] not know.

What were his dreams, his ambitions? Likely he shared those common to the millions: a life of peace and honest struggle, with such small success as comes to most who try; and at the end the place on the hillside among his fathers. Today to do honor at his last resting place come the greatest soldiers of the age, famous statesmen from other continents, the President, the high judges and the legislators of his own country, and many men who, like himself, fought for the flag. At his bier will gather the most remarkable group that America has seen. And the tomb which Fate reserved for him is, instead of the narrow cell on the village hillside, one as lasting as that of Rameses and as inspiring as Napoleon's.

It is a great religious ceremony, this burial today. The exaltation of the nameless bones would not be possible except for Belief. Where were Duty and Honor, the wellsprings of Victory, if mankind feared that death drew a black curtain behind which lay nothing but the dark? So all in whom the spark of hope has not died can well believe that we, to whom the Soldier is a mystery, are not a mystery to him. They can believe that the watchers at Arlington today are not merely a few thousands of the living but the countless battalions of the departed. "Though he were dead, yet shall he live"—there is the promise to which men hold when everything of this earth has slipped away.

All the impressive ritual of today would be a mockery if we did not believe that, out in an infinity which astronomers cannot chart or mathematicians bound, the Unknown Soldier and all the glorious dead whom we honor in his dust are looking down upon this little spinning ball, conscious of our reverence. And when noon strikes, signal for the moment of silent prayer, few of those who stand with bared head will lack conviction that the rites at Arlington are viewed by other than mortal eyes. Only in that spirit may we honor the Unknown Soldier and those who, like him, died for this Republic.

Unknown, but not unknowing!

MASTERS OF THE EDITORIAL

WILLIAM ALLEN WHITE:
MASTER OF NARRATIVE STYLE

In the realm of editorial writing, William Allen White stands out as perhaps the best and certainly the most versatile writer American journalism has produced. His stature rests on his mastery of a narrative style, his use of words, and his deep compassion for people.

He began and ended his editorial career at the same newspaper, the Emporia (Kan.) *Gazette*. He purchased the languishing newspaper in 1895 and moved back to the small town where he was born in 1868. From his indiscreet desk in the unimposing *Gazette* building, he began to pen the editorials that would eventually travel beyond the streets of Emporia and reach the hearts of people across the nation.

Those editorials were so powerful that today they are remembered as the mark of what, as *Christian Science Monitor* editor

Erwin D. Canham professed, "American journalism ought to be."

But what makes White's editorials worthy of such praise? A quick reading of editorials in any newspaper—whether great or mediocre—reveals that most come in the form of arguments or expositions. Although White worked under the same routine as other editorial writers, his works rarely fell into the routine. Whether the editorial is his argumentative "What's the Matter with Kansas?" or his beautifully narrative "Mary White," many of his writings could be considered editorial masterpieces.

White's writing genius can be explained in part by the simple and obvious fact that he wrote from the office of a small newspaper. All of his editorials were inspired, in one way or another, by the people and the places of Emporia. His audience was small town, middle class, and agrarian. He never became a metropolitan editor, slanted articles with a sensationalist edge or attempted to beat out competing newspapers. And he never wanted to be anything other than a small-town editor. At that, he was America's best. When he sat down at his typewriter, the words that appeared on paper were the words for *his* people. In his autobiography, he explained that "our affairs become common with one another, our joys mutual, and even our sorrows shared."

"Mary White," written in 1921 after his daughter's fatal riding accident, showed his love for his community. It mentioned "Charley O'Brien, the traffic cop" and "her pal at the *Gazette* office, Walter Hughes." The editorial tugged the heartstrings of Emporians and, soon, all Americans. Its ensuing publication in newspapers, as well as in literary magazines, throughout the country added to White's fame.

White's obituary editorials reveal his talent for writing about a person's life. He could, in few words, immortalize the human being, even when he didn't care for the deceased. Although not kind, White's editorial on publisher Frank Munsey is painstakingly honest in its succinctness: "Frank Munsey contributed to the journalism of his day the talent of a meat packer, the morals of a money changer and the manners of an undertaker."

White also had a penchant, like most editorial writers, for political writing. He, however, was more effective than most other editors because he geared his opinions to the people of his world. When he wrote on politics, he rarely ventured outside Kansas.

White never claimed to have all the answers. In fact, his changing opinions on politics provided him with more than a few critics, but he always fiercely supported what he believed in at the time.

"What's the Matter with Kansas?" is White's most famous political editorial. A minor incident on the streets of Emporia led him, in 1896, to write the editorial that would first make him known to millions of American readers. He wrote it in answer to a group of Populists who cornered him in Emporia over his conservative leanings. They asked him to defend his opinions. Overwhelmed with anger, he could not answer them coherently. He rushed to his desk and, in bold and opinionated language, gave them his answer. The editorial's sarcastically humorous description of Kansas's failings and the politicians responsible concisely expressed what other irate middle-class citizens felt.

Over the years, White's political convictions changed, and his dislike for Populists waned; his belief in justice, however, never faltered. He remained a Republican all his life, except for a brief interlude with the ill-fated Bull Moose party in 1912. After his political ideas matured during Theodore Roosevelt's presidency, he began to understand Populist causes and attempted to carry out changes through the Republican party. His 1922 editorial "To an Anxious Friend" was a "response" editorial similar to "What's the Matter with Kansas?" but it demonstrated his changed attitude. This time the response was to the Kansas governor's order that businesses could not display placards supporting striking railroad workers. White's editorial was concentrated, concise, and clearly reasoned. He wrote: "Either we have free speech and a free press in this country or we have not. Now is the time to find out." White clearly believed that the nation should "find out" and that by allowing freedom of expression right would emerge triumphant. The editorial, although certainly not White's best, won for him the 1923 Pulitzer Prize.

All of White's editorials ring loudly with a moral sense of what is right and just. He lived, personally and professionally, under a strong code of ethics. His political editorials, although sometimes angry, always reveal his faith in the future. His picturesque editorials about daily life in Emporia or about the passing of a "common" man also illustrate his constant belief in man's need always to strive, uplift, and crusade.

In a time when many editors dreamed of big circulation and large revenues, White never strayed from the simple conviction that his readers deserved honest responses to the news of the day. He believed that the character of the editor was the essence of a successful publication.

White interpreted the news of the day in a distinctive way. His writing style was unique in that it usually was narrative. His editorials read like the best of American literature, not surprising since he published many literary works, including the best-selling short story collections *The Real Life* and *A Certain Rich Man.*

White was a master wordsmith. He edited and re-edited his editorials until they were perfect. He cut out repetition and used whatever word was necessary, whether large or small, not preferring one over the other. "The short word," he said, "has received a great deal of attention that it doesn't deserve." Even when using large words, he was always pithy, but never boring. He also utilized many literary devices, including metaphor and alliteration.

The themes in White's editorials were universal. The emotions conveyed through his words, from grief to optimism to humor, touched something deep inside his readers. This fact, as much as anything else, accounts for the power of his editorials. His emotionalism and exuberance, for example, helped make "Mary White" a rare work in English literature.

With White's death on January 29, 1944, a pall passed over the journalistic world. It had lost an extraordinary writer and spokesman. Newspapers across the nation eulogized him with glowing words, and President Franklin Roosevelt called him one of the newspaper world's "wisest and most beloved editors."

In Emporia, his loss was felt more deeply and more personally. He had died on Kansas Day, and Emporia townspeople thought that fact appropriately symbolic of his love and concern for his state and its people.

•Written shortly after White bought the Emporia *Gazette*, the following editorial demonstrates his early talent to write in a descriptive manner.

THE END OF THE FIGHT
(Emporia *Gazette*, June 20, 1895)

There came through Emporia yesterday two old-fashioned "mover wagons," headed east. The stock in the caravan would invoice four horses, very poor and very tired, one mule, more disheartened than the horses, and one sad-eyed dog, that had probably been compelled to rustle his own precarious living for many a long and weary day. A few farm implements of the simpler sort were loaded in the wagon, but nothing that had wheels was moving except the two wagons. All the rest of the impedimenta had been left upon the battlefield, and these poor stragglers, defeated, but not conquered, were fleeing to another field, to try the fight again. These movers were from western Kansas—from one of those counties near the Colorado line which holds a charter from the state to officiate as the very worst, most desolate, God-forsaken, man-deserted spot on the sad old earth. They had come from that wilderness only after a ten years' hard, vicious fight, a fight which had left its scars on their faces, had bent their bodies, had taken the elasticity from their steps, and left them crippled to enter the battle anew. For ten years they had been fighting the elements. They had seen it stop raining for months at a time. They had heard the fury of the winter wind as it came whining across the short burned grass and cut the flesh from their children huddling in the corner. These movers have strained their eyes watching through the long summer days for the rain that never came. They have seen that big cloud roll up from the southwest about one o'clock in the afternoon, hover over the land, and stumble away with a few thumps of thunder as the sun went down. They have tossed through hot nights wild with worry, and have arisen only to find their worst nightmares grazing in reality on the brown stubble in front of their sun-warped doors. They had such high hopes when they went out there; they are so desolate now— no, not now, for now they are in the land of corn and honey. They have come out of the wilderness, back to the land of promise. They are now in God's own country down on the Neosho, with their wife's folks, and the taste of apple butter and good corn bread and fresh meat and pie—pieplant pie like mother used to make—gladdened their shrunken palates last night; and real cream, curdling on their coffee saucers last night for supper, was a sight so rich and strange that it lingered in their dreams, wherein they walked beside the still waters, and lay down in green pastures.

•Following is the editorial that bolted White to national fame and to prominence as a Republican spokesman.

WHAT'S THE MATTER WITH KANSAS?
(Emporia *Gazette*; August 15, 1896)

Today the Kansas department of agriculture sent out a statement which indicates that Kansas has gained less than 2,000 people in the last year. There are about 225,000 families in the state, and yet so many people have left the state that the natural increase is cut down to less than 2,000 net.

This has been going on for eight years.

If there had been a high brick wall around the state eight years ago, and not a soul had been admitted or permitted to leave, Kansas would be a half million souls better off than she is today. And yet the nation has increased in population. In five years ten million people have been added to the national population, yet instead of gaining a share of this—say, half a million—Kansas has apparently been a plague spot, and in the very garden of the world, has lost population by ten thousand every year.

Not only has she lost population, but she has lost money. Every moneyed man in the state who could get out without loss has gone. Every month in every community sees someone who has a little money pack up and leave the state. This has been going on for eight years. Money has been drained out all the time. In half a dozen money-lending concerns stimulating industry by furnishing capital, there is now none, or one or two that are looking after the interest and principal already outstanding.

No one brings any money into Kansas any more. What community knows over one or two men who have moved in with more than $5,000 in the past three years? And what community cannot count half a score of men in that time who have left, taking all the money they could scrape together?

Yet the nation has grown rich, other states have increased in population and wealth—other neighboring states. Missouri has gained over two million, while Kansas has been losing half a million. Nebraska has gained in wealth and population while Kansas has gone downhill. Colorado has gained every way, while Kansas has lost every way since 1888.

What's the matter with Kansas?

There is no substantial city in the state. Every big town save one has lost in population. Yet Kansas City, Omaha, Lincoln, St. Louis, Denver, Colorado Springs, Sedalia, the cities of the Dakotas, St. Paul and Minneapolis and Des Moines—all cities and towns in the West have steadily grown.

Take up the government blue book and you will see that Kansas is virtually off the map. Two or three little scrubby consular places in yellow-fever-stricken communities that do not aggregate $10,000 a year is all the recognition that Kansas has. Nebraska draws about $100,000; little old North Dakota draws about $50,000; Oklahoma doubles Kansas; Missouri leaves her a thousand miles behind; Colorado is almost seven times greater than Kansas—the whole West is ahead of Kansas.

Take it by any standard you please, Kansas is not in it.

Go east and you hear them laugh at Kansas, go west and they sneer at her, go south and they "cuss" her, go north and they have forgotten her. Go into any crowd of intelligent people gathered anywhere on the globe, and you will find the Kansas man on the defensive. The newspaper columns and magazines once devoted to praise of her, to boastful facts and startling figures concerning her resource, are now filled with cartoons, jibes, and Pefferian speeches. Kansas just naturally isn't in it. She has traded places with Arkansas and Timbuctoo.

What's the matter with Kansas?

We all know; yet here we are at it again. We have an old moss-back Jacksonian who snorts and howls because there is a bathtub in the statehouse; we are running that old jay for governor. We have another shabby, wild-eyed, rattle-brained fanatic who has said openly in a dozen speeches that "the rights of the user are paramount to the rights of the owner"; we are running him for chief justice, so that capital will come tumbling over itself to get into the state. We have raked the old ashheap of failure in the state and found an old human hoop skirt who has failed as a businessman, who has failed as an editor, who has failed as a preacher, and we are going to run him for Congressman-at-large. He will help the looks of the Kansas delegation at Washington. Then we have discovered a kid without a law practice and have decided to run him for attorney-general. Then for fear some hint that the state had become respectable might percolate through the civilized portions of the nation, we have decided to send three or four harpies out lecturing, telling the people that Kansas is raising hell and letting the corn go to weeds.

Oh, this is a state to be proud of! We are a people who can hold up our heads! What we need is not more money, but less capital, fewer white shirts and brains, fewer men with business judgment, and more of those fellows who boast that they are "just ordinary clodhoppers, but they know more in a minute about finance than John Sherman"; we need more men who are "posted," who can bellow about the crime of '73, who hate prosperity, and who think because a man believes in national honor, he is a tool of Wall Street. We have had a few of them—150,000, but we need more.

We need several thousand gibbering idiots to scream about the "Great Red Dragon" of Lombard Street. We don't need population, we don't need wealth, we don't need well-dressed men on the streets, we don't need cities on the fertile prairies; you bet we don't! What we are after is the money power. Because we have become poorer and ornerier and meaner than a spavined, distempered mule, we, the people of Kansas, propose to kick; we don't care to build up, we wish to tear down.

"There are two ideas of government," said our noble [William Jennings] Bryan at Chicago. "There are those who believe that if you just legislate to make the well-to-do prosperous, this prosperity will leak through on those below. The Democratic idea has been that if you legislate to make the masses prosperous their prosperity will find its way up and through every class and rest upon us."

That's the stuff! Give the prosperous man the dickens! Legislate the thriftless man into ease, whack the stuffing out of the creditors, and tell the debtors who borrowed the money five years ago when money "per capita" was greater than it is now that the contraction of the currency gives him a right to repudiate.

Whoop it up for the ragged trousers; put the lazy, greasy fizzle who can't pay his debts on the altar, and bow down and worship him. Let the state ideal be high. What we need is not the respect of our fellow man, but the chance to get something for nothing.

Oh, yes, Kansas is a great state. Here are people fleeing from it by the score every day, capital going out of the state by the hundreds of dollars; and every industry but farming paralyzed, and that crippled, because its products have to go across the ocean before they can find a laboring man at work who can afford to buy them. Let's don't stop this year. Let's drive all the decent, self-respecting men out of the state. Let's keep the old clodhoppers who know it all. Let's encourage the man who is "posted." He can talk, and what we need is not mill hands to eat our meat, nor factory hands to eat our wheat, nor cities to oppress the farmer by consuming his butter and eggs and chickens and produce. What Kansas needs is men who can talk, who have large leisure to argue the currency question while their wives wait at home for that nickel's worth of bluing.

What's the matter with Kansas?

Nothing under the shining sun. She is losing wealth, population, and standing. She has got her statesmen, and the money power is afraid of her. Kansas is all right. She has started in to raise hell, as Mrs. [Mary Elizabeth] Lease [a Populist campaign speaker] advised, and she seems to have an overproduction. But that doesn't matter. Kansas never did believe in diversified crops. Kansas is all right. There is absolutely nothing wrong with Kansas. "Every prospect pleases and only man is vile."

•The maturing of White's style is exhibited in the following editorial. The "child" in the editorial was White himself.

CHILD'S HISTORY OF KANSAS
(Emporia *Gazette*; July 4, 1907)

A child lives his own life, and the world of grown-ups is a thing apart. And when grown to man's estate, he recalls events that passed before his childish memories. Thus in Kansas, for instance, one child, now living, in a man's memory remembers the drought of '60, not by the anxiety on the faces of his parents, not by the waiting and watching for rain, but by the fact that a time was when they parceled out the biscuits at table, and a boy had to take his share and no more. The whole tragedy of the time to hundreds of men and women, when pride and want fought until want went to the "aid store" and took what was needed—all the bleakness and brownness of the land—these passed unnoticed under his eyes. For the things he saw were in the child's world. And so to one who came later into the world, history, as it was told by those who were a part of history, was told to a child, and recalled only with a child's understanding. Thus the child holds in his memory to-day not the stories he was told of the adventures of the army of the border, but he retains a curious wonder as to why those men had red legs. And of the statesman whose tragic end stirred Kansas in the early days, the child who heard the story of the drama's beginning, rise, and close a dozen times, only recalls that the man wore a buffalo skin over coat, and that men said he had dark, piercing eyes. All other things the man has learned, he has read, and it is the man's memory and not the child's that rises. And of the war between states, the child who must have heard the story a thousand times remembers best the songs—"Old Nicodemus," the "Year of the Jubiloo," "We Shall Meet But We Shall Miss Him," "Tramp, Tramp, Tramp," and the hanging of Jeff Davis to a sour apple tree. The tale that was told did not seem to stick; only the tale that was read found lodgment, but the songs cling like burrs to the memory.

As the child grew into his own consciousness, he passed through the drought of '73 and the grasshopper year. But of that strange calamity, so little remains in his memory. He remembers that men stood in the street looking at the sky, and that he turned his face toward the sky and watched the shimmering cloud of insects floating above him. But he does not remember how they came, nor when they went. He remembers that there was a time when boys caught grasshoppers by the bottleful and played with them, and made them "spit tobacco juice," and that for a certain number of pins another little boy would eat grasshopper legs; and that once the boys put up a fabulous purse of marbles and pins and precious treasure to get the little boy to eat them alive, and that he did eat a hopper and was very sick. But of the plague and its devastation the child remembers nothing, and of the drought of '74 he only remembers that the clouds were high and big and white and feathery one year, and the sky was bluer than ever, and the dirt in the road that passed before the house was warm to play in far after sundown. But of the withered corn, and the starving cattle he remembers only that one day an antelope came up to eat with the cattle in the feed lot. Also there is a recollection that the bone yard grew that year, and that the boy was not allowed to play there for a long time.

Of the politics that moved men in Kansas in the early days of the '70's the child, who must have heard men talk politics many long hours, remembers only that when he wore a Greeley scarf, another little boy grabbed one end and a big boy grabbed another, and choked the boy until he was black in the face, and the schoolteacher doused water in his face and brought him to. Later, when he was a big boy, he and four other big boys in the intermediate room at school, great hulks of fellows eight years old, lined up the four little Democrats in school one fall day, and threw watermelon rinds for Tilden one whole noon hour, and at recess again faced the school behind the woodpile for reform, and came in besmeared and spattered, but unconquered. "It was a famous victory." But what it was all about the boy did not know, except that his father was a Democrat, and that all Republican little boys were to be fought if they said much about it. It was years afterward that the boy knew what had become of Tilden, or why he smeared himself with watermelons in the lost cause. The fight in the boy world was a boy-world feud, and had only a remote connection with the contest in the world outside. Indeed, so confused was the boy's idea of the issues at stake in the upper world, that he confused Tilden with the man whose name was linked with Beecher's, and when they began talking about Tilden, then he would be sent out of the room for something, and when he came back be sent away for something else, and then told to run and play.

About this time a picture was put in the boy's memory of a trip to Topeka, to attend a Democratic convention. He remembers that his mother was some time ironing his father's nankeen trousers, and starching the pleats in his white shirt, and that there was talk in the family of cleaning up father's Panama hat. Then the record drops and the boy appears in a big, strange town, holding tightly to his father's hand, and it was a very fat, sweaty hand, and the boy lagged, and must have pulled, for the father prodded him with his cane. And then again the roll is blank, and the boy and his father are standing, looking at a long line of colored men—the first the boy has ever seen—and the father, seeing they are voting at some kind of a primary, snaps his silver tobacco box, after taking a big chew of fine cut, walking hurriedly off down the street, pulling the little boy after him, and the boy remembers that the father is very angry for a long time. And when some one in the convention says something about colored men voting, the father brought his cane down to applaud, and hit a little bare toe beside his, and then again the film is blank.

About this time events seem to begin to take definite shape. For the boy, who was used to going to revivals at the Methodist church just to be going, seems to remember meetings at which there was much abuse of the rum fiend, and the boy and all the other little boys in school appeared in blue ribbons, which the big boys pulled, and which caused fights, if a boy near enough your size pulled it to warrant taking offense. And then the boy remembers hearing St. John, and suddenly, as things happen in a dream, and without any particular cause, Jim Riley's saloon is gone, and the sawdust pile behind it, whereon the boy hunted for fishing corks, and whereon once Theodore Dunlevey found a dime—the sawdust dump had vanished, and the boy finds himself picking up empty bottles at the back end of the drug-store and selling them for marbles, and he remembers the awful scandal—the first story of graft and swollen fortunes that ever came into his life—when Ed Dupee and Dow Blair sold the druggist some bottles, and then slipped into his back door and got the same bottles in the back room and sold them to the druggist for marbles again. In spite of the admiration among the boys at the ingenuity and daring of the deed, there was a quiet feeling among the boys that the affair was not altogether honest. But no one said much about it, for Ed Dupee and Dow Blair would fight at the drop of the hat. Though a score of little Pharisees went home and told their parents about the transaction, and then preened on their own virtue.

But all this is beside the point; it has so little to do with the Emporia semicentennial celebration, which is occupying Emporia to-day. The boy whose mind is being unraveled for this story recalls Emporia only as a sort of fairyland. He learned his letters from the Emporia News which papered the kitchen walls, and Emporia names were familiar to him. But the town was only a place where lived the rich and the great Judge Ruggles, and his family used to come down on the stage at times to hold court, and there is a memory of a day when as a child the boy saw store sleds—dreams beyond his wildest fancies—in front of Miss Plumb's store, but the memory picture does not have any apparent connection with anything else. As the boy grew older, Emporia things came to him—the murders chiefly, because such things appeal to boys—and later the town was associated with the name of Plumb. To us in the little town he was the symbol of political strength. He was the mighty one. He could make a postmaster. He was greater than Tom Ryan, though not so imposing looking. And as the boy grew older the town came out of its blur and became a thing of streets, with railroad cars running through it. And then came the riot and the soldiers to mark the town, and then Emporia boys used to appear in the boy's town who were too well-dressed to fight, and then the place ceased to be fairyland and became fact.

And so, perhaps, it will be with all those things of which we dream to-day. When the mist shall clear away, we shall see them as they are, and truth will be far more beautiful than our dreams.

•Here is the editorial on the death on White's daughter. Among all editorials ever published in American newspapers, it comes closest to being a genuine classic of literature.

MARY WHITE
(Emporia *Gazette*; May 17, 1921)

The Associated Press reports carrying the news of Mary White's death declared that it came as the result of a fall from a horse. How she would have hooted at that! She never fell from a horse in her life. Horses have fallen on her and with her—"I'm always trying to hold 'em in my lap," she used to say. But she was proud of few things, and one of them was that she could ride anything that had four legs and hair. Her death resulted not from a fall but from a blow on the head which fractured her skull, and the blow came from the limb of an overhanging tree on the parking.

The last hour of her life was typical of its happiness. She came home from a day's work at school, topped off by a hard grind with the copy on the high school annual, and felt that a ride would refresh her. She climbed into her khakis, chattering to her mother about the work she was doing, and hurried to get her horse and be out on the dirtroads for the country air and the radiant green fields of the spring. As she rode through the town on an easy gallop she kept waving at passers-by. She knew everyone in town. For a decade the little figure in the long pigtail and the red hair ribbon had been familiar on the streets of Emporia, and she got in the way of speaking to those who nodded at her. She passed the Kerrs, walking the horse, in front of the Normal Library, and waved at them; passed another friend a few hundred feet farther on, and waved at her. The horse was walking, and as she turned into North Merchant Street she took off her cowboy hat, and the horse swung into a lope. She passed the Tripletts and waved her cowboy hat at them, still moving gayly north on Merchant Street. A Gazette carrier passed—a high school boy friend—and she waved at him, but with her bridle hand; the horse veered quickly, plunged into the parking where the low-hanging limb faced her, and, while she still looked back waving, the blow came. But she did not fall from the horse; she slipped off, dazed a bit, staggered, and fell in a faint. She never quite recovered consciousness.

But she did not fall from the horse, neither was she riding fast. A year or so ago she used to go like the wind. But that habit was broken, and she used the horse to get into the open, to get fresh, hard exercise, and to work off a certain surplus energy that welled up in her and needed a physical outlet. That need has been in her heart for years. It was back of the impulse that kept the dauntless little brown-clad figure on the streets and country roads of the community and built into a strong, muscular body what had been a frail and sickly frame during the first years of her life. But the riding gave her more than a body. It released a gay and hardy soul. She was the happiest thing in the world. And she was happy because she was enlarging her horizon. She came to know all sorts and conditions of men; Charley O'Brien, the traffic cop, was one of her best friends. W.L. Holtz, the Latin teacher, was another. Tom O'Connor, farmer-politician, and Rev. J.H.J. Rice, preacher and police judge, and Frank Beach, music master, were her special friends, and all the girls, black and white, above the track and below the track, in Pepville and Stringtown, were among her acquaintances. She brought home riotous stories of her adventures. She loved to rollick; persiflage was her natural expression at home. Her humor was a continual bubble of joy. She seemed to think in hyperbole and metaphor. She was mischievous without malice, as full of faults as an old shoe. No angel was Mary White, but an easy girl to live with, for she never nursed a grouch five minutes in her life.

With all her eagerness for the out-of-doors, she loved books. On her table when she left her room were a book by Conrad, one by Galsworthy, Creative Chemistry by E.E. Slosson, and a Kipling book. She read Mark Twain, Dickens, and Kipling before she was ten—all of their writings. Wells and Arnold Bennett particularly amused and diverted her. She was entered as a student in Wellesley for 1922; was assistant editor of the high school annual this year, and in line for election to the editorship next year. She was a member of the executive committee of the high school Y.W.C.A.

Within the last two years she had begun to be moved by an ambition to draw. She began as most children do by scribbling in her schoolbooks, funny pictures. She bought cartoon magazines and took a course—rather casually, naturally, for she was, after all, a child with no strong purposes—and this year she tasted the first fruits of success by having her pictures accepted by the high school annual. But the thrill of delight she got when Mr. Ecord, of the Normal annual, asked her to do the cartooning for that book this spring, was too beautiful for words. She fell to her work with all her enthusiastic heart. Her drawings were accepted, and her pride—always repressed by a lively sense of the ridiculous figure she was cutting—was a really gorgeous thing to see. No successful artist ever drank a deeper draft of satisfaction than she took from the little fame her work was getting among her schoolfellows. In her glory, she almost forgot her horse—but never her car.

For she used the car as a jitney bus. It was her social life. She never had a "party" in all her nearly seventeen years—wouldn't have one; but she never drove a block in her life that she didn't begin to fill the car with pickups! Everybody rode with Mary White—white and black, old and young, rich and poor, men and women. She liked nothing better than to fill the car with long-legged high school boys and an occasional girl, and parade the town. She never had a "date," nor went to a dance, except once with her brother, Bill, and the "boy proposition" didn't interest her—yet. But young people—great spring-breading, varnish-cracking, fender-bending, door-sagging carloads of "kids"—gave her great pleasure. Her zests were keen. But the most fun she ever had in her life was acting as chairman of the committee that got up the big turkey dinner for the poor folks at the county home; scores of pies, gallons of slaw, jam, cakes, preserves, oranges, and a wilderness of turkey were loaded into the car and taken to the county home. And, being of a practical turn of mind, she risked her own Christmas dinner to see that the poor folks actually got it all. Not that she was a cynic; she just disliked to tempt folks. While there she found a blind colored uncle, very old, who could do nothing but make rag rugs, and she rustled up from her school friends rags enough to keep him busy for a season. The last engagement she tried to make was to take the guests at the county home out for a car ride. And the last endeavor of her life was to try to get a rest room for colored girls in the high school. She found one girl reading in the toilet, because there was no better place for a colored girl to loaf, and it inflamed her sense of injustice and she became a nagging harpy to those she thought could remedy the evil. The poor she always had with her and was glad of it. She hungered and thirsted for righteousness; and was the most impious creature in the world. She joined the church without consulting her parents, not particularly for her soul's good. She never had a thrill of piety in her life, and would have hooted at a "testimony." But even as a little child she felt the church was an agency for helping people to more of life's abundance, and she wanted to help. She never wanted help for herself. Clothes meant little to her. It was a fight to get a new rig on her; but eventually a harder fight to get it off. She never wore a jewel and had no ring but her high school class ring and never asked for anything but a wrist watch. She refused to have her hair up, though she was nearly seventeen. "Mother," she protested, "you don't know how much I get by with, in my braided pigtails, that I could not with my hair up." Above every other passion of her life was her passion not to grow up, to be a child. The tomboy in her, which was big, seemed to loath to be put away forever in skirts. She was a Peter Pan, who refused to grow up.

Her funeral yesterday at the Congregational Church was as she would have wished it; no singing, no flowers except the big bunch of red roses from her brother Bill's Harvard classmen—heavens, how proud that would have made her!—and the red roses from The Gazette forces, in vases at her head and feet. A short prayer; Paul's beautiful essay on "Love" from the Thirteenth Chapter of First Corinthians; some remarks about her democratic spirit by her friend, John H.J. Rice, pastor and police judge, which she would have deprecated if she could; a prayer sent down for her by her friend, Carl Nau; and opening the service the slow, poignant movement from Beethoven's Moonlight Sonata, which she loved; and closing the service a cutting from the joyously melancholy first movement of Tschaikowski's Pathetic Symphony, which she liked to hear in certain moods, on the phonograph; then the Lord's Prayer by her friends in high school.

That was all.

For her pallbearers only her friends were chosen: her Latin teacher, W.L. Holtz; her high school principal, Rice Brown; her doctor, Frank Foncannon; her friend, W.W. Finney; her pal at The Gazette office, Walter Hughes; and her brother Bill. It would have made her smile to know that her friend, Charley O'Brien, the traffic cop, had been transferred from Sixth and Commercial to the corner near the church to direct her friends who came to bid her good-by.

A rift in the clouds in a gray day threw a shaft of sunlight upon her coffin as her nervous, energetic little body sank to its last sleep. But the soul of her, the glowing, gorgeous, fervent soul of her, surely was flaming in eager joy upon some other dawn.

FRANK BUXTON EXPLAINS 'WHO MADE COOLIDGE'

Shortly after Calvin Coolidge had become president on the death of Warren G. Harding, Frank Buxton of the Boston *Herald* wrote an editorial using a simple rhetorical device that answered the question "Who made Coolidge?" Repeatedly asking the question, the editorial each time gave a short answer.

Although the editorial is distinctive for its structure, the announcement that it had won the 1924 Pulitzer Prize was met with criticism. Critics said that its thought was superficial and its form simple. *Editor and Publisher* said of it: "The editorial prize winner seems to us a labored effort, freakish, without deep penetration and lacking qualities of spontaneity and purpose that one would expect in an editorial selected for distinguished merit from the year's production. The author might have carried his musical inquiry back to the biological source of human existence."

In response to the criticism, it can be pointed that the editorial was not typical of most editorial style or structure. Its mood is a pleasing combination of humor and adulation. Rather than being superficial, one could argue, its reasoning attempted to get at fundamental factors in Coolidge's rise to the presidency. This rise, the editorial implied, was the result of a combination of Coolidge's acquaintances, his character, and happenstance. It recognized the essentials of Coolidge's gaining national prominence: his honesty and frugality, his handling of the Boston police strike of 1919, the political astuteness of Frank Stearns and Senator W. Murray Crane, and the long line of accidents favoring his fortunes.

WHO MADE COOLIDGE?
(Frank Buxton; Boston *Herald*; September 14, 1923)

"Who made Calvin Coolidge?"

Margaret Foley, of course. When Levis Greenwood was President of the Massachusetts Senate he opposed woman suffrage. She opposed his re-election in his district and prevailed. Senator Coolidge became President Coolidge on Beacon Hill and the signals were set clear for the road to the Governorship.

"Who made Calvin Coolidge?"

Edwin U. Curtis, of course. When he was a sick man in that old brick building at the dead-end of Pemberton Square, the heedless policemen went on strike to the refrain, "Hail, Hail, the Gang's All Here."

The sick man showed the strength of the stalwart, until finally Governor Coolidge sent a telegram to Samuel Gompers that tapped its way into national prominence, and is today a sort of Magna Charta of the people's rights.

"Who made Calvin Coolidge?"

James Lucey, the Northampton cobbler, of course. No explanation or argument is necessary here, but merely a reminder. The *Herald* published a facsimile a few days ago of President Coolidge's letter to him, which said: "If it were not for you, I should not be here."

"Who made Calvin Coolidge?"

Frank W. Stearns, of course. With as close an approximation to second sight as we may expect in these days, and with an ability to see around the corner years before Einstein told us how rays of light are bent, this substantial, self-made, self-respecting Boston merchant, with his quiet sense of obligation to the community, discerned qualities which hardly anyone else glimpsed. To go to the Republican Convention he left a Governor only to come back to pay his respects to a potential Vice-President.

"Who made Calvin Coolidge?"

Senator Crane, of course. He made Coolidge by showing him, in precept and practice, the way of wisdom and by vouching for him in high places where his chance say-so was as good as his oath and bond. To the younger man he gave that mixture of personal attachment and respect of which he was none too prodigal, but always of mighty advantage to the few who won it.

"Who made Calvin Coolidge?"

The Republican Party of Massachusetts, of course, a canny organization, with some Bourbonism, some democracy, some vision, some solid traditions and no end of genuine appreciation of the merits of a trustworthy man. It always lined up behind him solidly even when he displayed that reticence which to the unknowing was some evidence of ingratitude, and to the knowing was merely Coolidgeism.

"Who made Calvin Coolidge?"

The people of Massachusetts, of course. They took him at more than his own modest valuation, whether he wanted to be a town officer or a Governor. They had that which thousands call a blind faith in him. More thousands called it a passionate intuition.

"Who made Calvin Coolidge?"

His mother, of course, who endowed him with her own attributes; a father that taught him prudential ways with all the quiet vigor of the old Greeks, who preached moderation in everything; his school and his college; his classmate, Dwight Morrow; and his guest of a day or two ago at the White House, William F. Whiting.

"Who made Calvin Coolidge?"

Calvin Coolidge, of course. From the reflective shoemaker and the furious Miss Foley to the complacent Frank W. Stearns and the watchful and discerning Senator from Dalton came some of the makings, but the man himself had the essentials of greatness. Give another man those same foes and friends and he might still be as far from the White House as most sons of Vermont.

WALTER LIPPMANN BLAMES SOCIETY FOR THE 'BOBBED-HAIRED BANDIT'

One of the greatest thinkers among American journalists, Walter Lippmann was also one of the best editorial writers of the 20th century. A writer for the New York *World* from 1922 to 1929 and editor until the paper died in a 1931 merger, he was erudite, even intellectual. He combined intelligence and detached reasoning with a polished writing style, thus allowing him to provide clear analysis of even the most complex issues.

Simplifying the issues, he felt, had grown in importance as society and its problems had increased in complexity. Even though problems had gotten "subtler and greater," he still thought in terms of fundamental principles and was able to isolate primary causes and effects from the vast confusion of details. His analytical ability resulted to a large degree from the fact that he did not get closely involved in issues, but remained detached, as if he were observing a drama rather than acting in it.

To make his analysis clear, Lippmann emphasized clarity in writing and excellence in style. A painstaking craftsman, he gave meticulous attention to his writing, tirelessly reworking and polishing it. He chose words precisely, so that his editorials became models of lucidity and vividness. When once he caught James M. Cain, a *World* writer and later a novelist, in a grammatical error, he exclaimed, "You, of all men!" Although most of his writing was scholarly and subtle, he could, when he wished, write with real power; and his masterful interpretive prose sometimes read, one critic said, like "a kind of ominous drum-roll."

Lippmann's best editorial, "Cecilia Cooney," thrives from his writing style and his incisive analysis, and is one of his editorials marked by passion rather than detachment. He wrote it two weeks after the 20-year-old woman had been arrested for a series of robberies. For several months, the attractive "bobbed-haired bandit" and her husband had made the front pages of New York's sensationalized papers. As Lippmann pointed out, however, the record of Cecilia's life was not nearly as glamorous as the picture reporters had painted. After detailing the young woman's background, he placed the blame on society for its failure to act when early in Cecilia's life her vicious environment had become apparent.

CECILIA COONEY
(Walter Lippmann; New York *World*; May 8, 1924)

For some months now we have been vastly entertained by the bobbed-haired bandit. Knowing nothing about her, we created a perfect story, standardized according to the rules laid down by the movies and the short-story magazines. The story had, as the press agents say, everything. It had a flapper and a bandit who baffled the police; it had sex and money, crime and mystery. And then yesterday we read in the probation officer's report the story of Cecilia Cooney's life. It was not in the least entertaining. For there in the place of the dashing bandit was a pitiable girl; instead of an amusing tale, a dark and mean tragedy; instead of a lovely adventure, a terrible accusation.

In the 20 years she has lived in this city she has come at one time or another within the reach of all the agencies of righteousness. Five years before she was born her father was summoned to court for drunkenness and neglect; the Charities Department recommended then that her older brothers and sisters be committed to an institution. That did not prevent her parents bringing, with the full consent of the law, three or four more children into the world. Cecilia herself, the youngest of eight, came at four years of age into the custody of the Children's Society. Six months later, on the recommendation of the Department of Public Charity, she was turned back to her mother, who promptly deserted her.

She was next taken to Brooklyn by her aunt and for ten years or so attended parochial school. At the age of 14 her mother brought her back to New York, took her to a furnished room, stole her clothes and deserted her. A year later, aged 15, Cecilia became a child-laborer in a brush factory in Brooklyn, and was associating at night with sailors picked up on the water-front. At 16 Cecilia was back in New York, living with her mother, working as a laundress for a few months at a stretch in various hospitals. At 20 she was married, had borne a child, had committed a series of robberies, and is condemned to spend the rest of her youth in prison.

This is what twentieth-century civilization in New York achieved in the case of Cecilia Cooney. Fully warned by the behavior of her parents long before the birth, the law allowed her parents to reproduce their kind. Fully warned when she was still an infant, society allowed her to drift out of its hand into a life of dirt, neglect, dark basements, begging, stealing, ignorance, poor little tawdry excitements and twisted romance. The courts had their chance and missed it. Schools had their chance and missed it. The church had its chance and missed it. The absent-minded routine of all that is well-meaning and respectable did not deflect by an inch her inexorable progress from the basement where she was born to the jail where she will expiate her crimes and ours.

For her crimes are on our heads, too. No record could be clearer or more eloquent. None could leave less room for doubt that Cecilia Cooney is a product of this city, of its neglect and its carelessness, of its indifference and its undercurrents of misery. We recommend her story to the pulpits of New York, to the school men of New York, to the lawmakers of New York, to the social workers of New York, to those who are tempted to boast of its wealth, its magnificence and its power.

EDWARD KINGSBURY GUIDES A TOUR THROUGH 'THE HOUSE OF A HUNDRED SORROWS'

The New York *Times*, like many other newspapers, at one time was in the habit of compiling a list of the neediest people in its city and sponsoring drives to help them during the Christmas season. The problem for the editorial writer who must write such a yearly piece is how to avoid cliché.

For his editorial urging help with the *Times'* "One Hundred Neediest," Edward M. Kingsbury won the 1926 Pulitzer Prize. Structured as if it were taking the reader on a visit to a building filled with people in need, the editorial has a distinctive approach. It also shows true sympathy and concern for the needy.

Kingsbury was the same writer who had authored "The Oldest Living Graduate" for the New York *Sun*. Edward P. Mitchell, editor of the *Sun*, said Kingsbury was unique for his "exquisite humor, fine wit, broad literary appreciation and originality of idea and phrase." The executive secretary of the Pulitzer Advisory Board said that although the Pulitzer Prize was awarded to Kingsbury on the basis of his "brilliant" previous work, the award was made primarily because of this one "beautiful" editorial.

THE HOUSE OF A HUNDRED SORROWS
(Edward M. Kingsbury; New York *Times*; December 14, 1925)

The walls are grimy and discolored. The uneven floors creak and yield under foot. Staircases and landings are rickety and black. The door of every room is open. Walk along these corridors. Walk into this room. Here is a sickly boy of 5, deserted by his mother, underfed, solitary in the awful solitude of starved neglected childhood. "Seldom talks." Strange, isn't it? Some, many children, never "prattle," like your darlings. They are already old. They are full, perhaps, of long, hopeless thoughts. There are plenty of other "kids" in this tenement. Here is one, only 3. Never saw his father. His mother spurned and abused him. He is weak and "backward." How wicked of him when he has been so encouraged and coddled! Do children play? Not his kind. They live to suffer.

In Room 24 is Rose, a housemother of 10. Father is in the hospital. Mother is crippled with rheumatism. Rose does all the work. You would love Rose if she came out of Dickens. Well, there she is, mothering her mother in Room 24. In Room 20 age has been toiling for youth. Grandmother has been taking care of three granddaughters who lost their mother. A brave old woman; but what with rheumatism and heart weakness, threescore-and-ten can't go out to work any more. What's going to happen to her and her charges? Thinking of that, she is ill on top of her physical illness. A very interesting house, isn't it, Sir? Decidedly "a rum sort of place," Madam? Come into Room 23. Simon, the dollmaker—but handmade dolls are "out"—lives, if you call it living, here. Eighty years old, his wife of about the same age. Their eyesight is mostly gone. Otherwise they would still be sewing on buttons and earning a scanty livelihood for themselves and two little girls, their grandchildren. The girls object to going to an orphan home. Some children are like that.

You must see those twin sisters of 65 in Room 47. True, they are doing better than usual on account of the coming holidays; making as much as $10 a month, whereas their average is but $6. Still, rents are a bit high; and the twins have been so long together that they would like to stay so. In Room—but you need no guide. Once in The House of a Hundred Sorrows you will visit every sad chamber in it. If your heart be made of penetrable stuff, you will do the most you can to bring hope and comfort to its inmates, to bring them Christmas and the Christ.

For I was ahungred, and ye gave me meat: I was thirsty, and ye gave me drink: I was a stranger, and ye took me in.

Naked, and ye clothed me: I was sick, and ye visited me: I was in prison, and ye came unto me.

GROVER HALL RIDICULES RACISM AND BIGOTRY

The revival of the Ku Klux Klan became a major problem in the 1920s. In few other places was it as bad as in Alabama, where the Klan gained gruesome control of government at all levels. By 1927, a year in which both of the state's U.S. senators were Klan members, the organization had become daringly bold. The ministry and the press, whose ranks contained a number of KKK sympathizers, remained silent at the Klan's outrages.

But the Klan had at least one opponent among Alabama's journalists, Grover C. Hall, editor of the *Montgomery Advertiser*. Born in Alabama in 1888, he joined the *Advertiser* in 1910 and was trained in its "tradition of tolerance." He was named editor in 1926.

In July of the following year, his anger and indignation ignited by the flogging of a young black man at a rural church, Hall opened fire on the Klan. He followed with a four-month campaign to bring the responsible Klansmen to justice, to expose the Klan as brutish and cowardly, and to get legislation enacted that would limit its activities, including a law to prohibit the wearing of masks in public.

State action did result. As a consequence of Hall's campaign, victims of floggings, too frightened before, talked to law officers and journalists; numerous Klansmen were convicted; and the number of floggings in Alabama declined dramatically.

For his campaign, Hall was awarded the 1928 Pulitzer, the first year in which the award was given for no specific editorial but for a series. The two editorials included here demonstrate the quality and power of Hall's writing. "We Predict a Freeze" is a fine example that an editorial can make a point forcefully with a minimum of words. "Our Tom" is scathing ridicule of Sen. Tom Heflin.

WE PREDICT A FREEZE
(Grover C. Hall; Montgomery *Advertiser*, August 14, 1927)

The fiery cross is not a permanent source of heat. It will burn out, leaving only charred remains fit only for use in 4 1/2 gallon kegs. Those politicians who thought it was to be as long-lived as the sun and accordingly resolved to keep themselves warm by it alone, will presently find themselves shivering in the cold. Then if they ask the faithful keepers of the constitutional home-fires for a blanket, they will be given a bedsheet and told to be on their way.

OUR TOM
(Grover C. Hall, Montgomery *Advertiser*, 1927)

A bully by nature, a mountebank by instinct, a Senator by choice. Conceited and vain as the peacock is, but not proud as the nobleman is, for a choicer spirit would be too proud to assail the weak. He is bombastic and blustery, but is wanting in high courage; certainly he is wanting in that valor which scorns advantage, otherwise he would not select the class with the fewest votes in Alabama on which to heap contumely and indignities. The Roman Catholics cast less than two per cent of the total vote in Alabama. If they had political power in this state Tom would be afraid of them, for he is quite the biggest 'fraid cat in the United States senate, even as he is about the grossest demagogue there. Tom has spent a lifetime studying the art of dodging dangerous issues and otherwise playing safe.

Heflin hates and suspects the personal honor of all men who oppose his boundless ambition. In controversy he is intellectually without scruples, he is slanderous, cruel, cheap and absurd, and without a generous emotion. The monkeyshine is the only light he is capable of casting on any serious public question. Dressed like an Al Field tenor, Tom is gifted with the humor of mimicry, as Bert Swor is, but is entirely wanting in the higher quality of wit, for while the sight of an audience is to him the signal to release a deluge of words, an art long practiced by him, Tom never in his life fashioned an epigram. His diction is too sloppy even if his intelligence could provide the thought on which to hang the dainty language that adorns the epigram. He is a ham actor metamorphosed into a United States senator by a sorry trick of fate that invested Tom with lofty aspiration and immense gall. He is a clown on the platform and only as an entertainer is he interesting, for he is ill-informed, inaccurate in thought and unreliable in statement. But a hero to thousands nevertheless! Yet all of his daring has been spent in killing phantom dragons and doing battle with armored straw knights.

Good taste? Sense of propriety? Such terms merely amuse Tom. Fairness? Courtesy? Such qualities under the Heflin code are but signs of weakness in men and need not be respected by a gent with a mission and without a muzzle.

Thus this preposterous blob excites our pity if not our respect, and we leave him to his conscience in order that he may be entirely alone and meditate over the life of a charlatan whose personal interest and personal vanity are always of paramount concern to him.

LOUIS ISAAC JAFFE WINS APPROVAL FOR ANTI-LYNCHING LAW

In the 1920s, when the revival of the Ku Klux Klan gave it a bigger heyday than it had enjoyed during Reconstruction, lynchings were considered local offenses. State prosecution had few supporters.

A leader of the movement for state anti-lynching laws was Louis Isaac Jaffe, editor of the *Virginian-Pilot.* In the mid-'20s he outlined plans for a law in Virginia and finally convinced Governor Harry Flood Byrd to propose a law to the legislature. When the bill was adopted in 1938, Byrd said Jaffe's editorials "had more to do than any other single outside urging in convincing me that I should make one of my major recommendations the passage of a drastic anti-lynching law providing that lynching be a specific state offense."

But Jaffe did not rest after enactment of the Virginia law. He urged a national law. Following a lynching in Houston, Texas, on the eve of the 1928 Democratic National Convention, he wrote "An Unspeakable Act of Savagery." Although Congress would delay in enacting anti-lynching legislation, Jaffe's editorial sparked national interest in such law. For his campaign, Jaffe received the 1929 Pulitzer Prize, with the jury specifically mentioning the following editorial.

AN UNSPEAKABLE ACT OF SAVAGERY
(Louis Isaac Jaffe; Norfolk *Virginian-Pilot;* June 22, 1928)

As the Democratic hosts prepare to rededicate themselves anew to fairness and justice, the bustling Southern city in which they are to meet is disgraced by an unspeakable act of savagery. There is no other way to describe the performance of the eight armed white men who yanked Robert Powell, 24-year-old Negro, from a hospital cot on which he lay with a bullet in his stomach, and hanged him from a bridge just outside the city. Powell was under the charge of killing a detective in a shooting match from which he himself emerged with an apparently mortal wound. In the event of his recovery, he was headed for the courts. But to this Texas mob neither Death nor Justice was an acceptable arbiter. Nothing would satisfy them but a loathsome act of murder carried out against a human being while he lay in agony with a bullet in his entrails.

Houston, which is said not to have had a lynching in fifty years, is understandably stirred by this foul thing laid on its doorstep just when it was most anxious to show itself to the world at its cleanest. The City Council made an immediate appropriation of $10,000 for an investigation to be carried out by a committee representative of both races. A grand jury has been ordered to drop all other business to conduct an immediate inquiry. The Governor has offered a reward for the capture of each participant in the lynching and sent a special detail of Texas Rangers to assist the Houston police in the hunt. Apparently the spotlight that beats on Houston at this particular time has had something to do with the energy with which the authorities have acted. Ordinarily, Texas proceeds in these matters with considerably less dispatch and excitement. But this is no time to inquire too closely into motives. One of the proudest cities of Texas has been polluted by one of the foulest forms of mob murder, and it is a matter for general satisfaction that the authorities are moving so energetically to repair the damage to Texas' good name. If the perseverance of the authorities is in keeping with their initial burst of energy, one or more of the group that bravely did to death a crippled man lying on a hospital cot may see the inside of the Texas penitentiary.

The year that saw four months pass without a single lynching has now accumulated five of them. Five lynchings in six months represent a proportional reduction in savagery from last year's record of sixteen lynchings in twelve months, but the year is only half gone and no one may be too confident. We have come a long way from the dark days of 1892 when America celebrated the 400th anniversary of its discovery with 255 lynchings, but we have not yet arrived at that social abhorrence of this crime that must precede its practical extinction. When eight presumably decent and rational beings can gain the consent of their conscience to rob a hospital bed for the purpose of executing summary vengeance, and when, as was the case a few days ago in Louisiana, two Negroes are torn from their guards and lynched because they were brothers of another Negro who was accused of murder, it must be recognized that the rise and fall of the lynching curve is governed by racial passions that remain still to be brought under civilized control.

Charles Ryckman Satirizes
'The Gentleman from Nebraska'

Effective satire is used rarely by editorial writers. Charles Ryckman's biting 1931 Pulitzer Prize winner gleams from the sea of analytical, reasoned ones. Even its title, "The Gentleman from Nebraska," was tongue in cheek.

As might have been expected, it also was controversial. From a conservative Republican newspaper, the editorial was—depending on whose interpretation you accept—either an attack on Nebraska's progressive Republican Senator George W. Norris or a poke at the paradoxical political behavior of the state's provincial voters. It was an attempt to explain humorously why Nebraska voters continued to send Norris to Congress when he seemed more interested in other parts of the world than in Nebraska. While Norris undertook such crusades as attempting to have the federal government sell electricity from federally built hydroelectric plants directly to consumers rather than to private electric companies and to prevent federal subversion of civil rights, Ryckman charged that he did little more for Nebraska than make himself objectionable to federal officials.

Liberals charged that the editorial was an underhanded, cruel, bad-tempered attack on Norris. Conservatives said it was a well-done explanation of the paradox of Nebraskans supporting the liberal Norris while their other political heroes were conservative. Nebraska's citizens thought it was an attempt to smear Norris and insult their intelligence.

THE GENTLEMAN FROM NEBRASKA
(Charles S. Ryckman; Fremont [Neb.] *Tribune*; November 7, 1930)

Senator George W. Norris, never lacking a mandate from the people of Nebraska in the course he has pursued as a member of the United States senate, now returns to Washington doubly assured of the unquestioned approval of his state and its people.

The senatorial record of Mr. Norris, with all its ramifications, has been endorsed in as convincing a manner as anyone could wish. Many reasons have been advanced as to why such an endorsement should not be extended to him. The opposition to Norris has been conducted as ably and as thoroughly as any group of capable politicians could do the job. The candidacy of as fine a statesman as Nebraska ever produced has been presented to the state as an alternative to that of Mr. Norris, and has been rejected.

Acceptance of the situation is therefore a matter without choice. To continue the argument is to waste words. The opposition to Senator Norris has been so completely subdued and so thoroughly discredited that further jousting with the windmill is more quixotic than Quixote himself.

There is not even good reason for being disgruntled over the result. For the purpose of the Nebraska political situation, 70,000 people can't be wrong. The will of the state is seldom expressed in so tremendous a majority, and it must be taken not only as an endorsement of Mr. Norris but also as at least a temporary quietus upon his critics and opponents.

The state of Nebraska has elected Norris to the United States senate this year, as it has many times in the past, mainly because he is not wanted there. If his return to Washington causes discomfiture in official circles, the people of Nebraska will regard their votes as not having been cast in vain. They do not want farm relief or any other legislative benefits a senator might bring them; all they want is a chance to sit back and gloat.

Nebraska nurses an ingrowing grouch against America in general and eastern America in particular. The state expects nothing from the national government, which it regards as largely under eastern control, and asks nothing. It has lost interest in constructive participation in federal affairs, and its people are in a vindictive frame of mind.

This grouch is cultural as much as political. Nebraska and its people have been the butt of eastern jokesters so long they are embittered. Every major federal project of the last half century has been disadvantageous to them. The building of the Panama canal imposed a discriminatory rate burden upon them. Various reclamation projects have increased agricultural competition. Federal tariff policies increase the cost of living in Nebraska without material benefit to Nebraska producers.

Nebraska voters have long since ceased to look to Washington for relief, and they no longer select their congressional representatives with relief in view. Neither George Norris nor any of his Nebraska colleagues in congress have been able to combat this hopeless situation. If Norris were forced to rely upon what he has done in congress for Nebraska, he would approach an election day with fear in his heart.

But Senator Norris has found another way to serve Nebraska. By making himself objectionable to federal administrators without regard to political complexion and to eastern interests of every kind, he has afforded Nebraskans a chance to vent their wrath. He is, perhaps unwittingly, an instrument of revenge.

The people of Nebraska would not listen to George Norris long enough to let him tell them how to elect a dog catcher in the smallest village in the state, but they have been sending him to the senate so long it is a habit. If he lives long enough and does not get tired of the job, he will spend more years in the upper house of congress than any man before him. Death, ill health or personal disinclination—one of these may some day drive him out of the senate, but the people of Nebraska never will!

The state asks little of him in return. It gives him perfect freedom of movement and of opinion. It holds him to no party or platform. It requires no promises of him, no pledges. He need have no concern for his constituency, is under no obligation to people or to politicians. He can devote as much of his time as he likes to the Muscle Shoals power site, and none at all to western Nebraska irrigation projects. He can vote for the low tariff demanded by cane sugar producers of Cuba, while the beet sugar growers of Nebraska are starving to death. He can interest himself in political scandals in Pennsylvania, and be wholly unconcerned over the economic plight of the Nebraska farmer.

He can do all these things, and be as assured of election as the seashore is of the tide. He could spend campaign year in Europe, and beat a George Washington in a republican primary and an Abraham Lincoln in a general election.

And yet, George Norris is not a political power in Nebraska. The people of other states believe he is revered as an idol in his own state. As a matter of fact, he is probably held in lower esteem in Nebraska than in any other state in the union.

His endorsement of another candidate is of no real value. He could not throw a hatful of votes over any political fence in the state. He gave his tacit support to La Follette as a third party presidential candidate in 1924, and the Wisconsin senator could have carried all his Nebraska votes in his hip pocket without a bulge. He came into Nebraska in 1928 with a fanfare of democratic trumpets and of radio hook-ups, stumped the state for Governor Smith—and Nebraska gave Herbert Hoover the largest majority, on a basis of percentage, of all the states in the union.

As far as the people of Nebraska are concerned George Norris is as deep as the Atlantic ocean in Washington, and as shallow as the Platte river in his own state.

The explanation of this fascinating political paradox is to be found not in an analysis of Norris, but of Nebraska. As a senator, Norris has given Nebraska something the state never had before. He has put the "Gentleman from Nebraska" on every front page in America, and has kept him there. A resident of Nebraska can pick up the latest edition of a New York daily or of an Arizona weekly, and find "Norris of Nebraska" in at least three type faces.

But the publicity Norris gets for Nebraska is not the whole story. His real strength in Nebraska is measured by the antagonisms he stirs up beyond the borders of the state. His people take delight in setting him on the heels of the ruling powers, whether of government, of finance or of industry. The more he makes himself obnoxious to a political party, to a national administration or to Wall street, the better they like him.

Nebraska is not interested in the smallest degree in what progress he makes, or what he accomplishes. It has been said of Norris that he has cast more negative votes against winning causes and more affirmative votes for lost causes than any other man in the senate. But every time he succeeds in pestering his prey until it turns around and snarls back at him, the chuckles can be heard all the way from Council Bluffs to Scottsbluff.

The summary of it all is that Nebraska derives a great deal of pleasure out of shoving George Norris down the great American throat. He has been an effective emetic in republican and democratic administrations alike, has worried every president from Taft to Hoover. His retirement from the senate, whether voluntary or forced, would be welcomed in more quarters than that of any of his colleagues.

The people of Nebraska know this, and enjoy it. Every time Norris baits the power trust or lambasts the social lobby, Nebraska gets the same amusement out of his antics that a small boy gets out of siccing a dog on an alley cat. When he shies a brickbat at a president, Nebraska has as much fun as a kid pushing over an outhouse.

You have to know the isolation of the hinterland to understand why this is so. Nebraska has sent many men to the senate who were more capable than Norris, as his predecessors and as his contemporaries. It has had other senators who have done more for the state and for the nation than he has.

But it has never had another senator who let the whole world know there was a "Gentleman from Nebraska" in the manner he has succeeded in doing. Nebraska could send a succession of great men and good men to the senate, and the east and west and south would never know there was a state of Nebraska or that such a state was represented in the senate. But Norris lets them know there is a Nebraska, and Nebraska does not care how he does it.

There is an instinctive resentment in the hearts of these people of the states between the Mississippi and the mountains against the failure of the far east to understand and appreciate the middle west. It crops up in politics, in religion, even in sports.

Nebraska is one of the richest of all the agricultural states and yet the wealth of its industries exceeds that of its farms. It has given such names as Gutzon Borglum, Willa Cather, John J. Pershing, William G. Dawes, William Jennings Bryan and a hundred others of prominence to the nation. It has unsurpassed schools, progressive cities and towns, people of intelligence and culture.

And yet the rest of the nation persists in regarding Nebraska as provincial, its people as backward. If the east thinks of Nebraska at all, it is as a state still in a frontier period. The national conception of a Nebraskan is that of a big hayshaker, with a pitchfork in his hands, a straw in his mouth, a musical comedy goatee on his chin, a patch on the seat of his overalls and the muck of the barnyard on his boots.

Nebraska has resented these indignities, but has given up hope of avoiding them. Its only hope is to pay back in kind. In the days of the real frontier, it vented its wrath on the occasional luckless tenderfoot from the east. Now it sends George Norris to the senate.

Norris does not represent Nebraska politics. He is the personification of a Nebraska protest against the intellectual aloofness of the east. A vote for Norris is cast into the ballot box with all the venom of a snowball thrown at a silk hat. The spirit that puts him over is vindictive, retaliatory. Another senator might get federal projects, administrative favor, post offices and pork barrel plunder for Nebraska, but the state is contemptuous of these. For nearly two decades Norris has kept Nebraska beyond the pale of federal favor, but his people consider him worth the price.

George Norris is the burr Nebraska delights in putting under the eastern saddle. He is the reprisal for all the jokes of vaudevillists, the caricatures of cartoonists and the jibes of humorists that have come out of the east in the last quarter of a century.

RONALD CALLVERT SINGS
A SONG TO AMERICA

As the world became slowly entangled in the tragedies that led to World War II, the American press—as it had done during the era of the first global war—again took on a cloak of patriotism. A presage of things to come was Ronald Callvert's editorial "My Country 'Tis of Thee...," a patriotic song of America. Like few other editorials, it was blatantly lyrical, an effect gained by its repetition of the phrase "in this land of ours, this America."

As luck would have it, Callvert wrote the editorial because another writer was unavailable. When he thought of the idea, Callvert said, "it occurred to me as a good editorial for Ben Hur Lampman to write." Lampman was noted for his lightness of touch as an *Oregonian* editorialist.

The editorial quickly drew the attention of readers and of churches, schools, and patriotic organizations. To meet the demand for reprints, the *Oregonian* issued the editorial in leaflet form and distributed more than 14,000 copies. It received journalism's highest honor when judges selected Callvert for the 1939 Pulitzer Prize and pointed out "My Country 'Tis of Thee... " as exemplary of his work.

MY COUNTRY 'TIS OF THEE...
(Ronald G. Callvert; Portland *Oregonian*; October 2, 1938)

In this land of ours, this America, the man we choose as leader dons at no time uniform or insignia to denote his constitutional position as Commander in Chief of armed forces. No member of his Cabinet, no civil subordinate, ever attires himself in garments significant of military power.

In this land of ours, this America, the average citizen sees so little of the army that he has not learned to distinguish between a major and a lieutenant from his shoulder straps. When the Chief Executive addresses his fellow-countrymen they gather about him within handclasp distance. Goose-stepping regiments are not paraded before him. When he speaks to the civilian population it is not over rank upon rank of helmeted heads.

In this land of ours, this America, there is no tramp of military boots to entertain the visiting statesman. There is no effort to affright him with display of mobile cannon or of facility for mass production of aerial bombers.

In this land of ours, this America, there is no fortification along the several thousand miles of the northern border. In the great fresh water seas that partly separate it from another dominion no naval craft plies the waters. Along its southern border there are no forts, no show of martial strength.

In this land of ours, this America, no youth is conscripted to labor on device of defense; military training he may take or leave at option. There is no armed force consistent with a policy of aggression. The navy is built against no menace from the Western Hemisphere, but wholly for defense against that which may threaten from Europe or Asia.

In this land of ours, this America, one-third of the population is foreign born or native born of foreign or mixed parentage. Our numerous "minorities" come from fourteen nations. The native born, whatever his descent, has all political and other rights possessed by him who traces his ancestry to the founding fathers. The foreign born of races that are assimilable are admitted to all these privileges if they want them. We have "minorities" but no minority problem.

In this land of ours, this America, the common citizen may criticize without restraint the policies of his government or the aims of the Chief Executive. He may vote as his judgment or his conscience advises and not as a ruler dictates.

In this land of ours, this America, our songs are dedicated to love and romance, the blue of the night, sails in the sunset, and not to might or to a martyrdom to political cause. Our national anthem has martial words; difficult air. But if you want to hear the organ roll give the people its companion—"America... of thee I sing." In lighter patriotism we are nationally cosmopolitan. Unitedly we sing of Dixie or of Ioway, where the tall corn grows, of Springtime in the Rockies, or of California, here I come.

In this land of ours, this America, there is not a bomb-proof shelter, and a gas mask is a curiosity. It is not needed that we teach our children where to run when deathhawks darken the sky.

In this land of ours, this America, our troubles present or prospective come from within—come from our own mistakes, and injure us alone. Our pledges of peace toward our neighbors are stronger than ruler's promise or written treaty. We guarantee them by devoting our resources, greater than the resources of any other nation, to upbuilding the industries of peace. We strut no armed might that could be ours. We cause no nation in our half of the world to fear us. None does fear us, nor arm against us.

In this land of ours, this America, we have illuminated the true road to permanent peace. But that is not the sole moral sought herein to be drawn. Rather it is that the blessings of liberty and equality and peace that have been herein recounted are possessed nowhere in the same measure in Europe or Asia and wane or disappear as one nears or enters a land of dictatorship of whatever brand. This liberty, this equality, this peace, are imbedded in the American form of government. We shall ever retain them if foreign isms that would dig them out and destroy them are barred from our shores. If you cherish this liberty, this equality, this peace that is peace material and peace spiritual—then defend with all your might the American ideal of government.

BART HOWARD DESCRIBES
THE EMPEROR OF EUROPE

Bart Howard was known for his skill at capturing a situation with a phrase and for the sparkle of his writing. He was especially fond of graphic description and alliteration. These characteristics are apparent in the editorials included in his entry for the 1940 Pulitzer Prize.

More than for his talent, however, Howard surpassed other editorial writers because, said a fellow staffer on the St. Louis *Post-Dispatch*, of his sincerity, his "deep and abiding convictions," and a "great faith in the dignity of the individual and in the validity of democracy."

The following editorial—analyzing Adolph Hitler's conquests —was typical of his work. It makes apparent his use of language and was prophetic in its vision of the destruction that Hitler would bring to Europe.

EUROPE'S EMPEROR
(Bart Howard; St. Louis *Post-Dispatch*; March 17, 1939)

The massive memory of Bismarck shrivels in the blazing sun of Adolf Hitler's conquests. The former won by "blood and iron" utilizing intrigue as a preface. The latter wins by strategy of conference, fortified by force, to be sure, and punctuated by the threat of marching armies.

Schuschnigg is summoned to Berchtesgaden for an afternoon in the torture chamber, and Austria is expunged from the map while Vienna becomes Berlin's scrubwoman.

How many a plotting hour ticked secretly across the clock as Hitler suggested and Henlein acquiesced may only be surmised. But at last the Sudeten Germans, under superb coaching, were letter-perfect in their parts, and the Reich was ready to rescue their brothers from the tyranny of "ruthless Czecho-Slovakia." What would the neighbors say—the great Powers pledged to safeguard that one green isle of democracy in stormy Central Europe? France was explicitly committed; Russia conditionally; England impliedly. Chamberlain made his pilgrimage to the Fuehrer's mountain retreat, and later, with Daladier, consented to the pillage of the little Republic at Munich's midnight.

With Austria and the Sudetenland securely possessed and the plunder respectably approved, Herr Hitler's hunger was satisfied, rapacity was foresworn, there would be no more raids in Europe. "The Sudetenland," said Hitler at the Berlin Sportspalast on September 26, 1938, "is the last territorial demand I have to make in Europe." And in an earlier September speech at Nuremberg, he said he had given the guaranty to Chamberlain: "We do not want any Czechs any more."

England believed, officially. So did France. Russia refused to be deceived, distrusting Hitler's vow and subsequently impugning the motives of both Chamberlain and Daladier. Russia's suspicions have been frightfully vindicated, and today London and Paris join with Moscow in pronouncing worthless the word of Hitler. And Mussolini's Rome, at the other end of the paper axis, sees in the once barred doors of the Brenner Pass an open gateway for a Colossus in growing pains.

In Dr. Tiso of Slovakia, Hitler seems to have found a craftier confederate than Henlein of the shriekingly managed Sudeten affair. Or perhaps Der Fuehrer has acquired a more polished technique. Surely the consummate skill of this latest coup, that caught the world flat-footed, may not be denied. Machiavelli could write it. Hitler does it. The revolt of Slovakia, inspired, promoted and directed in Berlin, is a masterpiece of statecraft. Moralists may deplore. Lights may burn late in sleepless chancelleries. The thing is done. A *fait accompli*, in the language of diplomacy, and the architect of the German Empire awakes in the historic castle of centuries-old Prague to breakfast contentedly and to count his gains.

He counts his gains realistically. Slovakia's independence lived but a day. Tiso, the politician, may now turn back to the priestly beads he seemingly had forsaken. The swastika is his country's flag.

What a vulturous Ides of March for the ravished, murdered homeland which Masaryk's genius had guided into the stature of a fine nation! The swastika flies over Bohemia and Moravia, and Hungary comes up from the south to seize Carpatho-Ukraine, with Poland ghoulishly hurrying to the feast of death.

The German Empire, territorially, is might today, and Hitler has inventoried the spoils with barbaric gusto.

The continental balance of power, deftly maintained, with grave lapses, of course, by Britain's ministerial jugglery, trembles under the tread of Europe's Emperor.

MASTERS OF THE EDITORIAL

BEN HUR LAMPMAN:
MASTER OF EDITORIAL POETRY

Readers of the Portland *Oregonian*, it was said, would turn to the editorial page even before they read page one news, sports, or the comic strips. Newsboys were known to hawk the newspaper by crying, "Ben Hur Lampman's done it again!"

The creator of such rare newspaper excitement made his reputation in the remote Pacific Northwest and, in editorial writing, by writing about subjects that newspapers often neglected. Dead dogs, missing cats, falling autumn leaves, and jumping fish in mountain streams were the subjects that found life in the works of Lampman, editorial writer for the *Oregonian* from 1922 to 1954. His writing, rhythmic to the point of being poetic, established him as America's foremost editorial essayist, in the 20th century at least, on nature subjects. Rarely has an editorial writer received such high praise from his peers as did Lampman. "He has written," a fellow *Oregonian* staffer declared, "many editorial articles... , all marked by sincerity, knowledge, facility, and by rare humor, and often by great beauty. The range of his topics is astonishing. He has a distinguished style, and he never fails to make his point." Lampman, a reviewer wrote, "tugs at your heartstrings and challenges your humanity in solid, exquisite writing."

Lampman was born August 12, 1886, in Barron, Wisconsin, where his father owned the weekly newspaper. In Neche, North Dakota, four years later, his father founded another weekly, *The Chronotype*. It frequently faced financial problems because the elder Lampman practiced a "hew to the line" editorial policy even when it angered advertisers. Although Ben had no formal training in writing—unless it was an early fondness for poetry—he found himself working, as his father had done, in the newspaper business. By the time he was 15, he had left school and was on his own, working in Canada and the western wheat country. When he was only 19, he started his own weekly, the Michigan (N.D.) *Arena*. He published it for seven years, until 1912 when he moved, with his young schoolteacher wife, to Gold Hill, Oregon. There he became editor and publisher of the Gold Hill *News* and captured a loyal following among the townspeople. His lyric nature paragraphs and poems attracted the attention of more than the 500 subscribers, and his readers named him "The Oracle of Gold Hill."

To supplement his income, Lampman also served as correspondent for the *Oregonian*. In 1916, that paper's editor, Edgar Piper, lured him to Portland as a reporter for a weekly salary of $25. As the paper's star police beat reporter, he attracted a following of readers who admired his approach to the human suffering he encountered. Six years later, Piper moved him to the editorial page as one of four associate editors. There he found his niche and a daily outlet for his works on nature, fishing, animals, and the humanity of people in the Northwest.

In the 32 years that Lampman wrote editorials for the *Oregonian*, until his death in 1954, he established for himself a large personal following among readers. Many *Oregonian* subscribers, it was said, read Lampman's editorials before ever looking at the front page. Readership studies ranked his editorials with its best-read features, and the editorial page was considered one of the prime factors in the *Oregonian's* passing its competitor, the *Oregon Journal*, in circulation in the 1930s.

As his editorials were reprinted in numerous newspapers, his fame spread throughout the nation, gaining for him a reputation as one of the nation's preeminent editorial writers on nature and whimsy. John Finley, then editor of the New York *Times*, listed Lampman as one of America's five best editorial writers; and Philip Parrish, editor of the *Oregonian*'s editorial page, called him "the country's greatest editorial writer on nature."

While human interest was his specialty, Lampman also ventured into serious pieces. In fact, Herbert Hoover had attempted to hire him as a speechwriter for his 1932 presidential campaign.

Lampman, however, preferred to write about what he knew and loved best—Oregon's interesting people and beautiful outdoors. People who knew him remarked that he would rather be fishing than participating in any other activity.

Just as he had favorite subjects, he also had a distinctive writing style. He possessed such an ear for the sound of words that he could memorize long poems with a single reading, and his pieces sometimes read as rhythmically as poetry. As evidence, a school principal scanned one of Lampman's editorials, "Where Are You, Soldier?" and easily transposed it into poetry form:

The taste of the day, of the wind,
Is of marsh and of woodland,
And is sweeter than wine.

In conjunction with his pieces' rhythmic quality were their rhyme and alliteration, metaphor and imagery, and overall simplicity. Lampman was a student of words and understood the quality of their sounds. Many of these elements are easily recognizable in these comments on Mount Hood and Mount Saint Helens: "When seen by moonlight these sisters of the range take on an appearance altogether familiar, almost unreal, yet beautiful as the mountains which live beyond the borders of faerie—the veritable mountains of the moon."

Lampman also made a practice of ending his editorials on the strongest note he could. He concluded with words that lingered in his readers' minds long after they had put down their evening paper. The *Oregonian*'s memorial to Lampman after his death (following a series of cerebral hemorrhages), described the approach as "that literary device which sets off an explosion in the reader's emotions as the last sentence penetrates his mind."

One of the other associate editors commented that there was "never enough space to do justice to Ben who, besides all this, is a real poet." Another editor declared that "whatever Ben pounded out on his ancient Royal typewriter emerged clothed in memorable magic, not just words, not just thoughts, but a happy blend of these, with feeling."

John Finley, the New York *Times* editor, before becoming acquainted with Lampman, assumed his editorials must have been written in longhand and with infinite care. Actually, although

Lampman did write with great concern for style, he composed at the typewriter and at such speed that, as Philip Parrish declared, he kept "his co-workers perpetually astonished."

Over the years, Lampman's editorials were so popular that they were reprinted in newspapers across the nation and in two anthologies. His best received was "Where to Bury a Dog," which was reprinted at the request of readers and, almost two decades after it first appeared, in *Reader's Digest.* Another editorial, "The Wind in the Flag," published on Memorial Day of 1947, created widespread demand because of the sentiment it attached to American soldiers who had died in World War II.

While known primarily as an editorial writer, Lampman also was an acclaimed author of short stories and poems. In addition to his collections of *Oregonian* editorials, *How Could I Be Forgetting?* and *At the End of the Car Line*, there were his literary works: *The Tramp Printer, Here Comes Somebody, The Coming of the Pond Fishes*, and *The Wild Swan.* Two of his magazine short stories won O. Henry memorial prizes.

Among his other honors were an honorary masters degree in 1943 from the University of Oregon and an honorary doctorate in 1947 from the University of Portland, even though he had never completed high school. In 1951 he received the Freedom Foundation certificate of merit for "outstanding achievement in bringing about a better understanding of the American way of life"; and Gold Hill in 1947 celebrated "Ben Hur Lampman Day" with a parade, races, baseball, dancing, free barbecue, and a tobacco spitting contest.

His proudest day came, however, in 1951 when he was named Oregon's poet laureate. Although he was never physically able to write many official pieces for his beloved state, it was appropriate that he had been given the honor. Many critics, during his lifetime, had agreed that he could have fled the *Oregonian* for more profitable, ostentatious positions. Never, though, did he want to leave Oregon, the home he had fallen in love with many years before.

His fellow staff members' response to the poet laureate award was an appropriate memorial. "No Northwest writer," they said, "has a greater personal following than Mr. Lampman. We who are his co-workers share the public appreciation of the depth and range of his work. He has earned the wreath of laurel."

•The following editorial demonstrates Lampman's nature writing at its best. Although the editorial has the feel of romantic poetry, it gives a practical view of the feeling of wanderlust.

IN OREGON WHEN AUTUMN COMES
(Portland *Oregonian*)

It is believed that the season of spring, most of all, causes mortals to wish and wish for another skyline. There is sorcery in the soft skies and magic in the soft breeze. Where would you go if you were footloose then? Sir, there are lands that must be seen if one would rest content. To such a land we would go in April, the turf underfoot, the geese overhead. So it is with spring. Yet this enchantment of restlessness, which makes its thrall a mildly discontented fellow, is not peculiar to spring, no matter what they say. The season of autumn weaves it, too.

What should be sad in the falling of spent leaves, of leaves that have decked themselves in bridal hues to keep a tryst with death? The leaves are glad enough. They spiral down from their parent twigs, and golden and red they are, to carpet the loam of which they must become a part. If a wind drives over them they are blithe to dance in the hazy sunshine of autumn. The leaves are not saddened by this most natural of fates. In death is found rebirth, and the tree lives. Nothing is lost in nature, nothing wasted. These leaves shall, in a manner of speaking, break from their waxen buds again or come back to us as flowers.

Yet the spent leaves sadden us, and the bare boughs touch our hearts. Something or somebody is going away, unseen, silent, wistful, and on a certain morning we shall wake to know a loss, to feel an absence. And we would go if we but could, out of the city and down the road, with a gray squirrel scolding and a crow drifting and a tang of wood smoke in the air.... We would go as the gypsies go. For, mark you, this must be the fact—that elsewhere one would find the days that never can return, the lost laughter, the golden hopes, the scent and presence of a dear morning in mid-May. We are forever certain that hidden in distance, away down behind the blue edge of the sky, is the past itself—the past purged of all care and worry and evil episode. Small wonder that each autumn wakes in us the spirit of the wanderer.

Give you good day, gypsy, and whither bound? To a lake in the southland, possibly, where there are white swans glistening? No; he knows little of white swans, this gypsy. He answers that he has heard of a horse for trade, and that there is money to be made by a shrewd fellow in distant parts. And you, geese that fly so far above the river, whither bound? For the wild geese must know of a region fairer than this, and thrice as fair. But the geese seek grain fields known to them of old, where geese may profit and attain fatness. Only the stay-at-homes have dreams. All the wanderers are practical creatures, bent on practical ends. So it is well worth while to stay at home, if only for the dreams one has.

Fall o' the year. Rain on the roof at evening and mist in the valley at morning. The air is new washed, crisp and tonic, and the thousand rivers have ceased to loiter. The sea trout are coming up from the sea. Are you restless now? Elsewhere there are restless ones who wish themselves in Oregon when autumn comes.

•The following editorial was the most widely reprinted one of all that Lampman wrote. It is simple in its presentation; and, with phrases such as "the grim, dim frontiers of death," it clearly showcases Lampman's literary talents. Its last sentence demonstrates his talent for strong, thematic conclusions.

WHERE TO BURY A DOG
(Portland *Oregonian*)

A subscriber of The Ontario Argus has written to the editor of that fine weekly, propounding a certain question, which, so far as we know, yet remains unanswered. The question is this—"Where shall I bury my dog?" It is asked in advance of death. The Oregonian trusts The Argus will not be offended if this newspaper undertakes an answer, for surely such a question merits a reply, since the man who asked it, on the evidence of his letter, loves the dog. It distresses him to think of his favorite as dishonored in death, mere carrion in the winter rains. Within that sloping, canine skull, he must reflect when the dog is dead, were thoughts that dignified the dog and honored the master. The hand of the master and of the friend stroked often in affection this rough, pathetic husk that was a dog.

We would say to the Ontario man that there are various places in which a dog may be buried. We are thinking now of a setter, whose coat was flame in the sunshine, and who, so far as we are aware, never entertained a mean or an unworthy thought. This setter is buried beneath a cherry tree, under four feet of garden loam, and at its proper season the cherry strews petals on the green lawn of his grave. Beneath a cherry tree, or an apple, or any flowering shrub of the garden, is an excellent place to bury a good dog. Beneath such trees, such shrubs, he slept in the drowsy summer, or gnawed at a flavorous bone, or lifted head to challenge some strange intruder. These are good places, in life or in death. Yet it is a small matter, and it touches sentiment more than anything else. For if the dog be well remembered, if sometimes he leaps through your dreams actual as in life, eyes kindling, questioning, asking, laughing, begging, it matters not at all where that dog sleeps at long and at last. On a hill where the wind is unrebuked, and the trees are roaring, or beside a stream he knew in puppyhood, or somewhere in the flatness of a pasture land, where most exhilarating cattle graze. It is all one to the dog, and all one to you, and nothing is gained, and nothing lost—if memory lives. But there is one best place to bury a dog. One place that is best of all.

If you bury him in this spot, the secret of which you must already have, he will come to you when you call—come to you over the grim, dim frontiers of death, and down the well-remembered path, and to your side again. And though you call a dozen living dogs to heel they shall not growl at him, nor resent his coming, for he is yours and he belongs there. People may scoff at you, who see no lightest blade of grass bent by his footfall, who hear no whimper pitched too fine for mere audition, people who may never really have had a dog. Smile at them then, for you shall know something that is hidden from them, and which is well worth the knowing. The one best place to bury a good dog is in the heart of its master.

•The following editorial covered one of Lampman's favorite topics—animals—and illustrated his talent for using precise verbs and descriptive words and phrases to evoke strong sentiment.

THE CAT CAN'T COME BACK
(Portland *Oregonian*)

Sometimes when the east wind leaps the kitchen porch to slat at the screen door, when the dishes are done and it's dark outside, they catch themselves thinking he is there. They think, before they have time to know better, that it is the old yellow cat asking in. For that is the way he used to tell them when he had come home from a cat's nocturnal concerns, with his eyes shining, his tail lifted—and sometimes it would be slightly puffed by recent adventure. How surely he swaggered! Then he told them about it. It is not to be wondered that, after so many years, they sometimes think the east wind is an old yellow cat who has returned, with a purr in his throat and love in his golden and ebony eyes. Instinctively almost they rise to open the door. Then their glances encounter and cling, each with the trace of embarrassment. It sounded like him, didn't it? But it was the east wind, instead.

He used to come out of the east wind, cobwebs in his whiskers, happiness in his heart, with that clean-cat smell of new-laundered linen, the way a healthy cat smells when he comes in from the cold. A leap to the couch, in lithe confidence, and the yellow cat found the crook of her arm. Put your magazine down. Here I am! Here I am! Your cat has come home from the darkness. How closely she held him then—cheek by cheek. So it is when of evenings the screen door slats in the east wind, they find they cannot get over the habit. The place he had in their hearts still is warm. Still is warm. As a cushion where a cat has been sleeping. It would be no manner of use to go call him. He was never the one to answer until he was ready—but now they know he can't come. Yet sometimes they will lift their eyes from book or paper, and quickly, to listen. It couldn't, of course, be the old yellow cat, and it never can be. How empty a house will seem where a cat has been! He used to come in from the east wind, smelling like fresh linen— he used to come in as of right; one of them.

Sometimes when it happens again, and their glances catch and linger, they speak of having another one. But never can they quite agree to, for, you see, there was only one of him, nor ever can there be such another. Don't you see? A cat that is loved isn't just a cat. He is something more than a cat. Why don't they, their friends ask, get another one? That's the easy phrase for it. But not yet. Not quite yet. It isn't so simple as that. Listen! Will they never cease starting when the east wind leaps the kitchen porch to slat at the screen door? O foolish! Go back to your book. The old yellow cat can't come home.

•Following is Lampman's Memorial Day editorial that gained widespread popularity and numerous requests for reprints.

THE WIND IN THE FLAG
(Portland *Oregonian*; May 30, 1947)

Then do not think of them as being yonder in alien earth with little white crosses above. They are not there. For these were boys who loved the homeland—her fields and forests, lakes and streams, her villages and cities. These were the boys who went to school here—and would they stay away when they were mustered out? These were the boys who fished our creeks and climbed our mountains; the boys who plowed our fields and harvested our wheat; who manned our factories and each enterprise of peace. It is not right to think of them as being where they seem to be. It isn't fair. Often they used to talk of going home, and surely—when death set them free—surely they came. Now we who knew them well must know they are not there who are forever here, inseparable from the land for which they died. No troopship brought them home, for they came home the quicker and the shorter way. Is it the wind that stirs the flag?

Nor should we think of them as being beneath the sea, where the plane plunged or the wounded ship went down, fathom upon green fathom. They are not there. For these were boys whose laughter scarcely hid from us the consecration which they felt, and when they said that they would soon get it over and come home, they meant it, every word. She called them from their classes and the ball grounds, she called them from the desk and lathe, and from the homes that meant as much to them as to any that ever loved his home with the full measure of devotion. They never thought to see the world, at least until they might be middle-aged, but soon they saw it, island after island, port after foreign port, and many an island was fenced round with flame, and there was one port that they did not fetch. They died too soon to reach it and to hear the bands and speeches. But we who knew them, surely we must know that they were here before that, for they had said they would come home the moment that they could. And so they aren't there, but here. The ship came back without them, if it came at all, but they were here, not there. Is it the wind that stirs the flag again?

And where they kept the bargain, they who died for land and liberty, it matters not at all, nor where they seem to rest—under the little white crosses or under the sea, or namelessly in the deep jungle. For they were boys who would not stay away when they were done with service, since often they had told themselves the first thing they should do would be to hasten home. And home they must have come. Where the trout rises or the grouse leaps into flight, or at the ball park, or along the seashore, these were the places that they loved—these that forever are our country, and to which they, by their passing, have confirmed our title. They are here surely enough, and shall be for so long as liberty and America are one, and the flag means still what they knew it meant— though they didn't say much about it. That was something they left to the orators and the politicians, and editors. Do not think of them as being elsewhere. For they are not there—who are here. Look. The light wind stirs the flag as though it caressed it, fold after fold. Look!

HODDING CARTER CALLS FOR RACIAL TOLERANCE

After serving in World War II on the *Stars and Stripes,* Hodding Carter returned to his newspaper in Greenville, Mississippi, and immediately began attracting nationwide attention. In numerous editorials he concentrated on building respect between races.

For such writing he was awarded the 1946 Pulitzer Prize. "I had been protesting editorially against racial and religious injustices for a long time before our editorials won a Pulitzer Prize," he said. "But... the Pulitzer prize induced more people at home to concede that there might be some merit in what we were saying."

The most popular editorial of his prize-winning series was "Go for Broke," written shortly after V-J Day. Although it was outwardly a challenge to white Americans to treat Japanese-Americans as equals, there is little doubt that Carter intended it to call for racial tolerance for blacks also. "Go For Broke" was widely reprinted and is one of the most frequently quoted Pulitzer Prize editorials in the history of the award.

GO FOR BROKE
(Hodding Carter; *Delta Democrat-Times*; August 27, 1945)

Company D of the 168th Regiment which is stationed in Leghorn, Italy, is composed altogether of white troops, some from the East, some from the South, some from the Midwest and West Coast.

Company D made an unusual promise earlier this month. The promise was in the form of a communication to their fellow Americans of the 442d Infantry Regiment and the 100th Infantry Battalion, whose motto is "Go For Broke," and it was subscribed to unanimously by the officers and men of Company D.

In brief, the communication pledged the help of Company D in convincing "the folks back home that you are fully deserving of all the privileges with which we ourselves are bestowed."

The soldiers to whom that promise was made are Japanese-Americans. In all of the United States Army, no troops have chalked up a better combat record. Their record is so good that these Nisei were selected by General Francis H. Oxx, commander of the military area in which they are stationed, to lead the final victory parade. So they marched, 3,000 strong, at the head of thousands of other Americans, their battle flag with three Presidential unit citationed streamers floating above them, their commander, a Wisconsin white colonel, leading them.

Some of those Nisei must have been thinking of the soul-shaking days of last October, when they spearheaded the attacks that opened the Vosges Mountain doorway to Strasbourg. Some of them were probably remembering how they, on another bloody day, had snatched the Thirty-Six Division's lost battalion of Texans from the encircling Germans. And many of them were bearing scars from those two engagements which alone had cost the Nisei boys from Hawaii and the West Coast 2,300 casualties.

Perhaps these yellow-skinned Americans, to whose Japanese kinsmen we have administered a terrific and long overdue defeat, were holding their heads a little higher because of the pledge of their white fellow-soldiers and fellow-Americans of Company D. Perhaps, when they gazed at their combat flag, the motto "Go for Broke" emblazoned thereon took on a different meaning. "Go For Broke" is the Hawaiian-Japanese slang expression for shooting the works in a dice game.

The loyal Nisei have shot the works. From the beginning of the war, they have been on trial, in and out of uniform, in army camps and relocation centers, as combat troops in Europe and as frontline interrogators, propagandists, and combat intelligence personnel in the Pacific where their capture meant prolonged and hideous torture. And even yet they have not satisfied their critics.

It is so easy for a dominant race to explain good or evil, patriotism or treachery, courage or cowardice in terms of skin color. So easy and so tragically wrong. Too many have committed that wrong against the loyal Nisei, who by the thousands have proved themselves good Americans, even while others of us, by our actions against them, have shown ourselves to be bad Americans. Nor is the end of this misconception in sight. Those Japanese-American soldiers who paraded at Leghorn in commemoration of the defeat of the nation from which their fathers came, will meet other enemies, other obstacles as forbidding as those of war. A lot of people will begin saying, as soon as these boys take off their uniforms, that "a Jap is a Jap," and the Nisei deserve no consideration. A majority won't say or believe this, but an active minority can have its way against an apathetic majority.

It seems to us that the Nisei slogan of "Go For Broke" could be adopted by all Americans of good will in the days ahead. We've got to shoot the works in a fight for tolerance. Those boys of Company D point the way. Japan's surrender will be signed aboard the Missouri and General MacArthur's part will be a symbolic "Show Me."

Reprinted with permission of the *Delta Democrat-Times*.

HOW AN EDITORIAL
CALLED A NATION TO PRAYER

Carl Saunders received the 1950 Pulitzer Prize for Editorial Writing. The judges based his selection on a 1949 editorial that led to Congress' resolution that Memorial Day be made permanently a national day of prayer for peace. Saunders' efforts actually began with an editorial published in 1948. Perhaps no other recent editorial has had such a direct national impact as that editorial. In the modern post-World War II age of journalism, when editorial writers and critics alike have bemoaned the decline of editorial influence, Saunders' was a rare editorial.

His campaign began from a conversation with his clergyman following a potluck dinner. Tension between America and Russia was building, and the Cold War was starting to heat up. Uncontrollable forces seemed to be pushing the nation toward war. But what could any individual do?

Saunders, the editor of the *Citizen Patriot* in Jackson, Michigan, made a suggestion: "Why don't we—all of us in America—pray for peace? We've tried rattling our tanks and planes; we've tried calling names; we've tried the United Nations. Let's put first things first—let's have a day of prayer for peace."

Shortly afterward, he wrote an editorial urging the President and Congress to set aside a day (which he recommended should be Memorial Day) and a particular time for the nation to go to prayer. Two of Michigan's Congressmen introduced a joint resolution in the U. S. Senate and House of Representatives, where it received unanimous approval. In an executive proclamation, President Harry Truman called the nation to prayer.

Saunders then composed a "Prayer for Peace" and published it in the *Citizen Patriot*. It was so well received that the paper had to publish thousands of copies of the prayer to meet the demand. Most of Jackson's churches used the prayer in services preceding Memorial Day. It was recited in ceremonies at the Tomb of the

Unknown Soldier on Memorial Day. A nation-wide radio hookup carried the program.

Saunders repeated his appeal in 1949, and the following year Congress, at his urging, unanimously adopted a resolution calling on the President to "issue a proclamation calling upon the people of the United States to observe EACH Memorial Day... by praying." Truman agreed.

Following announcement of the award of the 1950 Pulitzer Prize, the *Citizen Patriot* received so many requests for copies of the winning 1949 editorial ("Firsts Things First") and of Saunders' "Prayer for Peace" that it reprinted them in a four-page brochure.

Saunders, who had served as editor of the *Citizen Patriot* from 1937 to 1961, died in 1974. Why had his call for prayer been so effective? The answer is not because his editorial had been brilliantly crafted or because Saunders believed in some modern editorial "duty" to provide detached analysis of issues. Instead, he appealed to a deep need and a faith widespread among readers in his community and throughout the nation. Reprinted below are his original 1948 editorial and his "Prayer for Peace."

SUPPOSE ALL AMERICA PRAYED FOR PEACE
(Carl M. Saunders; Jackson *Citizen Patriot*; May 16, 1948)

The United States is generally classified as a "Christian nation."

If that means anything at all, it means that the vast majority of our people accept the basic tenets of the Christian faith. Beyond that there is a large minority of Americans who worship in the Hebrew faith. Both Christian and Hebrew believe in God as the maker of Heaven and earth.

Yet as a nation we seem utterly unaware of God or of his place in the making of history.

As individuals many Americans worship. Many pray to God daily or more often.

Why then should not America pray as a nation in a time when as a nation we are in dire need of help and guidance?

We do have one day in the year supposedly dedicated to thanksgiving when we as a people are expected to offer thanks to the Supreme Being for the blessings showered upon us.

But we have no day or hour or minute when as a people we turn to prayer.

If we are a Christian nation, isn't a national moment of prayer a logical, natural course?

Differences in creed or systems of worship or dogma need not enter into this discussion if as a people we believe that there is a God who shapes the course of our lives.

It should be possible for Protestants, Catholics, Jews and others to join in a common appeal to a common God.

***

The world is troubled today. America is deeply troubled. The threat of war hangs over all of us. Yet we want peace. We are not a warlike people. We cherish the lives of those young people who become sacrifices in war. We are ready to be tolerant of all nations which do not menace us regardless of divergent ideologies.

So far as this newspaper is concerned, it believes that the preparation for defense of our country is wise and is not in contravention of basic religious beliefs. We appreciate, of course, that some good people disagree with us. They do not believe a fire department is needed to protect us from war's flames even though conflagration threatens.

But first things should come first.

And the first defense against disaster should be prayer. The first appeal for peace should be to the Omnipotent Master of the universe.

We as mortals do not know what are His plans for us and for the world.

We know only that, as the poet has said:

"God moves in a mysterious way

His wonders to perform."

But a troubled Christian nation should turn to prayer. Its people should lift their voices as from a single throat in supplication to the Divine Architect of our destinies, remembering always "Thy will be done."

***

Through the medium of newspapers and the radio we have great opportunities for mass supplication. We as a nation can duplicate the mass prayers of the early Christians who gathered, a small handful, to present their appeals.

Suppose that Congress were to set aside a day and an hour and a minute as the time to Pray for Peace.

Suppose that by request from Congress all newspapers on that day were to publish the appeal for prayer at the set time and were to print the proposed words for prayer.

Suppose that every radio station at the same moment broadcast the Prayer for Peace.

Suppose that millions of Americans turned their radios high at that same moment.

The voices of prayer would echo and re-echo from the White mountains of Maine to the Black mountains of California, from the warm currents of the Gulf stream to the cold fogs of the Bering sea.

All America asking for guidance, appealing for peace, pleading that our leaders be made wise and blessed!

***

We are not thinking that a 150,000,000 person pressure group can force God to create a peace disregarding His own great purpose. We would not want to be interpreted as anticipating that merely for all of us to rub the lamp of prayer will produce some white magic peace out of the heavenly mists. But we are suggesting that when 150,000,000 people by common consent turn their minds and hearts to the Spirit which created this world rather than leaning wholly upon the materialism of man's own strength, then something is bound to happen to those people—something which conceivably will make easier the accomplishment of God's purpose. Not knowing what that purpose is, whether in His great scheme of things we are to have peace or war, to survive or pass into the limbo of broken nations—not knowing, we still will have the inner warmth and cleanliness which is brought to prayer.

Inevitably would not such a moment of consecration raise us up? Would it not in a measure at least lend authenticity in a moment of travail to our proud claim to being a Christian nation?

***

We suggest that the President or Congress, or both, set a day and a moment for a national Prayer for Peace. Perhaps the early evening of May 30th would be a most fitting time. We suggest that in proclaiming such a period of supplication, all mediums of information—newspapers, radio, etc.,—be asked to join.

"and pray unto the Lord for it; for in the peace thereof shall ye have peace."—Jeremiah 29:7.1

PRAYER FOR PEACE
(Carl M. Saunders; Jackson *Citizen Patriot*; February 20, 1949)

O Lord, Father of All Men, We come to Thee in humble supplication.

Thou knowest we have strayed much from Thy laws.

Yet, O God, Thou hast blessed us abundantly, and our children.

Thankful for these blessings and hopeful in the promise of Thy forgiveness, we now beseech Thy special guidance and care.

Again in this world of mortal men wars and threats of wars beset us.

Jealousies and rivalries of nations plague us.

Fears are all about us.

We turn to Thee, O God, to ask that in Thy good time peace may be restored to all nations of men.

We ask that men may live together in understanding and respect.

We ask that governments may rule in Thy wisdom.

We ask that intolerance, bigotry, and greed as between nations, and men, and races, may be overcome by the force of Thy will.

We ask that this United States and its people may be guided by Thee and that its mothers may be spared the sorrows and its sons the sacrifices of further wars.

Bless our leaders with wisdom.

Show us the way to better understanding one with another among our own people.

To that end we seek Thy benediction and light, ready always in faith that Thy will be done and confident that in the end Thy good purpose will triumph. Amen.

Reprinted with permission of the Jackson *Citizen Patriot.*

LOUIS LACOSS LAMENTS 'THE LOW ESTATE OF PUBLIC MORALS'

"The Low Estate of Public Morals" may have evoked more public response than any other Pulitzer Prize editorial. Now, four decades later, an era that has been marked by scandal in government and in public life—an era in which we perhaps have come to accept cheating among our officials, our students, our university sports programs—it may be difficult to comprehend how Louis LaCoss's editorial could have elicited so strong a public response. Numerous letters and telegrams to the St. Louis *Globe-Democrat,* however, applauded LaCoss's stand, and the paper received around 50,000 requests for reprints.

The editorial was inspired by a cheating scandal at the West Point Military Academy, but LaCoss tied the scandal into the climate of dishonesty and low morals throughout America. "The editorial," LaCoss surmised, "said nothing particularly new—I had written many times previously on the general subject—but, as reader response indicated, it packaged the thinking of many Americans."

Following publication of the editorial in 1951, the *Globe-Democrat* received a volume of suggestions from readers that resulted in a series of articles by leading Americans on solutions to the problem of public immorality.

THE LOW ESTATE OF PUBLIC MORALS
(Louis LaCoss; St. Louis *Globe-Democrat,* August 6, 1951)

The discharge of 90 West Point cadets for cheating at examinations is only one facet of the many-sided problem of moral disintegration nationally that is causing many persons to wonder whether America is going down the path of decay that caused the Roman empire to fall. It is a sobering thought. But the facts must be faced.

The West Pointers were dishonest. They cheated. Some did so because they couldn't play football and keep up with their studies. Others who were not athletes cheated because that was the easy way to make passing grades.

The excuse of the athletes accents the abnormality of thinking in many institutions of higher education as to the part sports should play in college life. The necessity of having a good team to assure big revenue to build a bigger stadium to make more money, has led many of our colleges into the evil devices of buying players, of competing in the open market for a star half back. Some colleges have recognized the error and have de-emphasized sports, as should be done.

At West Point the incentive was a bit different because Uncle Sam foots the bills there, but there was the incentive for the individual to "make" the team that was tops or near it in the nation. So, if practice on the field interfered, cheat a little and make the necessary grades.

But fundamentally what happened at West Point reflects a present distorted attitude toward old-fashioned honesty and integrity that obtains not only in our schools but in America's social and political life.

It is seen in the high places in government, which after World War II practiced plain deception on the people. We were told no secret agreements had been made with anybody. Later, we discovered pacts were signed at Tehran, Yalta and Potsdam that made the Korean war inevitable.

In the New Deal era was born the idea that an administration can perpetuate itself in power by buying the voters with handout money. Remember how Harry Hopkins tapped the WPA till to win an election in Kentucky? During that era was born the fiction that cities and states as well as individuals need not look to their own resources or ingenuity to survive—let Washington do it. Out of the mating of depression and political trickery came the insidious thinking by millions of Americans that hard work is positively silly; that if one does work, do the least possible, draw the biggest pay possible—and strike for more.

The youths, such as the West Pointers, with whom we are concerned today, were babies then. They have grown into manhood in an environment of take-it-where-I-find-it entirely alien to the American tradition. They are the unpretty fruit of the mistakes of the past two decades.

What do we see in Washington today? Corruption and scandals. The close link between the underworld and politics was revealed by the Kefauver committee. The Fulbright committee turned the spotlight on the RFC and the influence peddlers, some within the shadow of the White House, who sold their contacts for a price.

We hear of doubtful goings-on in the government department that collects our income taxes.

We hear of patronage bought and sold like so much goods over the counter.

An Army General sees no wrong in accepting gifts from those with whom he does government business, nor in diverting government materials to private use.

The chairman of the Democratic National Committee yells "smear" when it is discovered that he is on the pay roll of a St. Louis company for the ostensible reason that he has influence on RFC loans.

The close personal friend of the President, a Major General, has a desk in the White House where he conveniently hands out receipts for deep freezers presented him gratis and which he distributes where they will do good politically.

Campaigns for the Senate in Ohio and Maryland last year were conducted along lines that set a new political low.

So, when 90 West Point cadets stray from paths of honesty, when nauseous revelations are made of the bribing of college basketball teams, when youths charged with robbery stand up in court, as they did in New York, and brazenly admit their guilt, but excuse it by saying that "everybody's doing it," when teenagers become delinquent via the narcotics road, when too many youths of both sexes flout the laws of chastity and decency—when these derelictions of the youths of our land are totted up, there comes a time for sober questioning among the adults.

Where does the fault lie? In the home? Perhaps. In the schools? In part. In the churches? In part. But in the main the fault lies in that nebulous field of public morals and spirituality which was so highly cultivated by the founding fathers and which of late has been so scantily tilled. Among too many of us the accepted premise is that anything is fair unless we are caught; that each of us is entitled to something for nothing; that the world owes us a living; that an honest day's work for an honest day's pay is almost unethical; that gypping the other fellow before he gyps you is the only policy that pays off.

The level of public morals is low. Unfortunately, the good example is not set in Washington. The President is victimized by his friends, but a false sense of loyalty prevents him from moving forthright against them. His reluctance condones wrong-doing. Leadership in both parties is weak, because it is consistently attuned to the next election, not to what is best for the public welfare. In fact, public morals are low because politics at all levels is played at an historic low. The one is the coadjutor of the other.

Yet, we strut the earth telling everybody else to look at us and see democracy in fairest flower—and please copy; we'll foot the bill. We wonder, for instance, what Pravda will have to say about the 90 West Point cadets.

The time is here for moral regeneration. West Point is just one item in the sad chronology. The Roman empire fell, not because it was overwhelmed from without, but because it decayed from within. If this is an appeal for a return to the day-by-day practice of old time religion, and respect for God's moral law, so be it. When the moral fabric of a nation begins to unravel, it is time to do some patching before the entire garment is gone. The cause and effect of this deterioration nationally will be issues in next year's presidential campaign.

Reprinted with permission of the St. Louis Mercantile Library Association.

RUSSIANS ACCEPT LAUREN SOTH'S INVITATION TO VISIT IOWA

Rare are the editorials that have an effect on a major public event. Lauren K. Soth's "If the Russians Want More Meat... " was one of those rare editorials.

During the midst of the Cold War, he suggested that the U.S.S.R. send a delegation to Iowa to study agricultural methods. The invitation was made casually, and Soth did not believe it had a chance of being accepted. It was, though; and it opened up a program of exchanges between the Soviet Union and the United States, helping to thaw the Cold War a little. A Russian delegation visited Iowa farms and later introduced Iowan methods to their country's agriculture. In return, an American delegation was invited to Russia. Soth, who toured with the group, wrote that the Soviet Union remained secretive but that "the freedom we had was a far cry from the way foreigners have been treated in Russia during most of the last ten years."

IF THE RUSSIANS WANT MORE MEAT...
(Lauren K. Soth; Des Moines *Register and Tribune*; Feb. 10, 1955)

Nikita Khrushchev, who seems to be the real boss of the Soviet Union now, signaled his emergence to power by a well-publicized speech before the Central committee last month, lambasting the performance of the Soviet economic managers. In this speech Khrushchev especially attacked the management of agriculture. And in doing so, he took the rare line of praising the United States.

Khrushchev advocated the development of feed-livestock agriculture as in the United States. "Americans have succeeded in achieving a high level of animal husbandry," he said. He urged Soviet collective and state farms to plant hybrid corn to provide more feed for livestock. And he demanded an eightfold increase in corn production by 1960.

Speaking as an Iowan, living in the heart of the greatest feed-livestock area of the world, we wish to say that, for once, the Soviet leader is talking sense. That's just what the Russian economy needs—more and better livestock so the Russian people can eat better.

We have no diplomatic authority of any kind, but we hereby extend an invitation to any delegation Khrushchev wants to select to come to Iowa to get the lowdown on raising high quality cattle, hogs, sheep, and chickens. We promise to hide none of our "secrets." We will take the visiting delegation to Iowa's great agricultural experiment station at Ames, to some of the leading farmers of Iowa, to our livestock breeders, soil conservation experts, and seed companies. Let the Russians see how we do it.

Furthermore, we would be glad to go to Russia with a delegation of Iowa farmers, agronomists, livestock specialists, and other technical authorities. Everything we Iowans know about corn, other feed grains, forage crops, meat animals, and the dairy and poultry industries will be available to the Russians for the asking.

We ask nothing in return. We figure that more knowledge about the means to a good life in Russia can only benefit the world and us. It might even shake the Soviet leaders in their conviction that the United States wants war; it might even persuade them that there is a happier future in developing a high level of living than in this paralyzing race for more and more armaments.

Of course the Russians wouldn't do it. And we doubt even that our own government would dare to permit an advance in human understanding of this sort. But it *would* make sense.

HAZEL BRANNON SMITH FIGHTS RACIAL INJUSTICE IN MISSISSIPPI

Hazel Brannon Smith was a small-town editor who worked energetically against racial injustice in the 1960s. Like several Southern editors who took stands against the racial system in the 1950s and 1960s, she gained high journalistic recognition for her work. The judges who selected her for the 1964 Pulitzer Prize commended her for "steadfast adherence to her editorial duty in the face of great pressure and opposition." The statement was inadequate to describe her real dedication.

Mrs. Smith's problems began in 1954 when she criticized a sheriff who shot a young black man. A local court awarded the sheriff a $10,000 libel verdict. Although an appeals court overturned the decision, pressure on Mrs. Smith began to mount. The White Citizens' Council encouraged an advertising boycott of her newspaper. Local residents were induced to drop their subscriptions. Opponents supported the founding of a competing paper. After opponents gained control of the local government, Mr. Smith was removed as administrator of the area hospital. The Smiths' financial situation grew critical. They drew from their savings to support their newspaper; they mortgaged their home and built up a debt of $80,000.

Still, Mrs. Smith continued her attacks against racists, corrupt local politicians, slot machine operators, gamblers, and liquor racketeers. For her stands, she received the 1960 Elijah Lovejoy Award for Courage in Journalism and the 1963 Golden Quill Editorial Award from the International Conference of Weekly Newspaper Editors.

When Mrs. Smith was given the 1964 Pulitzer, she described what she saw as her role as an editor: "All we have done here is try to meet honestly the issues as they arose. We did not ask for, nor run from this fight with the White Citizens' Councils. But we have given it all we have, nearly 10 years of our lives, loss of financial security and a big mortgage. We would do the same thing over, if necessary.... I could not call myself an editor if I had gone along with the Citizens' Councils—feeling about them the way I do. My interest has been to print the truth and protect and defend the freedom of all Mississippians. It will continue."

Included here is the editorial for which Mrs. Smith received the Golden Quill award and which was one of the editorials in her Pulitzer entry.

ARREST OF BOMBING VICTIM
IS GRAVE DISSERVICE
(Hazel Brannon Smith; Lexington *Advertiser*; May 16, 1963)

It is not moral or just that any man should live in fear, or be compelled to sleep with a loaded gun by his bedside.

Holmes County Deputy Sheriff Andrew P. Smith's action in arresting a 58-year-old Negro farmer, Hartman Turnbow, for fire bombing his own home has come as a numbing shock to the people of Holmes County.

It is a grave disservice to our county and all our people in these days of increasing racial tension and strife.

White and Negro citizens of Holmes County alike simply could not believe that something like this could happen in our county, that a man and his wife and 16-year-old daughter could be routed from sleep in the small hours of the morning and be forced to flee their home literally in terror, only to be shot at by intruders outside—then to have the head of the family jailed the same day for doing the dastardly deed by an officer sworn to uphold the law and protect all citizens.

The only evidence presented against the aged Negro man at the preliminary hearing was testimony given by Deputy Smith and that was only an account of the bombing and shooting incident, as reported by Turnbow, to him. Mr. Smith added his own opinions and suppositions, as did County Attorney Pat M. Barrett, who prosecuted the case. As a result the man was bound over under $500 bond for action by the Holmes County Grand Jury in October.

Mr. Barrett, who said he was "not a demolition expert," nevertheless told the Court that "it just couldn't have happened. There is no way on God's earth for that situation over there to have happened like he said it happened."

Four other Negroes, who had been arrested the same day in connection with the same case, were released for lack of evidence. Not one shred of evidence was presented against them. But they had been held in jail five days and five nights.

This kind of conduct on the part of our highest elected peace officer has done serious injury to relations between the races in Holmes County—where we must be able to live in peace and harmony, or not live at all.

It is distressing that no statement has come from Mr. Smith saying that he is continuing his investigation. Perhaps he is. We hope so.

But irreparable damage has been done, and let no one doubt it.

We have always taken pride in being able to manage our affairs ourselves. When we become derelict in our duty and do not faithfully execute our obligations, we may rest assured it will be done for us.

FBI agents and U.S. Justice officials have already made an exhaustive investigation of this bombing and shooting incident.

A suit has already been filed against Deputy Smith, Mr. Barrett and the District Attorney, stating these Negroes were arrested "on false and baseless charges," which were in effect an effort to coerce and intimidate Negro citizens of Holmes County and get them to cease voter registration activity. The Federal suit asks for a permanent injunction to prohibit these officers from interfering with voter registration activities, including the prosecution of the charges filed against Turnbow, who attempted to register to vote here April 9, and Robert Moses, director of SNCC, a voter registration project.

This kind of situation would never have come about in Holmes County if we had honestly discharged our duties and obligations as citizens in the past; if we had demanded that all citizens be accorded equal treatment and protection under the law. This we have not done.

But if we think the present situation is serious, as indeed, it is, we should take a long, hard look at the future.

It can, and probably will, get infinitely worse—unless we have the necessary character and guts to do something about it—and change the things that need to be changed.

Mrs. T.M.B. Hicks Writes
an Elegy to a Fallen President

Hired writers on daily newspapers produce most of the best

contemporary editorials. One of the reasons is that they devote much if not most of their workday focusing on editorial writing. On small dailies and weekly newspapers, on the the the other hand, the people who write the editorials usually perform a number of other chores. On weeklies, the editorial writer is the owner-publisher—and editor, reporter, columnist, advertising manager, and salesperson, sometimes even the press operator.

Thus, the editorial work of weekly writers such as Hazel Brannon Smith and Mrs. T.M.B. Hicks becomes even more impressive. For the following editorial, the latter received the Golden Quill Award in 1964. The staff of the International Conference of Weekly Newspaper Editors selected the award by examining editorials in every weekly newspaper it received throughout the year, a total of approximately 80,000 in 1963. From that number, it selected almost 1,200 for further consideration. Mrs. Hicks' editorial, "The Living Flame," was selected, according to the official Golden Quill announcement, "based on an appreciation of the time when it was composed, on the depth of emotion it expressed, and on the fact that... this piece of writing should be preserved throughout the future as an example of great writing. It expressed the thought and soul of America."

Mrs. Hicks wrote the editorial immediately after viewing the funeral procession for the assassinated President John F. Kennedy.

THE LIVING FLAME
(Mrs. T.M.B. Hicks; Dallas [Pa.] *Post*, November 25, 1963)

The hollow and alien sound of hooves on Pennsylvania Avenue. The six grey battle horses and the outrider on the seventh.

The flag-draped casket on the caisson.

The riderless horse with its empty saddle, dancing feet spurning the pavement, restive under the rein, but obedient.

The Navy Band—Hail to the Chief—America the Beautiful... The Navy Hymn.

The unending procession of mourners filing past the bronze casket, high on the catafalque in the vast and echoing rotunda of the Capitol, the same catafalque where Abraham Lincoln had lain in state almost a hundred years ago.

Dark faces among the grieving multitudes and among the chosen service men who guarded the casket, North and South and East and West, at the four points of the compass.

Notables from other countries, heads of State, delegations, arriving at Dulles Airport during the evening hours of the day before the State funeral.

Royalty joining the family and the new President of the United States, the Cabinet, and high officials of the government on the symbolical walk behind the caisson from the White House to St. Matthew's Cathedral.

The Mass of Requiem.

The procession from St. Matthew's to Arlington Cemetery, sleek black limousines creeping behind the caisson.

The Funeral March.

Anxious secret service men guarding the new President.

The Lincoln Memorial at the entrance to the bridge spanning the Potomac.

The endless procession, reaching back as far as the eye can see.

Onward Christian Soldiers—And again, the muffled drums.

The caisson, emerging from the shadows of the buildings into eternal sunshine.

The Memorial Bridge, and the grey horses laboring up the hill to the yawning grave.

Dry leaves scudding before a freshening breeze, in the bright November sunshine.

The Black Watch, and the wailing bagpipes.

Two colored soldiers, young and dignified, in the uniform of their country, helping six other servicemen to carry the coffin from the caisson to its final resting place.

The solemn ceremony.

Jet planes screaming overhead in formation, saluting their fallen chief.

The Irish Guard, saluting and leaving the site of the grave.

Haile Selassie, the Lion of Judah, from Ethiopia, small and somehow pathetic in his bedizened uniform, dwarfed by General DeGaulle, imperturbable in his Field Marshall's cap.

A breathless hush.

Cardinal Cushing... I am the resurrection and the life.

The 21-gun salute, echoing over the graves at Arlington, and over the Tomb of the Unknown soldier, where the President of the United States had placed, so short a time ago, a wreath in memory.

And over the grave of John Fitzgerald Kennedy.

The firing squad, three short bursts of fire.

Taps.

The flag, held taut above the casket by eight service men, folded now with beautiful precision, and passed ceremonially from hand to hand, to be presented formally to the black garbed widow.

The Navy Hymn—Almighty Father, strong to save.

The eternal flame, kindled by Mrs. Kennedy.

The decorous departure of visiting dignitaries, foreign heads of State, the new President of this Nation, and two former Presidents.

The lengthening shadows, throwing into stark relief the white gravestones of the Nation's heroic dead.

The "little people," filing past the casket, still not lowered into the kindly earth.

A cathedral hush, lone light slanting through the trees.
Dusk, and a newly mounded grave.
The living flame.

Reprinted with permission of the Dallas *Post.*

JOHN HARRISON FIGHTS
FOR BETTER HOUSING FOR POOR

John R. Harrison has been one of the most highly decorated of recent editorial writers. Along with the Pulitzer Prize that he received in 1965, he also has won the national Walker Stone Award given by the Scripps Howard Foundation on two occasions, 1974 and 1976.

The Pulitzer Prize recognized the editorial campaign he waged to get a minimum housing code passed in Gainesville, Florida. Civic leaders had been trying for 10 years to get the code adopted before Harrison came to the rescue. When the Pulitzer Prize was awarded, judges commended Harrison for serving as a leader for citizens who were helpless by themselves to get the machinery of government to turn for them.

Typical of Harrison's writing was "Memo to McKinney," published near the middle of the month-long campaign. Both descriptive and argumentative, the editorial begins with a scene in one of Gainesville's inadequate housing areas and follows with a criticism of the city's mayor for dragging his feet on housing reform.

MEMO TO MCKINNEY
(John R. Harrison; Gainesville *Sun*; November 20, 1964)

The road was dusty, and the small Negro boy strained under the weight of the bucket he was carrying. He had brought it more than two blocks from the fountain that was provided "as a courtesy," the sign told us. Three to five times a week the child makes the trip.

The child lives in a house eighteen feet by twenty-four feet along with three other people.

On several of the open windows there are no screens.

There is no front door at all.

Sunlight comes through the roof in two places.

The child and his family share with another family the outhouse in the backyard.

Not only is there no lavatory in the house, there is no tub, shower or hot water supply.

The siding on the house had deteriorated, the chimney needed replacing, the foundation was out of level.

The water lapped over the side of the bucket as the child stepped up a concrete block into the house.

Now, Mayor McKinney, that's a third to a fifth of the family's weekly supply of water.

To drink.

And that family lives in the Northeast section, within the city limits, of Gainesville, Florida, and they pay $5 a week rent. That's Florida's "University City," Center of Science, Education and Medicine.

Now, tell us again, Mayor McKinney, as you have since last August, that a minimum housing code for Gainesville is unnecessary. Tell us again that you want more discussion of the minimum housing code as you did last week. After all, the League of Women Voters and the Citizens' Housing Association of Gainesville, Inc., have, since 1955, documented by studies housing in Gainesville that has no indoor plumbing or piped-in drinking water.

That's ten years, Mr. Mayor.

But tell the child that carries the drinking water down that dusty road that the minimum housing code is unnecessary.

In our mind's eye we'll try to console him with Emerson— "The dice of God are always loaded. For everything you have missed, you have gained something else. The world, turn it how you will, balances itself.... Every secret is told, every virtue rewarded, every wrong redressed, in silence and certainty."

Reprinted with permission of John R. Harrison.

THEO LIPPMAN EXPLAINS
NUDE DANCING'S LEGAL HISTORY

Only rarely have editorial writers been adept at using humor. Many may consider the editorial column a place for serious, somber reflection, and humor inappropriate there. Humor, however, can be an effective means to attract readers to the editorial and, in the hands of the right writer, can provide a way of making incisive comment on serious issues.

Among contemporary editorial writers, none has used humor better than Theo Lippman Jr. of the Baltimore *Sun.* His editorial specialties include politics, government, the courts, and civil rights, among others. The following editorial demonstrates his humorous approach to the topic of the constitutional right of freedom of expression. It was one of the works for which he received the American Society of Newspaper Editors' 1982 award for commentary.

EXERCISE OF FREE SPEECH
(Theo Lippman, Jr.; Baltimore *Sun*; June 8, 1981)

The Supreme Court ruled 7-2 last week that a New Jersey adult book store's nude female dancers were engaged in a form of free speech protected by the First Amendment. A lot of people were surprised by this logic, but actually, it is not all that new.

Many legal experts have long said the same thing. Gypsy Rose Lee pointed out in her autobiography that, "the wimps at the American Civil Liberties Union were my best customers."

And Bubbles Gumm, in her famous course on the First Amendment at the Yale Law School, often said "res adjudica' nihili bonum!" ("take it off").

Dorina and Her Doves made the point in another way in the Oliver Wendell Holmes Lecture at Harvard Law School. "In conclusion," she opined, "it ain't what you say, it's how you say it."

And, of course, no one in Baltimore has to be reminded of Blaze Starr's article "The Blackstonian Concept of Bumps and Grinds," in the *Maryland Law Review* (Fall, 1938).

The Supreme Court has never gone as far as it did in last week's New Jersey decision, but it has certainly been moving in that direction for years. For instance, in *Illinois vs. Paris Burlesque* 213 U.S. 105 (1959), Justice Hugo Black said for the court, "we agree this act 'doesn't play' in Peoria but, look, it's not bad, especially the LaVonne sisters."

In *Ex parte Peaches O'Hara*, 144 U.S. 62 (1968) Justice Felix Frankfurter, speaking for the majority, said of Miss O'Hara's act, "You're talking our language." The court was bitterly divided on this issue in those days. That was a 5-4 decision. In a stinging dissent, Justice John Marshall Harlan referred to Justice Frankfurter as "a weenie."

Some scholars trace the idea that nude dancing is a form of free speech all the way back to the Founding Fathers. That is wrong. It is based on a misreading of this passage from the journal of the Constitutional Convention:

James Madison. There is nothing like a dame. Nothing in this world.

Alexander Hamilton. There are no books like a dame.

Charles Cotesworth Pinckney & Gouverneur Morris. No! No!

Madison. And no one cooks like a dame.

Pinckney & Morris. No! No!

Hamilton. And nothing looks like a dame.

Pinckney & Morris and others. No! No!

Madison & Hamilton. There is nothing you can name, that is anything like a dame....

Actually, they were not talking about the First Amendment, but the Nineteenth, which they all opposed.

Reprinted with permission of Theo Lippman, Jr.

Ann Daly Goodwin
Remembers America's Dead

Ann Daly Goodwin of the St. Paul *Pioneer Press* has twice won the national Walker Stone Award for editorial writing given by the Scripps Howard Foundation, and in consecutive years, 1988 and 1989. Like most editorial writers, she writes on a variety of topics, ranging from public issues to education to cigarette smoking. (The 1988 Stone award especially recognized her campaign to encourage smokers to stop.) She is able to write about such topics with a versatile style, but it is distinguished by a human touch, allowing readers to see issues in personal terms. She "shares an opinion," the Stone awards have pointed out, "with clarity and finesse, and indulges readers with her mastery of language."

The following editorial, one of those for which she won the 1989 award, demonstrates her ability to present a cliché topic— Memorial Day, requiring the annual editorial in almost every newspaper—in an original and poignant way.

UNCOMMON SERVICE, UNCOMMON TRIBUTES
(Ann Daly Goodwin; St. Paul *Pioneer Press*; May 29,1987)

In countless cemeteries, unnumbered hearts and innumerable ways, America remembers its dead today.

With love and gratitude, America remembers its military and civilian dead, its dead who were close as blood ties and marital bonds, its dead who were known only as commended names on casualty lists and in obituary columns.

In solemn ceremony, America remembers its unknown dead. With the laying of wreaths, with the firing of volleys, with the playing of taps at Arlington National Cemetery, the nation acknowledges its debt at the tomb where "lies in honored glory an American soldier known but to God."

As happens every day the year long, America remembers its most recent war dead with offerings brought to "the Wall"—the Vietnam Veterans Memorial. With a mother's letter: "America has had no better than you, and you were ours." With a son's message: "Well, what do you know? I also joined the service.... Why? To do what my father did—protect this great country of ours for democracy and freedom."

As happens every day, America remembers uncommon individuals in singular ways:

•As at a baptism, where a mother and father give to their infant son the names of uncles he will never know: their brothers who died in battle.

•As on a Minnesota farm, where a family enjoys the agreeable shade of trees planted through succeeding decades to commemorate cherished ancestors.

•As in a local nature preserve, where a plaque offers respect to a benefactor who had walked and loved those very woods.

•As in a concert hall, where a bereaved young conductor strides onstage, lifts his baton, spins out the expectant silence while he whispers in his heart, "This one's for you, Grandpa," and then gives the downbeat.

•As at a funeral, where the close survivors play songs their loved one had composed and crooned to his children.

•As on the anniversary of a death, when the family of a plucky girl who could not walk, but raced her snowmobile and entered teen-age beauty pageants, reprints the poem she wrote when she was 14:

If we believe
(just a little)
in magic
the world would be
a lot
better off.

With the healing magic of these and boundless other tributes, public and private, conventional and uncommon, America remembers its dead.

Reprinted with permission of Ann Daly Goodwin.

SAMUEL FRANCIS JUSTIFIES
EXECUTION OF SERIAL KILLER

Samuel Francis of the Washington *Times* is the only writer who has won the American Society of Newspaper Editors' award for editorial writing on two separate occasions, first in 1989 and again the following year. The awards recognize in Francis a combination of talents. They are the same talents that always have accounted for superior editorial writing. One finds in his editorials an ability to analyze a situation or issue in an original way, a distinctive and strong point of view, and writing that is interesting and forceful.

Francis came to editorial writing only recently and, one might say, late in his career. After earning a doctorate in history from the University of North Carolina, he worked as a policy analyst at the Heritage Foundation in Washington, D.C., and then served as a legislative assistant to a U.S. senator. In 1986 he joined the Washington *Times*, a newspaper published by the Unification Church, as an editorial writer and later was named deputy editorial page editor. That non-journalism background may provide a clue to the reasons for his success as an editorial writer, as it helps him to look at issues in a way unobscured by standardized journalistic thinking.

The following editorial provides a stark argument in favor of the execution of Ted Bundy, a serial killer, because, Francis reasons, people are morally responsible for their actions.

JUSTICE REBORN
(Samuel Francis; Washington *Times*; January 26, 1989)

When 2,000 volts of lightning slammed into the body of Ted Bundy Tuesday morning, America suddenly became a little bit cleaner and a little bit safer. For nearly a decade, the notorious serial killer had exhausted his fertile imagination in exploiting every conceivable legal and public relations maneuver to avoid execution. But neither the ingenuity of Bundy and his lawyers, the pedantry of judges, nor the lachrymose quackery of death penalty opponents could stop this week's grim ceremony in Florida's death house. The killer's progress to the hot seat was met with the cheers of citizens impatient that justice be done.

The nation's pundits, for the most part, have not yet weighed in, but the more courageous opponents of the death penalty may soon wax solemn about the viciousness of capital punishment and the ghoulishness of those who celebrated Bundy's death. With celebrants brandishing frying pans, wearing "Burn Bundy" T-shirts, and guzzling beer and doughnuts outside the Florida prison, what seems to have developed into the social event of the season may well have gone too far.

Yet most of those who exuberated over the execution were not ghouls, and their conduct ought to tell us something worrisome about what many decent people have come to believe about the state of criminal justice in the United States. The visitation of strong punishment upon criminals clearly known to be guilty is regarded as unusual, and when it occurs many citizens consider it the exception rather than the rule and the occasion for making merry.

Some may sermonize that Bundy's death will not restore to life any of his victims, and they will fallaciously equate his own death with those he caused. Yet nothing that the state of Florida did to this creature at all resembled what he did to his victims. Florida's executioner did not lacerate Bundy's face and hands with a hacksaw as he admitted he did to the body of 18-year-old Georgann Hawkins. It did not beat him to death with the branch of a tree or leave toothmarks on his corpse as he did to the bodies of two sorority coeds. It did not rape him, kill him, and pitch his corpse into a pigsty as he did to 12-year-old Kimberly Leach of Lake City, Fla. None of these victims will be resurrected because Bundy is now dead, but then, no more will go to their graves because of him either, and the ghosts of the young women he hunted will now perhaps be stiller.

Bundy's execution was the occasion for much biographical wallowing: He was born out of wedlock, his father remains unknown, his grandfather was violent, he early showed the signs of "sociopathic" behavior. Some will seize on these factoids to argue that he was not morally responsible and that therapy, not punishment, was the "proper" way to deal with him. But to deny even Ted Bundy his moral responsibility, and the rewards and punishments that responsibility obliges, is to deny the very concept of what is proper. If human beings are not responsible for their actions, then there is nothing "proper" to be done with any of us. Justice, even in a black leather hood at dawn, is kinder and gentler, more merciful and more humane, than the pseudoscience that seeks to replace it.

Ted Bundy died because he deserved to die. Some of the admittedly tasteless celebrations of his death recognized this truth, but they also were hailing its recognition by those public authorities who sent Bundy to his fate. For years many of our leaders have been blind to this truth, and if they now are beginning to grasp it more firmly, that is cause for celebration.

Reprinted with permission of Samuel Francis.

MASTERS OF THE EDITORIAL

PAUL GREENBERG: MASTER OF VERSATILITY

Among the hundreds of editorial writers working on American newspapers today, none is more honored or respected than Paul Greenberg. Editorial page editor of the *Commercial* in the small town of Pine Bluff, Arkansas, he has built his reputation on a combination of talents. He has the rare ability to pierce unerringly to the heart of an issue, he holds an unflinching belief in his duty to comment on the world around him as he honestly sees it, and he presents his ideas in a versatile and always interesting writing style.

Assessing the editorials of writers who lived 100 years ago is an easy task—easy, that is, compared with estimating the editorials of a living writer. Time solidifies critical opinions and reveals which editorials will remain to be read for years to come. Today's writers are writing even as readers hold this anthology in their hands. The writers' volume of lifelong work is not yet completed. Add to all that the ever-changing attitudes about what constitutes "good" writing, and the task becomes even more difficult.

As judged by his peers, however, Greenberg already has been acknowledged with most of the accolades that an editorial writer can be given. He received the Pulitzer Prize in 1969, and in 1978 was recommended for it by the selection jury and again was a finalist in 1986. Along with the Pulitzer, he has received the American Society of Newspaper Editors award for commentary, the Walker Stone Award for editorial writing, the H. L. Mencken Award, and the William Allen White Award, among others. Scores of newspapers publish his thrice-weekly syndicated column, and he is frequently called on to speak about the craft of editorial writing.

Except for a brief stint as an editorial writer for the Chicago *Daily News* in 1966-1967, Greenberg has spent his entire career at the Pine Bluff *Commercial*. He was born in Shreveport, Louisiana, in 1937 and lived there until he went to the University of Missouri to study journalism and history. He began work for the *Commercial* in 1962 as the editorial page editor, the same position he holds today. The fact that he has spent his career on a small daily newspaper has greatly influenced his editorial writing. He has been compared to William Allen White, more for the obvious small-town reason than for any other. Both men presented their ideas from a local, intimate community in middle-America, away from the hustle and bustle of big-city journalism. Like White, Greenberg also has enjoyed widespread success not limited geographically. Even though he writes primarily on local events, his words are read by people across the nation.

More than most editorial writers, Greenberg has spoken and written frequently on the subject of writing. He is a writer who has thought critically and at length about technique. The most important of his ideas is that editorial writing must be done with a clear, important purpose in mind. "Don't sit down to write an editorial," he declares, "but to say something.... Write the only editorial in the country that will appear from your particular point of view, a product of your unique experience, knowledge, wisdom, viewpoint."

Being able to "say something" is one of the reasons he has chosen to spend his career with a small newspaper in a small town. The location, he believes, gives him a clearer vision of the important things. "There is something in us all," he has written, "that seeks not just what we can get but what we can give. There is a chance to know and shape a small town—in a way it would never be possible to know and shape a great city."

To produce words that get readers to think, Greenberg employs many techniques, so that it is impossible to say that his editorials are in the "Greenberg style." Instead, his style is marked by a variety of styles. He does not hesitate to write editorials with different tones and personalities. On one day, his editorial may be filled with metaphors and whimsical anecdotes; on another it may be a serious analysis based on carefully researched facts and figures. One editorial may be an indictment of the public education system; another, a reflective musing on nature.

Indicative of his varied repertoire is his frequent use of humor. Even when dealing with serious subjects, he sometimes injects it. Humor, by making an editorial more attractive and accessible, can touch the reader as few other devices can. Greenberg's humor often comes in the form of caricature. Although he has said "Be tough on ideas, easy on personalities," he can be a harsh critic. He often attacks politicians by branding them with a satirical nickname. Arkansas' governors Frank White and Bill Clinton, for example, became "Governor Goofy" and "Slick Willie" in Greenberg's editorials. He rarely forgets an individual's past mistakes and by repetition of the caricature is able to stick a satirical label to the politician and to readers' images of the politician. His caricatures are, however, always done as a backdrop to some central message, never as a means in and of themselves to poke fun. That ability to capture the essence of a personality accounts for many of the marvelous editorial profiles of local and world figures that he has produced over the years. A number of them were collected in the book *Resonant Lives.*

Greenberg's success at writing editorials is linked with his method of writing. Above all else, he believes that strong editorials stem from emotion, not the intellect—at least not in the initial stage. Even when one of his editorials is based on solid issues, the seed for its idea is planted by some emotional reaction. Describing the process involved in writing a column entitled "On the Beach," he explained: "I had a very strong emotional feeling that did not change from the moment I conceived of [the editorial] till I read the piece in the newspaper. The first feeling was completely wordless. The next question was to put it into words."

Intertwined with this emotional inspiration is the laborious process he goes through to produce a finished product. Starting from emotional, abstract ideas and going to concrete, understandable words often can be a complicated process. Greenberg often goes through several drafts before settling on the final version of an editorial. Writing and rewriting are part of the same job.

As with many editorial writers, one of Greenberg's favorite topics is politics—usually either community or state. He believes in giving preference to local issues because, quite simply, he is closer to them. In dealing with political issues, he has revealed a consistency of viewpoint over the years which has confused many readers. Some find his political mind to be a puzzle. Some call him a conservative; others, a liberal. The solution to the puzzle seems to be that while partisan stands shift with the times and with whatever stand appears at the moment to be most advantageous, Greenberg has applied fundamental principles to the issues. While partisan viewpoints have changed with, it sometimes seems, daily regularity, he has held firm to beliefs in human equality, liberty, democracy, and the other values that Americans traditionally have clung to. That firmness of beliefs has allowed him to subject daily events and issues to a sharp scrutiny.

Naturally, his close inspection and often sharp criticism have made some dislike him. He has plenty of admirers, but a number of detractors as well. That, he says, is a sign of good journalism. "I must have offended everybody at some point," he once declared. "...An editorial writer who does his job is just bound to have [written] things that offend people." Journalism, he proclaimed to an audience of journalists at one of his speeches, "should be an unfraternal conspiracy on behalf of the laity." A survey of Pine Bluff town leaders in the 1980s ranked the *Commercial*, Greenberg is fond of pointing out, second among "services needing improvement"—just ahead of the town's sewage system—while residents in general put the paper near the top of the city's features.

Despite community leaders' complaints, loyal readers and those same leaders recognize Greenberg's talent for writing hard-hitting and eloquent editorials. They take pride in the fact that their hometown newspaper is his home. Even those who disagreed with his editorials dissecting George Wallace and the racial conflicts in the 1960s were proud of the Pulitzer Prize he earned for writing them. In a way, he believes, it and the other awards he has received have been a recognition of the entire Pine Bluff community.

What Greenberg has said about the craft of editorial writing could fill an entire course. One suggestion, however, taken from his list of "37 Ways to Write an Editorial," may reveal where his award-winning, audience-involving inspiration comes from. "Aim for a masterpiece," he advises, "not just another editorial."

•The following editorial is one of those for which Greenberg received the American Society of Newspaper Editors' award for writing in 1981. It demonstrates his talent for incisive character study.

A TRIP IN TIME
(Pine Bluff *Commercial*; October 2, 1980)

We were driving to Little Rock to hear Orval Faubus. Just like the old days. But Tom Parsons, who was behind the wheel, wasn't a cub reporter any more but managing editor. Years ago, decades ago, it had been John Thompson, the newspaper's laconic man at the legislature, who had introduced this new editorial writer to the cockpit of Arkansas politics. I remember how he had summed up Redfield on the way up to the state Capitol: "A Faubus box." If you were limited to a three-word description of Redfield in July of 1962, those three would be hard to beat.

But driving up this fall afternoon, everything was wrong, or anyway different. This wasn't a snaky two-lane obstacle course but a four-lane expressway. The most over-promised and under-built road in the state finally had been completed—long after Orval Faubus (who had done most of the promising) had left the scene. Several New Souths had come and gone since then. The

Governor's Mansion had been handed over to a succession of Moderates and there hadn't been a hard edge to state politics for years.

Now we were headed for Little Rock to stir up all those old memories, and grudges. The press had been invited to preview a television documentary on the life and times of O.E. Faubus, Eternal Incumbent, Peerless Leader, and footnote in American history books under Law, Defiance of. I felt like Jack Burden in *All the King's Men,* assigned to turn over rocks and poke into the malice of time once more. Thus literature robs experience of its original perception, replacing it with somebody else's art.

And like Jack Burden toward the end of Willie Stark's saga, I wasn't looking forward to the job. It wasn't fun any more; it was a history assignment. But when anybody begins explaining How It Really Was, somebody else needs to be around to see that the footnotes aren't misplaced. He who is allowed to control the present, as any revisionist historian knows, controls the past, and he who controls the past sways the future. History isn't just a quasi-science, and it's more than an art; it's a political weapon.

At the television station, it was like a subdued opening night, with a small bar, old friends, a comfortable board room with cushy chairs and an outsized screen on which to watch the show. And there was Orval Faubus, chatting amiably. When the hurly-burly's done, when the battle's lost and won, we'll all get together and have a drink, History, where is thy sting?

The scenes from the documentary were almost as comfortable, with a few exceptions. Like some Depression Era pictures that could have come from old WPA files. Nothing testifies to the unchanging mutability of human affairs like old photographs. But most of the documentary had the depth of a travelogue, and it came swathed in music that might have been written expressly for organists in all-you-can-eat buffeterias. It sounded both ominous and confectionary. It sounded—yes, it was—the theme from the movie *Jaws* somehow rendered toothless.

The old adrenalin didn't start to flow till well into this candy-coated production. That's when Orval Faubus up there on the screen was saying: "I think that's part of the proof that the American dream is still possible." He was talking about his own rise in politics, not his part in denying that dream to a whole race of Americans. Then the unlined Orval Faubus of 1957 was telling an incredibly young Mike Wallace in a television interview that the troops he had just called out to bar black students from Central High "will not act as segregationists or integrationists." They were there, you see, only to keep the peace. Law and order would be maintained by having the proper authorities do the mob's bidding.

As for those troops that enforced the law of the land when he wouldn't, Governor Faubus made them sound like some Foreign Legion. There he was in a newsreel of the time telling the local populace: "We are now an occupied territory." Nothing inflammatory about *his* performance in 1957.

For a brief moment, just what Orval Faubus stood for in 1957 came rushing back, along with the worldwide name he gave Arkansas that year. Then the lights came on and it was 1980 again. And one was seated next to a 70-year-old man nibbling peanuts, reminiscing about old times, and rubbing his hands together as he explained why he had retired to Houston, Texas: "I've always suffered from cold weather," this Orval Faubus was saying. Besides, he added, Houston had a lot of medical facilities. He talked of his two recent operations and the medication he took for his heart.

The old passion faded out almost a quickly as the television screen had. One recalled that in his last two times out in the gubernatorial races, Orval E. Faubus hadn't done much better than Frank Lady or Monroe Schwarzlose. He was scarcely a clear and present danger now. The second volume of his memoirs was being published by Democrat Printing & Lithographing Co. in Little Rock, which ain't exactly Harper and Row.

This Orval Faubus was repeating all the old lines, unchanged since 1957, but they no longer inspired anger. Only a certain tiredness. It is wearing to be in the presence of history's condemned, and not just because they keep repeating their brief. But because they cannot even enter a room without dragging all that irrevocable history after them, filling every space with suffocating judgment. Their unchanged routine, like an old photograph, brings home how much everything else has changed.

This Orval Faubus, for example, is still the master of the great unintended self-revelation, as when he assured those of us around the table: "I'm out of politics. I'm not running for anything. I don't have to lie to you." (Any more?) This new line may be the most revealing since the one that became the unofficial motto of his administration: Just because I said it doesn't make it so.

The sneak preview is over now, but Orval Faubus is still going strong, surrounded by reporters, rehashing old campaigns, reaching back for the names of old friends and foes. He obviously relishes it. At 70, he still enjoys the game. He will yet justify the unjustifiable, if only history would listen. He'll look better, he said, "in the perspective of history when animosities and prejudices have faded with time...." It is another great quote from a politician who used animosities and prejudices so adroitly. And won six terms as governor. That seemed a long time then. Now it is the shortest, like yesterday when it is past. Stepping outside into fresh air, I am struck again at this season by how suddenly it gets dark.

•The following editorial, which combines humor with critical social commentary, was one of those for which Greenberg won the Walker Stone Award in 1987.

FAREWELL TO JOE BOB
(Pine Bluff *Commercial*; April 24, 1985)

Oh, no. The *Dallas Times Herald* is canceling a column that has given American pop culture a character who ranks with Archy and Mehitabel or anyway with Westbrook Pegler's average American, George Spelvin. He's Joe Bob Briggs, supposed author of "Joe Bob Goes to the Drive-In," a weekly offering that was a small delight in a columniating world otherwise grayed out by the likes of Joseph Kraft, James Reston, and all the other deep, uh, thinkers.

Joe Bob never developed those kinds of airs; he wouldn't know Deng Xiaoping from any other Chinaman and, if somebody started telling him how great Margaret Thatcher is, he'd probably ask what her breast measurement was. He still thinks Joe Louis was a Credit to His Race and, when he gets ready to sell his old pick-up truck, he doesn't appreciate being gypped or jewed down. Not only doesn't Joe Bob know too much, but he doesn't suspect an awful lot—though at times he displays a certain native shrewdness that can illumine subjects other commentators are too deracinated to touch. In short, he is rude, uneducated, lecherous, and more than something of a jerk—and that is but to mention some of his better qualities. Ol' Joe Bob is a meandering complex of gaucheries.

But Joe Bob is also honest (to a big fault) and can be a delight as well as an outrage, the way Archie Bunker was at first, before he became an overworked, heavy-handed institution. Joe Bob has stayed outrageous enough to amuse and just real enough to remind the reader of the twisted little know-it-all bigot who resides deep down in just about all of us. He is, in short, a great new character in American literature or anyway in American newspapers.

Correction: Joe Bob *was* a great character. Sad to report, he was done in this week by a lynch mob of some 300 enraged protesters with the consent of his supposed patron and good buddy, the *Dallas Times Herald*. Before that, Joe Bob had gone after just about every race, creed, color, and national origin within Dallas's limits, not to mention various sexual preferences and political viewpoints. But when he parodied "We Are the World," the record industry's contribution to famine relief in Ethiopia, he became an endangered species. Apparently only Garry Trudeau's *Doonesbury* is allowed to do that. Then he had to go and condescend to blacks—and that did it. Hundreds of angry people descended on the *Times Herald*, which in this small crisis displayed all the backbone of a cream puff. "We made a mistake," editor Will Jarrell told the mob, offering it Joe Bob's mangy corpus. The column will also be discontinued by the Los Angeles Times Syndicate—which distributed it to 57 newspapers willing to run something other than Ann Landers as an example of American pop culture.

The protesters had complained that Joe Bob was racist, which of course he was, as well as being xenophobic, ignorant, jingoist, bigoted in general, and a male chauvinist of the more porcine variety. If he had been just a bit more organized, he might have qualified as a fascist, too. But the only folks really maligned by this bit of social criticism disguised as a review of the more exploitative kind of movies are... rednecks, of course. Joe Bob is his own best parody, like Sinclair Lewis's Babbitt. But rednecks tend to laugh at themselves, even to take a certain contrary pride in their faults.

To take offense at Joe Bob's barbs at any other group is to reveal the kind of philistinism that has just about turned a great, brawling, popular culture that would do justice to Walt Whitman into a polite, empty nothing. Censorship has triumphed once again, this time in the name of progress, and of liberalism—which just ain't what she used to be in America. Perhaps only when blacks and whites can laugh at Joe Bob together will American race relations have improved to the point some of us optimists thought already had been reached. Now *that* would be progress.

If this same mediocre standard had been enforced in an earlier America, no newspaper would have dared print James Russell Lowell, Joel Chandler Harris, Ring Lardner, Langston Hughes, Mark Twain, or anybody else who slipped into dialect. Lest some ethnic group somewhere, or rather its more literal-minded members, take offense.

The people crowding into that conference room at the *Times Herald* in Dallas brought to mind the sort of oh-so-sensitive souls who want to ban Huckleberry Finn because one of its heroes—so admirable a character he's really a little hard to believe—is named Nigger Joe. Because of that, they would protect innocent little minds from reading the great American novel—and from meeting Joe and Huck and feeling what they felt, and knowing what it is to be a slave, and what it is to be that other variety of slave called a minister.

They're the sort of reformers who want to ban Shakespeare's *Merchant of Venice* because the supposed villain is a miserly Jew. Never mind that Shylock, more sinned against than sinning, speaks some of the most moving, human lines in the play. The same sort of reformer turns up at any meeting called to demand that something or other be censored for the most high-minded of reasons. But usually the librarian or publisher being accosted doesn't cave in like a tower of Jello.

The folks, protesting at Dallas had to be ignorant of what satire, at least the best kind, is about. It is not gentle or conventional or fashionable. It stirs. At its best and most insightful, it captures the reader's attention the way a two-by-four does a mule's. The editors of the *Times Herald* surely can't plead such ignorance. They had to know that Joe Bob is the alter ego of their gifted critic, John Bloom, who must have spent many a mosquito-bitten night diligently taking notes on beery conversations at Central Texas drive-ins. Or maybe he does his research in honky-tonks and country cafes.

Now the *Times Herald* has decided to sacrifice his creation to an angry crowd. When Goethe said there was nothing more frightening than ignorance in action, he may not have considered what ignorance can do in combination with spinelessness. Wimpishness, thy name is the *Dallas Times Herald*; its spirit in this instance is the same one that has turned a great, fighting, discordant chorus of 19th Century newspapers into today's pallid press. Much of modern life and fashion conspires against such élan. But with the possible exception of the kind of dunderheaded judges who assume that the purpose of the First Amendment was to make the American press a nice, respectable institution that never offends the right people, the greatest threat to robust American debate comes from editors who censor their own papers before government can, and who bow to only the loudest pressure groups and call it upholding unity and enlightenment. With editors like that, American newspapers need no censors.

Here's hoping that at the last minute Joe Bob's dangling body can be cut down and his spirit revived. Surely it wouldn't be too much trouble for John Bloom to take his elegant leave of the *Times Herald* in the best George Jean Nathan manner and escort his good buddy Joe Bob the five or six short blocks over to the *Dallas Morning News,* a paper with guts. 'Cause it's gonna get awful lonesome on all those Dallas freeways without ol' Joe Bob ridin' shotgun.

•The following editorial demonstrates Greenberg's ability to take a commonplace topic, recognize its underlying meaning, and use it as the basis for social commentary.

MERRY CHRISTMAS:
IT'S STILL A WONDERFUL LIFE
(Pine Bluff *Commercial*; December 24, 1989)

To many Americans, this season would not be complete without at least a few scenes from "It's a Wonderful Life." The movie wasn't much of a hit when it was first released just after the Second World War, but it has slowly acquired an immense popularity—and even a certain critical acclaim. Perhaps that is because it represents a peculiarly American vision. It is not so much a vision of Christmas—despite that last, tear-wrenching scene in front of the tree—but of a society, and how it ought to be.

A brief analysis of the movie by a professor of American Studies at Boston University got us to thinking not so much about the movie as about the consistent misunderstandings of professors. Professor Ray Carney has written a book about Frank Capra's films entitled *American Vision.* He says the movie shows that, while life can be "an enriching Norman Rockwell experience, it also can be smothering, where you end up marrying the girl you went to high school with, and you never get to go to Europe.... It tells us George is one of the most sad and lonely and tragic characters ever imagined. I cry when I see it."

George Bailey a lonely and tragic character? We confess to having shed a few tears over "It's a Wonderful Life" ourselves, but not for the professor's reasons. Nothing in the movie seems as sad as the professor's analysis of it. Why, George Bailey would be the richest man in town if he didn't have a penny—as his brother says at the end of the movie. He makes Mr. Potter, that old miser, look like a pauper—because George Bailey has loved and sacrificed and built and given, and stood alone a time or two, and, well, lived. He has not gone through life as a tourist.

Not getting to go to Europe does not strike us as the kind of experience that qualifies for tragedy, possibly because we know some Americans who were born there. To them, not coming to America would have been the tragedy.

Surely only an American would be so bereft of the tragic sense of life as to consider marrying your high school sweetheart a tragedy. These latitudes are simply not hospitable to the tragic art, though in the go-getting American spirit, we can compete with the best of foreigners in that department. (See *The Great Gatsby.*) But "It's a Wonderful Life" is not an entry in the Tragedy category.

Maybe we misunderstood, but the message of the movie we saw is that George Bailey has *not* led a sad, lonely or tragic life, much as he might think so in his more self-pitying moments. Can the professor, like so many Americans, be using "tragic" as a synonym for sad? It is a common American misusage, and says much about the nature of our history. Lacking much experience with the real thing, we call everything a tragedy from a fender-bender to a bankruptcy.

On these shores, tragedy in its original, legitimate Greek sense flourishes only with care and feeding, while in Europe, where the concept originated, it seems to come naturally. Perhaps it is the American insistence on happy endings, onstage and off, that makes our definition of tragedy decidedly less than Aristotelian.

If there is a moral to Frank Capra's movie, it may be the comment from Clarence, George's bumbling guardian angel: "Strange, isn't it? Each man's life touches so many other lives, and when he isn't around he leaves an awful hole to fill, doesn't he? ... You see, George, you really had a wonderful life. Don't you see what a mistake it would be to throw it away?" That's a lot more Eugene Field than Aristotle.

The movie is a celebration of the usual American virtues, which have never been usual enough. To quote Nancy Dillon, a writer who can remember watching the film with her father: "We laughed, and cried, a lot that afternoon, and at the end I no longer saw my father as being at all ordinary." There are few things more extraordinary than the ordinary virtues of small-town, middle-class America.

Nancy Dillon, it might be noted, lives in Worthington, Ohio—which sounds not unlike the movie's Bedford Falls. The values of Bedford Falls are those our professional intellectuals are supposed to see through. Sometimes they are so busy seeing through them that they don't see them at all. Or they confuse the happy with the sad, the lonely with the interconnected, and, strangest of all, the triumphant with the tragic. Just as George Bailey did for a while.

Equally undiscerning are those who would idealize small towns; they don't see the potential Pottersville inside every Bedford Falls. Just one man, like George Bailey, can make the difference. Think of all those who made a difference in this town—Harvey McGeorge and Wiley Branton, Walter Trulock III and George Makris Sr., Jimmy Joyce and Earl Chadick Sr.—and of all those who continue to make a difference, the Jack Joneses and Cliff Roafs and Havis Hesters and Edna Mayses.

The most unsettling aspect of the popularity now accorded "It's a Wonderful Life" is the realization that nostalgia for certain values tends to set in just when they are disappearing. Happily, nostalgia can bring them back, for there are fashions in values just as there are in clothes.

Jimmy Stewart, the actor who is George Bailey's alter ego, was once asked to explain the movie's popularity, and responded: "In spite of all the things that have happened and the things that seem to be going wrong, I think it shows that George Bailey's values are still prevalent in this country and are in no danger of being knocked down." That does not sound like a tragic character talking. It sounds like George Bailey after Clarence has straightened him out.

The distinguished professor's view of George as a tragic figure strikes us as sadder than anything in the movie, but at least it's not tragic. It's more comic, this being America. We wish the professor a merry Christmas, a happy new year, and a wonderful life.

•The following editorial demonstrates Greenberg's ability to analyze a much discussed and debated issue from a fresh and insightful perspective.

THE FLAG WAR:
THE DESENSITIZING OF AMERICA
(Pine Bluff *Commercial*; June 28, 1990)

The failure of Congress to propose a constitutional amendment that would protect the flag can be seen in different ways. To some, it is a triumph of reason: Given sufficient time to think about the issue, more and more Americans refused to be provoked into adding words to the Constitution, that great charter and ordering of our freedoms. This district's congressman, Beryl Anthony Jr., started out in favor of a constitutional amendment but thought better of it—a course doubtless followed by many Americans. In turning down such an amendment, it is said, the House and Senate reflected mature and sober American opinion. We are in the presence of a happy ending.

And yet, and yet, it does not feel that way. Some of us are unpersuaded about that happy ending—for reasons not as glib and ready as those offered by the prevailing side in this debate, yet reasons that will not go away, that remain like a hard stone in the pit of our being. It is as if something unspoken within had been assaulted.

Only a year ago the country was shocked by the Supreme Court's decision permitting the desecration of the flag as a lawful form of protest; now the shocking has become the accepted. Is this the result of calm reflection, or just one more step in the desensitizing of American society? One after the other, lines that once defined the limits of what was permissible have been crossed; now the one inviolable symbol of the country may be violated with impunity. The rage of a year ago has given way to a sense of loss all the greater because more and more of our leaders seem incapable of sharing it fully. After all, they assure us, the flag is only a symbol.

There are symbols and there are Symbols. And there are some that go beyond the symbolic and become something else, something transcendent, something so real it would be wrong to treat it as only a symbol. Maybe a story will explain: As a promising young writer, Flannery O'Connor was once invited to a soiree at the home of Mary McCarthy, by then a Big Name in American literature. As the elegant talk wound on into the night, somehow the subject of the Eucharist was raised. Mary McCarthy mentioned, doubtless with some amusement, that when she was a child and saw as a child, she thought of the Host as the Holy Ghost, the most "portable" member of the Trinity. But now that she was grown, she added, she thought of it as a symbol—and implied that it was a mighty effective one, too. Doubtless she meant such condescension as praise. But all young Flannery O'Connor could say was, "Well, if it's a symbol, to hell with it."

Because to Flannery O'Connor, the Eucharist was not a symbol but a Presence. It was the one thing, she said, that was indispensable in her life; all the rest she could live without. To some of us, the American flag is more than a symbol; it is a presence. And to stand by while it is mutilated and do nothing—to be able to do nothing by law—is not simply to let the mob express itself; it is to join the mob, to aid and abet it by our silence, our permission, our impotence before the law. It is to become an accessory to the desensitization of America.

John Paul Stevens, in his dissent from the Supreme Court's latest ruling on this issue, noticed how swiftly the flag's significance can be lost. "A formerly dramatic expression of protest is now rather commonplace," he wrote. "The symbolic value of the American flag is not the same today as it was yesterday. Events during the last three decades have altered the country's image in the eyes of numerous Americans, and some now have difficulty understanding the message that the flag conveyed to their parents and grandparents—whether born abroad and naturalized or native-born." To an earlier generation the flag was not just a symbol; it was.... The Flag. It had transcended the symbolic. It was important of itself. It was a presence.

For that matter, it is unfair to the protesters not to punish them for desecrating the flag; it reduces a solemn act of civil disobedience to an unremarkable, risk-free, less and less meaningful gesture. Remove the penalty and you remove the significance of the act—as Henry David Thoreau would surely understand. It is not just the flag that has been devalued by these events but the desecration of it. When anything is permitted, nothing signifies. (Perhaps that explains the awful emptiness of some modern philosophies.)

Granted, to revere the flag as something to be protected by law requires a certain moral imagination, a quality that grows less and less discernible in this society. The importance of that quality can scarcely be over-estimated. To quote Russell Kirk: "All great systems, ethical or political, attain their ascendancy over the minds of men by virtue of their appeal to the imagination; and when they cease to touch the chords of wonder and mystery and hope, their power is lost, and men look elsewhere for some set of principles by which they may be guided."

But the quality of moral imagination is not easy to explain in 1990. Robert Bolt, the playwright, did not find it easy to explain in this modern period why a medieval churchman like Sir Thomas More would choose to lose his head rather than repeat a few words under oath that he might not agree with in every detail. The author of "A Man for All Seasons" had to add a preface in which to explain why men once had such a fear of committing perjury. But that has changed. As the author put it, "There are fewer and fewer things which, as they say, we 'cannot bring ourselves' to do." And now we have brought ourselves to another: Standing by while the flag is defiled. The press is even advised not to pay much attention to such scenes. Maybe if a flag desecration isn't reported, it isn't happening, or at least we won't have to bother with it. After all, it's not as if something real were being destroyed; it's only a symbol, isn't it? And if we keep telling ourselves that, maybe we'll believe it. Maybe we won't even feel it after a while. This is the very definition of desensitization.

Speaking of which, perhaps the most insensitive comment in this whole sad war over the flag was made by a spokesman for the

American Bar Association in the course of explaining why the flag should not be protected by law. "We don't want to set a precedent," he said, "for criminalizing peaceful political protests in the course of which someone defaces a privately owned piece of property, the American flag." This person, Randolph W. Thrower, is apparently under the impression that it is possible to privately own the American flag—in the way one might own, say, a blanket, a house, a car, or any other personal possession. But we know in our hearts that is not possible, that the flag does not belong to any single individual. The flag belongs to all of us—the way the Lincoln Memorial does, and the flag, too, should be protected by law.

Besides, in this highly organized society an American may not be able to do as he wishes even with his private property—not with zoning laws and environmental standards and traffic regulations and many another restriction in effect. Shall the law protect only a public interest that can be estimated in dollars and cents, but not one that is inestimable, invaluable? Perhaps so. Perhaps that is the real message of the vote in Congress. It is a simple enough message: There seems to be less and less of the moral imagination that we can bring ourselves to protect.

Editorials are reprinted with permission of Paul Greenberg.